Establishing
Equilibrium

Establishing Equilibrium

How to Attain Balanced Health and Healing Using the Counter Chakra Road Map

Erin Garay

Love. Heal. Thrive.

Published 2023
Printed in the United States of America
Paperback: 979-8-9889487-0-4
E-ISBN: 979-8-9889487-1-1
Library of Congress Control Number: 2023917269

Interior design by Leah Lococo

DISCLAIMER

This book is not intended to replace medical advice.
Seek help from your physician or other health professional in
matters relating to your health, particularly with respect to any
symptoms that may require diagnosis or medical attention.

DEDICATION

This book is dedicated to my
Love. Heal. Thrive. community of Thrivers.

May you continue to reach for a truth
that exists just beyond where you are so that you
are always growing, learning, and expanding.

Love yourself enough to heal.
Heal yourself enough to thrive.

CONTENTS

INTRODUCTION

YIN. YANG.

Low. High.

Absent. Present.

Stagnation. Movement.

Illness. Health.

Is not. Is.

Imbalance. Equilibrium.

The world is balanced by opposites.

We are balanced by opposites.

The principle of polarity states there is an opposite for everything in our world. One thing does not exist without its opposite.

One cannot exist without the other.

The dark makes the light brighter, and light makes the dark appear darker.

Opposing forces allow us to remain on course. One keeps the other from getting too out of balance.

In Ayurveda, the microcosm is considered a reflection of the macrocosm. The individual is a mirror of the Universe. Our state of health is the result of our stories, our surroundings, and the beliefs we have created as a result of living them. But just as we must partner with the Universe, we must partner with ourselves. Our internal energetic system has its own alignment of partnerships in place to establish its own powerful healing.

Each energetic center, known as a chakra, has a stand-alone function to balance and heal a certain aspect of the body that will be detailed later. However, these energy centers do not heal in isolation. Each of these energy centers also has a counterpart that helps bring strength, balance, and interdependent optimization for each chakra pairing and the system in its entirety.

Each of our energy centers is stabilized by an equal and opposite counter chakra. In order to bring balance to one energy center, we must bring balance to its counter chakra. My hope is that in our time together I teach you precisely how to create powerful healing within your body by establishing collective balance within the system.

Energy can never be destroyed. It can only be transformed and redirected and, in partnership, balanced. This is what I intend to teach you throughout this process—the precise system I have used for years to bring true healing to my clients. Beyond my healing practice, I have worked with and experienced energy my entire life.

The movie *The Sixth Sense* felt more like my autobiography for me than a scary movie. Much like young Haley Joel Osment did in the movie, as a child I would stand in my bedroom doorframe in the middle of the night and build up the courage to sprint to the bathroom by way of the lingering spirits in the hall.

One morning, when my mom asked me how I slept, I decided to be brave enough to ask her what I should do with the spirits in the hall.

She freaked out and said, "In the name of Jesus Christ, get out."

While I assumed my well-meaning mother was talking about the spirits, my little self couldn't help but feel outcasted that day as well. Did she want me out? That little girl was never quite sure, so she never mentioned anything again about the energy and spirits she'd see regularly. And so the intense solo journey of discovering my energy gifts was initiated that day, and I have spent every day since learning, connecting, meditating, and intuiting systems and procedures to help truly understand the energy body and all it is capable of.

In my thirties, I came home to visit my family, and while sitting at the dinner table talking over dessert, I noticed a gray hue emanating around my mom. I asked if she was feeling okay. She said, "Yes, I'm fine, just a little tired."

A month later, her doctor discovered she had breast cancer, and five months later she died.

I see this gray hue a lot.

If I am close enough to the person, I ask if they are well. If I am not close to them, I will send a blessing and ask for the highest blessed outcome for that person. I will often hear a story about the illness they recovered from since I had last seen them or that they have transitioned onto their next phase of being.

I do not consider my gifts unique. I believe with the correct understanding and daily work, anyone can see what I see. Like all things, it takes dedication, focus, and a road map to help you get there.

Consider this book your road map.

I want to help you define your experiences. I bet you have experienced this same energy and just don't know it yet.

- Or maybe you know that you are sensitive but have no idea how sensitive you are.
- Or perhaps you have been struggling with your sensitivity and are looking for guidance.
- Or you are sick and have not found your remedy and are still looking for answers and healing.

For all these reasons, you are being called here to understand and learn how to establish your own equilibrium so you can bask in the peace and joy that emanates from this place of balance and health.

The framework of this process is the chakra system, and these words are my mantra:

Our thoughts trigger emotions, emotions move energy,
and energy manifests physically.
What we do with our energy matters.
If our energy isn't weak, our body doesn't weaken.

With this energetic road map, you are about to embark on a healing journey. With each page you turn, you are going to learn about the chakra system and the power of the partnerships that exist within this system, and how to apply this system to obtain healing.

I have spent more than a decade studying the chakra system and have shared this wisdom with thousands of people in person, at my healing center, and via online courses.

Simply put, there are seven major chakra centers that affect our daily life, and I believe this knowledge ought to be one of the cornerstones of fundamental learning when studying the human body and how it works. I'm thrilled to share my findings and my passion with you and to teach you how this system can bring you the healthiest version of you, as you will start discovering in this chapter.

The chakra system originated in India between 1500 and 500 BC and is a true and essential understanding of the human body's energetic system. However, what I'm sharing is a result of my proven clinical experience and clinical reasoning from years of working with clients and discovering and connecting patterns between the chakras that I found to be true through a series of sessions.

We are all unique and require unique healing. My hope is that you are guided to your ultimate truth about the healing that lies within you and hope to guide you and help you find your way to this place that is calling to you. It is the intimate and compassionate understanding and knowing of yourself that will bring the healing you've been searching for. Together, we will journey through the chakra system within your body, and you will learn the location and function of each chakra and how they work in solidarity. It is in teaching these very techniques that I have had students tell me they no longer experience stress or illness after incorporating these tools into their daily routines. These are techniques that I have used for my own healing and when Western medicine left my clients without a viable solution.

The chakra system allows us to piece together our physical, emotional, energetic, and spiritual bodies in one complete story so that we can understand the big picture of our health and life. We journey to find the root cause of our problem or illness and heal it, thus eradicating destructive patterns from our lives, harmonizing physical and emotional struggle, and experiencing a life that is vibrant, connected, and healthy. This is a beautiful, comprehensive system that I use daily to heal myself as well as my clients. By utilizing this integrated chakra system, you can connect why you do the things you do to why your body is ill the way it is right now and to how your symptoms reveal themselves. It's all rooted within you.

Establishing Equilibrium will become a daily energetic process, much like brushing your teeth, that will guide you back to the healthiest and happiest version of you.

CHAPTER 1

The Principle of Polarity

"**EVERYTHING IS DUAL**; everything has poles; everything has its pair of opposites; . . . opposites are identical in nature, but different in degree."

This fourth great Hermetic principle was drawn from *The Kybalion*, written by the Three Initiates in 1908, and teaches that every manifested thing, experience, and feeling has two sides, two aspects, two opposites with varying degrees between the two opposites. This influential text expands on the ancient teachings of Hermes Trismegistus and describes how opposites are different in degree in that heat cannot be transformed into sharpness or loudness but transformed into cold only by lowering its vibration. By shifting vibration, this state is changed. This will be a critical understanding as we move forward and as you learn to shift your vibration and alter that state of your being. Healing is found in the shifting of the vibrational state.

It is in the understanding of this degree of opposites that your healing journey begins. When comparing two opposites, how far apart are they and to what extent are they opposite? What causes them to be opposite? Which opposite is "louder" and which opposite "quieter"?

The silent aspect of any situation often guides us to the foundational solution to the problem to bring about balance and healing.

What is not being seen, heard, or shown but exists as the opposite of what we see? Just as in the schoolyard, there can be loud bullies and silent children, often at odds with each other. Both children need attention in different ways and need to be guided toward a mutual solution but for different reasons. Often the child in greater distress is the silent child who needs exponentially more attention and healing than the louder and excessively vocal child. Collectively, the relationship between these children will not be healed without them reaching shared compromise, reconciliation, and balance.

The same is true for our energy system. Many use the presenting symptoms of each chakra as their focus for healing. However, true healing and balance is achieved only when you have healed and balanced the counter chakra, the silent chakra who partners with the presenting symptoms revealed by the chakra and whose emotional and energetic imbalance is at the root cause of the state of the body.

Within the chakra system, one energy center cannot exist without its partner. If one energy center exists, its opposite must exist.

Yin and yang together form a complete symbol and share in mutual energetic consumption when balanced. Together, these two opposing energies create a union of equal completeness. For one to exist, the other must also exist. Similarly, the chakra system is unified and whole but also must be healed in a complete and holistic manner through a balancing of the partnerships found within this system. When energetic equilibrium is established within the chakra system, there is even and equal distribution and absorption of energy between each center.

The principle of polarity will be our guide on our road map to healing. I have found this system to work very effectively with my clients, time and time again, and am thrilled to share this process here.

You are going to learn how *Establishing Equilibrium* is your road map to your healthiest, happiest, and most joyful self with specific markers to notice at every stop along your journey.

CHAPTER 2

The Holistic Understanding of Energy: Introducing Chakras

AFTER I WAS ATTUNED for Reiki for the very first time, we were placed in groups of three to take turns healing each other. I allowed my other two partners to go first as I watched the energy move and dance around their bodies. I was fascinated by the colors and the feeling of it all. When it was my turn to finally heal another person for the first time, the moment I touched him, I saw a pickax on his shoulder. This seemed crazy to me, but I listened to my intuition, cleared the energy, and continued on. Afterward, I told him about the ax I had seen on his shoulder. His jaw dropped and he said years prior, he and his dad had gone mountain climbing and along their climb, he had lost his pickax and could no longer ascend the mountain with the group. He said this moment in his life had halted his progress and he had been stuck since then because he let down his dad and himself. He had lost all confidence to move forward in relationships and his career. This is when I knew for sure I needed to immerse myself into all this wisdom and learn everything I could learn about healing our body, mind, soul, and energy. It was at that precise moment I confirmed for myself everything I had suspected: we hold our stories, our emotions, and the road map to our own healing within our own bodies.

What Are Chakras?

Remember when you were little and used to play with spinning tops? You would spin them, see how fast you could rotate them, and turn them in both directions. You might have noticed how fast or how slow they would spin. This simple toy offered sheer delight for hours.

Chakras function and appear similarly to spinning tops. There is energy within you, located in seven main central areas within your body. When healthy, this energy flows clockwise and nourishes the organs. Once the organs are fed, all seven chakras then release energy out of the body to create an electromagnetic field called the aura. (The aura also absorbs energy from its surroundings, but this will be addressed in greater detail in the next section.) This vortex of releasing energy looks much like a spinning top. The tip of the spinning top is found in the center of the chakra within the body. The circling energy widens as it moves out and away from the body. This energy can spin clockwise, or it can spin counterclockwise. If the energy spins clockwise, the energy is healthy. If it spins counterclockwise, this tells us the energy state within this chakra center is unhealthy. If the chakra is still, the energy is stagnant and not moving at all.

Why does this matter? Well, our chakras feed our organs with the energy supply they need to complete their primary function. We know which organs are fed by the chakra by looking at where the tip of the spinning energy releases from the body. The organs that are located within the range of the release point are the same organs nourished by this energy center.

Where are the chakras located, and what do they nourish?

The major chakras are energy centers located throughout the cavity of the body from perineum to crown. As mentioned above, the energy is released out of the body to create the aura. Chakras 1 and 7 have only one expelling/absorption energy vortex. In chakras 2 to 6, one energy vortex expands from the front of the body and one energy vortex expands from the back of the body, creating a dual release/absorption for each of these chakras. The energy expelling and absorption patterns for each chakra are as follows:

- **THE FIRST CHAKRA (ROOT CHAKRA)** is located at the very base of the cavity of the body, also called the pelvic floor and perineum. There is one vortex of releasing/absorbing energy that expands downward between the legs. This energy center feeds the adrenals, anus, and pelvic floor and lays the foundational energy for the health of the entire physical body.
- **THE SECOND CHAKRA (SACRAL CHAKRA)** is located two to three inches below the belly button. There are two energy expelling/absorption points that exist in this chakra, as will be the case in the subsequent chakras except for the crown chakra. The sacral chakra supports the kidneys, bladder, sexual organs, and gonads.
- **THE THIRD CHAKRA (SOLAR PLEXUS CHAKRA)** is located between your belly button and directly below your rib cage and supports your stomach, liver, pancreas, spleen, and gallbladder.
- **THE FOURTH CHAKRA (HEART CHAKRA)** is located in the center of your chest and nourishes your heart, thymus gland, and lungs.
- **THE FIFTH CHAKRA (THROAT CHAKRA)** is located at the V that makes up your collarbone and nourishes your thyroid, mouth, tongue, teeth, and ears.
- **THE SIXTH CHAKRA (THIRD EYE CHAKRA)** is located in between and just above your eyebrows and nourishes the pituitary gland and manages intuition and sleep patterns.
- **THE SEVENTH CHAKRA (CROWN CHAKRA)** is located just above the crown of your head and releases energy from the crown of your head as it opens up to the sky. This chakra nourishes the brain and thepineal gland.

What makes the chakra spin? How much joy did it bring you to have your spinning top whirl and move? How sad or exasperated did you feel when it stopped or wouldn't spin? Just as you experienced a multitude of emotions while playing with your spinning top, your emotions determine how fast or slow your chakras move. Your thoughts trigger your emotions, your emotions move energy, and energy manifests physically. When the chakras are not spinning, energy becomes stagnant and we become ill, dissatisfied, and anxious.

If we are upset or hurt, the energy moves slower. If we are in shock or trauma, the energy may become stagnant because it doesn't even know if it is safe to move. When we are in love and are feeling joyful, our energy is spinning, flowing, and moving . . . just like the squeals of delight when you were able to get a great turn out of your childhood spinning top.

Chakras themselves are energy transfer centers that send and absorb energy throughout the body to nourish our physical organs and cells with the vital energy necessary to maintain a healthy body. The energy absorbed in each chakra is received from the people we interact with daily, the food we eat, the sun we enjoy, and the five elements we experience: earth, water, fire, air, and ether. We enjoy the nutrients from the earth, we drink and cleanse our bodies with water, we receive healing from the sun, and we breathe in the air through oxygen. Ether is the lightest of the elements and refers to the space for our body to exist. If our bodies did not contain ether, they would collapse. It is ether that allows our lungs to remain structured throughout our exhale when there is no oxygen in them. It is ether that offers the space within our veins so that blood can flow through them. Without ether, or any of these elements, we would perish.

Chakras also hold certain life themes and purpose. Our emotional responses to these themes dictate the health and vitality of each energy center. We have seven major chakras in our bodies and thus seven major themes. We can think of these as floors of a building you can move among via an elevator. These seven chakras are located from our perineum to the crown of our head on a central line parallel to the spine. As an elevator opens to allow people in and out on each floor, so the chakras open and close to nourish the organs and cells in our body (of that "floor," figuratively speaking). The latent energy that resides in the root chakra is called Kundalini energy. As the Kundalini energy is awakened, it rises up through the chakras until it reaches the crown of the head. Much like an elevator, though, upon first awakening, the Kundalini energy may rise and fall several times until it flows past the heart chakra ultimately to connect with the crown chakra before joining with Universal energy through meditation. How much energy you experience in each chakra determines how healthy or unhealthy the organs may be.

Our cumulative health is based on the balance and integration of the three bodies that exist within us.

- **PHYSICAL BODY/GROSS BODY.** This is the body we know, see, feel, and touch. It is also the physical part of our building metaphor. It is our essence, and in qigong, it is referred to as *jing*.
- **SUBTLE/ASTRAL BODY.** This is the energy depicted by the energetic layer of the body where the chakras exist within and by the aura around the body. As you will learn, the aura senses your surroundings and can extend many feet/meters around you. This energy, or vitality, is termed *qi* in qigong.
- **CASUAL BODY.** This is the seed or the Universal force that allows the other two bodies to exist. This is where our higher self exists as well as our karma. This body encircles both of the other two bodies. This is where and how you see the aliveness in someone's eyes and experience this moment of deep connection with one glance. In qigong, this spirit witnessed in someone's eyes is referred to as *shen*.

All three of these bodies connect through the chakras in the realization of the physical manifestations of our thought, emotion, and energy. Intention arises out of the causal body. The force that creates this intention precedes even our thought.

Our thoughts trigger emotions, emotions move energy,
and energy manifests physically.
What we do with our energy matters.
If our energy isn't weak, our body doesn't weaken.

How the Chakra System Works

The chakras absorb energy from the food we eat. They also receive a continuous flow of energy from the sun, elements, and Universe. This is one reason why meditation is so important. It is an opportunity for us to open the skylight on the top floor of our "building" and allow the light to flow in. The energy from the chakras then feeds the organs connected to each chakra and uses it to perform the various body functions, such as breathing or heartbeats. Upon completion of the bodily function, the organ releases the unused energy out of each individual chakra. It is important to remember the law of conservation of energy, which states, "Energy can neither be created nor destroyed—only converted from one form of energy to another. This means that a system always has the same amount of energy, unless it's added from the outside." The release of energy follows this route.

The crown chakra and the root chakra release through only one energy outlet (the crown of the head and the perineum, respectively). The energy centers between the crown and the root have one release in the front of the body and one in the back of the body. It is believed the front release is connected to our feelings and our current life, while the energy released at the rear of the body is connected to our will and our past lives.

If your organs are healthy and functioning efficiently, less energy is needed to heal and complete their physical bodily tasks. As a result, a generous amount of energy should be released through the chakra connected to that particular organ area. For example, if your stomach and intestines are healthy, digestion should be easier, and plenty of energy should release from this chakra near the stomach.

If the organs connected to the energy center are not healthy as a result of our thoughts and emotions, more energy will be required to complete their bodily functions, so less energy will be released from the energy center. The energy is already used up performing its physical task. Returning to our building analogy, the air conditioner in the building draws in air from the outside, filters it, and sends it through the air ducts and into the rooms on each floor to provide cool air. The air conditioner also releases air outside of the building. The more muddied the air conditioning filter, the less air flows through the system of the air conditioning unit. This is why we often see a filter message on the thermostat when it's time to clean the filter. The cleaner the filter, the more the air flows.

As we travel together, you will learn how to "clean your own filters," discover what has been at the root of their congestion, and reconnect to your true source of power, resulting in parasympathetic dominance within your system.

Your energy system works in the same way, although it gives you a different sign than a clear "change filter" message. Your body's messages will look like pain and illness. Your body takes in energy through food, sunlight, and meditation, uses the energy to make your heart pump, your lungs breathe, and the cells to move throughout your body. The healthier your thoughts, emotions, and physical body (which would translate to a cleaner filter), the less energy it takes to perform their functions. The more unused energy released out of the chakra points, the more vibrant your aura becomes.

By determining how much energy is flowing out of your system, you are able to diagnose the clarity of your energy system.

Have you ever experienced the same struggle showing up in your life over and over again? Same problem, with a different face? Each energy center carries a unique life theme. When a certain theme continues to show up in your life repeatedly, such as a particular relationship pattern or illness, there's a good chance the energy in that particular chakra is imbalanced. By sourcing the problem and healing it, you are able to stop the incident from showing up repeatedly. As mentioned, we source the problem by discovering the event that started the thought process. Once you source the original thought that caused your emotions to be triggered, you will have the knowledge necessary to heal the emotion and thought causing the physical manifestation to occur.

Our thoughts trigger emotions, emotions move energy,
and energy manifests physically.
What we do with our energy matters.
If our energy isn't weak, our body doesn't weaken.

Chakra Themes

Here is a brief summary of the chakra themes in the order of how they are found in the body. We will expand upon each energy center in future chapters.

- **SEVENTH CHAKRA—CROWN:** The center of Universal consciousness and where we trust and know all things happen for good reason.
- **SIXTH CHAKRA—THIRD EYE:** The home of our intuition. This center sees beyond the physical into the energy of things.
- **FIFTH CHAKRA—THROAT:** The center that conveys our truth, feels truly heard, and the knowing that we deserve to be fully heard.
- **FOURTH CHAKRA—HEART:** The source of our love . . . love for self and love for all. This center allows us to give and receive freely with a knowing that we are worthy of receiving love.
- **THIRD CHAKRA—SOLAR PLEXUS:** Where we powerfully know who we are, what we stand for, and what we are meant to be and have the faith to bring it to fruition.
- **SECOND CHAKRA—SACRAL:** The warehouse of our emotions. This is where our emotional equilibrium exists. It is our center for desire, creativity, and connection.
- **FIRST CHAKRA—ROOT:** The center of acceptance, safety, security, and physical needs. This is where we experience feeling tribal acceptance (or need to heal

from tribal rejection), feel safe and secure, and feel that all needs physical—physical body and physical needs—are abundantly provided.

We will get into the fascinating detail of this as we address each chakra individually in the following chapters.

There are twenty-one minor chakras found throughout the body, including the hands, shoulders, and feet, along with eighty-six micro chakras, but that is not the focus of this book. The simple road map I have laid out for you allows you to focus on the seven major chakra centers and how they function together and bring holistic balance into your body and life. As you complete this process, you will come to know yourself in a way you may not have known before. I assure you, it will literally be life-changing.

CHAPTER 3

The Holistic Understanding of Energy: Your Energy

What we do with our energy matters.

WHAT IS TRUE for something as simple as blushing is true for all of our bodies' ailments, as well. As you begin to look deeper into your thoughts, emotion, and energy, you will begin to heal your body in ways you never knew were possible. And I understand if you feel overwhelmed or unsure about these new concepts. I get it. No problem.

I invite you to experiment with me. Read through and complete the exercises and journaling through and including all of chakra 1. Once you begin to incorporate these tools into your life, you will have verifiable proof this works. You will find that your sleeping improves, you are more present in conversations, and you may even stop losing your keys! You will begin to witness your life shifting.

This life shift begins with an awareness of how your thoughts and emotions affect your physical body. This understanding comes down to the following concept: the basis of my practice.

Our thoughts trigger emotions, emotions move energy,
and energy manifests physically.
What we do with our energy matters.
If our energy isn't weak, our body doesn't weaken.

I have found this to be undeniably and consistently true, both in my personal life and with every client I see. The chakra system allows us to reverse-engineer the solution from a physical ailment or emotional eruption by discerning the root cause of the problem. Once the origin of a thought is discovered, an energetic imprint can be illuminated based on the feeling that arose from that situation. The reemergence of this imprint can be followed throughout the course of your life as the feeling and situation continue to repeat themselves until the imprint is healed. You can use your tools and techniques to heal those imprints and injuries to reach a healthier state. One little thought that arose, maybe in a brief time of trauma, possibly triggered a series of connected events within your body—an emotional release followed by an energetic release, culminating in a physical manifestation. You may be surprised what the root cause of your illness turns out to be. Often, many of my clients are amazed. By utilizing this system as your own step-by-step guide and decoder, you can heal your body and your life. In doing so, you will not only shift your health but your entire reality—thoughtfully, emotionally, energetically, and ultimately physically.

Let's describe how the simple example of blushing to see how this works.

You find yourself at an associate's party and you are politely making small talk when suddenly a good friend enters the circle and reveals something personal that perhaps the circle of colleagues may not have known. This ignites a thought: *Oh, that's embarrassing.* This thought of embarrassment triggers the emotion of embarrassment and you find yourself *feeling* embarrassed. The embarrassment emotion shifts the energetic vibration of your cells to the frequency of embarrassment, which in turn launches your physical cells into motion to move the blood and energy to your face and chest where you then . . . blush.

Our thoughts trigger emotions, emotions move energy,
and energy manifests physically.
What we do with our energy matters.
If our energy isn't weak, our body doesn't weaken.

Whether we are blushing or experiencing pain, our thoughts and emotions are moving our energy to create a physical response. But what is energy, anyway?

"An atom is 99.99999 percent energy and 0.00001 percent physical substance," says Dr. Joe Dispenza, author of *Breaking the Habit of Being Yourself: How to Lose Your Mind and Create a New One* and *Evolve Your Brain: The Science of Changing Your Mind*.

According to Bruce Lipton, best-selling author of *Biology of Belief: Unleashing the Power of Consciousness, Matter & Miracles*, "The average 'membrane potential' for a cell is 70 millivolts OR .07 volts (this is the electrical charge difference between the inside of the cell, separated by the cell membrane, from the charge just outside the cell membrane). There are 50 trillion cells X .07 volts = 3.5 trillion volts."

3.5 trillion volts of energy—this is a powerful force of energy to be coursing through us all at once! Imagine what extraordinary things you could accomplish by directing all that energy toward one object, one mission, or one purpose.

Truly amazing things could happen.

Alternatively, what happens if that amount of energy remains scattered, disheveled, or at the mercy of our emotions? Well, the energy could manifest as several different physical ailments as it bumps around trying to find its way through the body. It might look a lot like overwhelm and stress.

Our nervous system plays a key role in our health, and our body has four different parts to its nervous system, essentially the body's electrical wiring for its building.

1. The cranial nervous system connects the brain to the eyes, mouth, ears, and other parts of the head.

2. The central nervous system is the command center of the body, consisting of the brain, spinal cord, and retina.

3. The peripheral nervous system consists of clusters of neurons that connect the central nervous system to our arms, hands, feet, and legs.

4. The autonomic nervous system is composed of nerves that connect the central nervous system to the lungs, heart, stomach, intestines, bladder, and sexual organs. This system is divided into three parts:

   a. The sympathetic nervous system stimulates our fight-or-flight response, which is activated when the body feels threatened. It speeds up the heart rate to pump more blood to the limbs, relaxes the bladder to lighten our load so we can run faster, and dilates the pupils because more mental effort is being used.

   b. The parasympathetic nervous system calms us and maintains normal body functions, inhibiting overuse. For example, this system controls the bladder and slows down heart rate.

   c. The enteric nervous system (ENS) is confined to the gastrointestinal tract, often called the "second brain."

Within the chakra system, it is understood there are three main energy lines, termed *nadis*, that also correlate with the sympathetic and parasympathetic nervous system. The *sushumna nadi* runs through the center of the body, parallel to the spine, while the *pingala nadi* and *ida nadi* flow crisscross back and forth around and through the central line, meeting at each chakra. This model has also been popularly used as the medical symbol, the caduceus.

Please refer to the appendix for a more detailed description of this energy system according to tantric tradition. For the purpose of establishing equilibrium, this movement of energy is the most important concept to grasp. My goal is to create a streamlined and efficient means for you to heal and obtain a life that feels empowered and joyous.

While we have drawn the illustration of how the "electrical wiring" functions in your body, each stop of your journey along your road map will teach you how to maintain your electrical wiring, keep your energy centers clear, and harness and balance the source that feeds the energy into this wiring to maintain a state of parasympathetic dominance.

When our energy is imbalanced, our sympathetic nervous system can be hyperactivated, leading to a state of fight or flight, along with the aforementioned symptoms of high blood pressure, poor digestion, and loss of bladder control. When our energy is balanced, our parasympathetic nervous system activates and reaches a place of "rest and digest." Our heart rate slows, our blood pressure lowers, healthy digestion returns, and our organs are functionally more efficient. The techniques you will learn will give you a myriad of choices and options to incorporate this balance and healing into your everyday life so you can live an empowered life that allows your parasympathetic nervous system to regulate your system.

CHAPTER 4

The Holistic Understanding of Energy: Your Aura and the Energetic Road Map to Healing

EACH MAIN CHAKRA RELEASES ENERGY from its own center and creates one layer of your aura. Thus, our aura is made up of seven layers; you can imagine a large gossamer forming around your body. Kirlian photography uses sensitive equipment to read the energy field surrounding a person and their vibrational frequency. In these photographs, the aura can be seen. See chapter 46 to learn how to see it for yourself.

Your aura's function is to sense your surroundings, process what is happening, and bring the knowledge discovered back to your body and chakras. Your aura can range from half an inch to more than sixty-five feet wide, depending on many different factors.

Each layer of your aura is produced from the energetic release of each of the seven main chakras contained within the body. If your internal energy center is imbalanced, you will also have an imbalance in the way you see and experience the world. When this stagnation takes effect, the filter by which you are bringing information back to your system becomes clogged. You will continue to see experiences, but they will be tainted by the filter of your imbalanced auric layer. What you are sensing may not be the truth of what is *actually* happening.

It certainly is *your* truth, yes. But is your truth as clear as it can be? Is your perception really accurate about the truth of the situation? Or do you think your health and your life might be better served if you spent some time clearing and balancing your energy centers so you can discover the truth beyond any misguided perception caused by an auric distortion?

We've all experienced situations with people where we think to ourselves, *What are they thinking? How can they possibly be interpreting this situation this way?* This is why. It *is* their truth they are experiencing. They are merely determining their truth via the stagnant energy filters in their chakra system and aura. The more distorted the filter, the more distorted the aura, the more distorted the interpretation of the truth, leaving you with a distorted interpretation of reality.

You will learn how to clean your filters and have a clearer interpretation of the events taking place in your life. My hope is this will help you to have more compassion for those whose perspectives seem a bit askew. We know now it's energetic, and as you shift your energy, it will have a resounding effect on their system as well.

Aura size can influence perception, too. The larger your aura, the greater the amount of information and energy you take in. The aura wraps around our body 360 degrees. If someone's aura is nine feet wide, the result is a person gathering energy, emotion, or intelligence from anyone who walks through their nine-foot-wide aura, resulting in a twenty-eight-foot circumference of intel. Taking in this much information and taking on all these external emotions can lead to anxiety, nervousness, and depression. The result of a larger aura can be your own energy dispersed too widely, and you are left feeling scattered, ungrounded, and anxious. You will learn how to master your aura toward the end of this road map once you have greater understanding of the chakra system and how it is affecting your life.

Here's a great example of how aura healing works. I had a client, a young boy, who often had tantrums at school and at home. When he came to my office, we used the same *Establishing Equilibrium* techniques you will learn on your journey here to determine the size of his aura. His aura was over 10 feet wide. This meant he was taking in the energy and emotions from the students in his classroom and all the energy surrounding him within a circumference of 31.4 feet, and he was experiencing and absorbing energy and emotion 5 feet in every direction. His emotional and energetic body couldn't handle all that energy. His body needed to release this energy, so he did so the only way he knew how—through tantrums. He and I worked together, and he learned all the road map tools and mastered his aura.

He has now been able to have fewer tantrums and outbursts. If you have children who are prone to having tantrums, it could be they are just energetically sensitive and need to learn the tools to manage their energy. Make it a fun game and teach your young ones the *Establishing Equilibrium* principles. It will be a gift of a lifetime for you all.

What belief or truth have you been holding on to from a stagnant auric layer that ignited a thought, triggered an emotion, and moved energy that has now made you physically ill?

Our thoughts trigger emotions, emotions move energy,
and energy manifests physically.
What we do with our energy matters.
If our energy isn't weak, our body doesn't weaken.

Armed with all this information, you are about to learn the tools and techniques to clear and balance your chakras. This rebalance will shift your perception of the world and your role in it by empowering and strengthening each of your energy connection points, aura, and health.

CHAPTER 5

The Holistic Understanding of Energy: Where Is My Energy Stagnant? A Chakra Questionnaire

YOU WILL BEGIN to learn more about everything encompassed in this questionnaire, but it is a good idea to begin this process with a general idea of where your energy may be stagnant. Just as you would before a trip, circle which questions resonate with you to map out where you need to go on this journey.

Root Chakra
Have you been . . .

- constantly losing your keys or double-booking your calendar?
- dealing with a loss of smell?
- struggling with hemorrhoids?
- experiencing multiple miscarriages?

Sacral Chakra

Have you been . . .

- struggling with bladder infections or erectile dysfunction?
- feeling overemotional?
- blaming others for everything?
- experiencing a swollen tongue or sore throat?

Solar Plexus Chakra

Have you been . . .

- struggling with eye issues?
- suffering from digestive problems?
- dealing with toe or feet fungus?
- acting overly aggressive?

Heart Chakra

Have you been . . .

- struggling with skin issues?
- experiencing high/low blood pressure?
- dealing with pain in your hands?
- a people pleaser?

Throat Chakra

Have you been . . .

- experiencing ear infections or laryngitis?
- too afraid to speak up for yourself?
- struggling with thyroid issues?
- dealing with canker sores in your mouth?

Third Eye Chakra

Have you been . . .

- dizzy or feeling out of touch with your life?
- feeling overly sensitive to your surroundings?
- experiencing headaches?

Crown Chakra

Have you been . . .

- experiencing deep grief about world events?
- ruminating in your thoughts?
- felt fearful or anxious?

Notice which chakra holds the most circles for you. Our goal with this process is to balance all of our energy centers, but it is helpful to begin with this initial starting point before diving in deeper.

CHAPTER 6

The Toolbox: The Science
Behind the Techniques

THIS CHAPTER SHARES with you the reasoning behind why I encourage you to incorporate proven tools and techniques into your life that will help you heal your body, your emotions, and your life. This chapter is the *why* chapter and the left-brain chapter. There is a great amount of science that backs my recommendations, and my personal and clinical success supports you giving these a try. I understand that, for many, there is a strong need to understand the motivation behind each of these ideas before getting started. I have provided the science and my personal interpretation here, hoping it will satisfy your questioning and inspire you to experiment with these powerful tools. These tools function like weights in the gym. We use them to strengthen our energy; we do not become dependent on them. We allow them to nourish us and raise our vibration so that we walk around with "in-shape," powerful, strong energy.

Color and Clothes

The healing mechanism of chromotherapy utilizes the power of the visible spectrum of light to heal physical diseases. This healing practice dates back to ancient Egypt around 1500 BC, when Egyptians built solarium rooms within their pyramids. The structure was built with a colored crystal embedded in the frame, designed to reflect sunlight through the crystal to cast colored light into the room for a specific therapeutic purpose. Light is energy, and color is the result of energy combining with matter. Each color is made up of a specific wavelength and frequency that helps balance our energy. When we wear a specific color, we absorb that color's energy frequency and strengthen the area of our body where the vibrational frequency is a match.

Element

In Ayurvedic philosophy (an alternative medicine system that treats body, mind, and spirit in conjunction with each other), there are five elements upon which the Universe is built. The five great elements are earth, water, fire, air, and ether. All these elements are found in the body, and they also nourish our bodies physically, energetically, and metaphorically. The elements begin in your root chakra, beginning with the densest element: earth. As you rise through the system, the elements—water, fire, air, and ether—become less dense until they reach the lightest of them all. This is a very powerful tool to help diagnose the body's ailments and bring continual constitutional balance into it.

Our Five Senses

Our senses allow us to enjoy a fully integrated sensory experience in life. Sound energy moves slower than light energy, so we see something happen before we hear it happen. Our taste and touch require the object of interest to be touching, or almost touching, the body. Our body can smell from far away and uses this signal to determine its level of safety, i.e. the smell of fire or a skunk. The first five energy centers are connected to one of our five senses. It is important to develop a deep understanding of this connection to our senses, as it will be one of the most important diagnostic tools in healing your body.

Organ of Action

Just as our senses are felt through one of our physical body parts, each of our energy centers is experienced through an organ of action in our life. This organ is how we experience each energy center physically in this life. Knowing the organ of action for each energy center helps guide us to the root cause of our illness, and you will begin to find signs and symptoms manifesting in these organs when their corresponding energy center is disrupted.

Food

As Greek physician Hippocrates preached, "Let food be thy medicine, and let medicine be thy food."

Certainly, we need nutrition for our bodies to function properly. We also need the energy produced by nature's food to help heal our body. The food we pick freshly off a tree will have the greatest amount of life force energy contained within it. Like all things cut off from source, it begins to lose the life force energy the more time it spends off its energy source. As we consume the freshly picked food, our body absorbs the energy and completes its function. The higher the frequency, the healthier the food is for our body. This road map will offer different food recommendations for a myriad of reasons, but in every recommendation, it is preferable to choose the most freshly picked and organic food available. Our energy matches the vibration of the food or drink we consume, so what we consume either upregulates or downregulates our energetic frequency. What we eat matters not just physically but also energetically.

Essential Oils

Essential oils are extracts derived from plants. In the production process, certain parts of the plants are pressed or steamed to release the compound necessary to create the oil. Essential oils have the capability to cross the cellular membrane of the cells within our body directly. Only oxygen, carbon dioxide, alcohol, and some drugs are able to perform this same function. This allows for the essential oils to work powerfully and effectively on the cellular level and can heal our physical, energetic, and emotional states. Essential oils are absorbed through the skin and into the bloodstream and then metabolized by the liver.

In 1910, French chemist René-Maurice Gattefossé discovered the effectiveness of lavender when he was badly burned in a cosmetic lab and put his hand in the closest liquid to him—lavender essential oil. He was amazed by how quickly his burn healed and began his lifelong research on the effectiveness of essential oil.

Much research and testing remain to be completed on the overall effectiveness of essential oils. When you are deciding which oil would best suit you, you may use a simple form of manual muscle testing. Muscle testing is a form of applied kinesiology that uses the body's energy system to deem whether something is beneficial for it. A simple standing sway test will help you find the essential oil that is best for you. Stand with your toes forward and feet shoulder-width apart. Ground your energy. (See chapter 12 for my grounding technique.) Hold only one essential oil bottle up to your solar plexus. If your body sways forward, this essential oil is beneficial to you. If your body pushes backward, it is not beneficial for you at this time. Muscle testing is an excellent way to test the effectiveness of not only essential oils on your body, but also food and supplements.

When you are applying the oil to the chakra, rub the oil on with your right hand clockwise to energize the deficient chakra and counterclockwise to decongest the excessive chakra. Make three to five slow circles on each chakra. For chakras 2, 3, 4, 5, and 6, apply the oil on the front of the body and the back of the body to ensure you are rubbing oils on the chakras that leave the front and back side of the body.

Crystals

The use of crystals dates back to the Mesopotamian age, almost six thousand years ago. Crystals heal by emitting the positive energy frequency of the particular crystal while absorbing negative energy when placed on the body. This helps clear any blockages, so that our body's energy flows more freely and our body heals. This is also how crystals can be very helpful to shift energy in physical places. As you are working with specific crystals, you may choose to program your crystal for your specific purpose. Most crystals are made up of a crystalline structure that can hold information. By setting clear intention for what you need from your crystal, you can direct the energy to a clear and focused purpose.

It is important to distinguish the use of crystals as a strengthener of your energy, rather than a crutch for your energy. Think of using crystals like as you would think of lifting weights. You utilize the weights to strengthen your muscles. You do not continue to carry the weights around throughout your day. It is unnecessary to carry them around because you've built the muscles. While crystal therapy may call for you to carry your crystals around throughout your day, it is not because you are dependent on this crystal. It is because you need to absorb the crystal's energy for that quantity of time for your energy frequency to reach its necessary state. Our entire book is about strengthening your energy, and we do not want to give our power away to any outside object. Crystals are your energetic barbell set and will train your energy system to up-level to its frequency. When your energetic frequency reaches a new level, it will be time for a different crystal "barbell" set.

Mantra

Sound can affect our bodies positively or negatively and is an established part of many kinds of meditation. Mantra, a repeated word or chant, helps balance the left and right hemispheres of the brain and ignites healing energy to flow. According to Jonathan Goldman, author of *The 7 Secrets of Sound Healing*, "Such chanting will also help oxygenate the brain, reduce our heart rate, blood pressure and assist in creating calm brainwave activity." Jonathan Goldman has also produced a very helpful phone app called Chakra Tuner that applies the sound and mantra healings should you want to download it to use in your practice.

The National Center for Biotechnology Information (NCBI) ran a study and found when their participants sat in silent meditation utilizing mantras, their brain activity quieted, confirming this with the use of MRI and blood-oxygen-level-dependent (BOLD) contrast imaging to determine the state of the brain. Chanting also tones the vagus nerve, which is critical in building our resiliency to stress.

Sound changes our molecular structure. Our bodies are made up of two-thirds water. Researcher Masaru Emoto conducted an experiment where he exposed water to negative messaging, prayers, mantras, and positive messaging. The ice crystals in water that received the negative messaging produced tarlike and horrendous-looking formations while the water that received the prayers and mantras produced exquisitely beautiful formations. What we tell ourselves matters. It not only calms us, it changes us.

If you would like company reciting your mantras, log onto www.LoveHealThrive.com and you will find recorded mantras for each chakra. We can complete the mantras together.

Please refer to the appendix for more detailed information on the *bija* mantras.

Environmental Shift

Allowing the physical energy around our living environment to flow smoothly and be in energetic balance is extremely important. A cluttered home often represents a cluttered mind. Leaning into each of the elements and drawing more of them into your home in a balanced manner will bring balance into your life.

Yoga

According to Bessel van der Kolk, clinical psychiatrist, in his interview "Overcome Trauma with Yoga," trauma is the result of your body getting stuck in heartache and in an emotional state that is intolerable. Yoga can help alleviate such emotional trauma by reestablishing a timeline. When you are experiencing trauma, you may feel that it will never come to an end. In yoga, when you are in an uncomfortable pose, you breathe through it and it does come to an end. Thus, this practice reestablishes the understanding that "this too shall pass." Utilizing the breath for a set number of breaths teaches students they can use their breath to endure pain, building a sense of confidence and reconnecting to a sense of self once they've successfully made it through the uncomfortable yoga position. According to van der Kolk, a steady yoga practice for a traumatized person is more effective than any medication studied. I offer yoga positions for each energy center. There are many great YouTube videos that walk you through each step of the pose. I encourage you to look up each pose and follow along with your favorite yoga teacher.

Archangels

Coming from the Greek *archangelos*, meaning "chief angel," archangels are believed to be extensions of God and to aid in the healing of our energy, body, and lives. Archangel Michael is written
about in the Bible, Torah, and Quran. Archangels aid in healing a
particular life theme or energy vibration in our body and are very
much connected to our personal experience. Often, when we can
let go and hand our struggle over to something greater than us,
we place ourselves in a receptive mode, and once we do, healing
occurs. I have found this concept to work regardless of religious
affiliation. This healing functions on an energetic frequency. The
different archangel names can be looked at simply as different
frequencies. So if archangels do not resonate with you, you can
approach this concept as the name of an energetic frequency.

Ten-Second Rescue

My personal belief system in all spiritual practices is that whatever
tool you use needs to fit into your life. Sometimes we have time
to sit and meditate for thirty minutes, but if you do not have that
time, or are in an extreme emotional moment, I want to give you
the ten-second rescue. This is a tool or technique that can be utilized on the spot to give you an immediate energy shift to get you
through the moment. Ideally, your long-term habits and practices
will remedy the need for a ten-second rescue because you will have
shifted your energy frequency so high you will no longer attract
situations that call for a rescue.

Homework

You got to do the reps. Neural connections are strengthened through repetition. The homework given in each chapter offers you an opportunity to incorporate that chapter's learning into your everyday life, so you begin to master it and adjust it to best fit into your lifestyle and, ultimately, create a positive habit.

Journal

As we journal, we begin to release our emotions and detach from them. We become a witness to our story, and the identity we used to attach to the story becomes less personal. We must tell our story over and over again to heal our life grief. Journaling is a powerful way to detail our story. Scientific evidence also suggests other benefits to journaling. A renowned expert in this field, University of Texas at Austin psychologist James Pennebaker, believes journaling strengthens immune cells and reduces stress. Journaling also improves memory and mental sharpness, boosting both the analytical and rational left brain, as well as the more creative, intuitive right brain.

God

On occasion, I will reference God in this book. This word can mean what God means to you: an all-knowing source of wisdom or something that loves you as unconditionally as a puppy cuddling with you. I have suggested to clients who do not believe in a God to refer to this space as their sacred center. Once you find your internal sacredness, you receive all that you need regardless of belief. Choose your own definition that feels best for you here, within or outside these parameters.

CHAPTER 7

The Childhood Connection to Your First Chakra Marker: The Root Chakra

EVERY SUMMER, my family would pack into our station wagon with a bag of white bread and a cooler of bologna, cheese, and mustard to make our annual pilgrimage from California to North Carolina to visit my grandparents.

The summer before I started kindergarten, we drove along Interstate 40 through emergency broadcasts of tornadoes and bolts of lightning illuminating the broad skies that reached forever across the desert flatlands. We spent hours in the hot, sticky back seat, comprised of one long bench, playing Mad Libs and the license plate game on the way to Grandmother's house. Looking back, I realize these natural disasters were probably warning signs and were grounding me so I could be prepared for what was to come.

One night during the middle of our visit, I was put to bed before the sun had even set. Being the third child with much older siblings, this never even happened at home. You can imagine my disillusionment at being put to bed early while visiting the East Coast where our circadian rhythm was set to a bedtime three hours later. As my head rested upon on the pillow, a ray of light squeezed in between the window sill and drawn window shade to beam directly into my eyes as I wallowed in confusion and frustration at my early tuck-in. About thirty minutes after being tucked into my sleeping bag with my blanket and blue bird, I surrendered to my wakefulness and walked back out into the TV room where my family sat eating ice cream sandwiches. It was as if time stood still for all of us. I walked in and it felt as though they were chewing their treats in slow motion while their eyes widened by being "caught" by me. My tiny little body showed up as a painful reminder to them that you can never "get away" with anything.

My grandmother said, "We didn't have enough for you, so we sent you to bed."

I ran to my room, sobbing. My mom came in to comfort me and told me she would share hers with me and brought me out to the TV room, but that ice cream sandwich was flavorless to me. You will learn why in chapter 16.

The five-year-old me struggled to believe I could be outcast like that over ice cream or that ice cream was more important than being a cohesive tribe. This was a powerful childhood imprint of exclusion that took years to heal.

From that point on, I had challenges when it came to trusting groups of people. I did have groups in elementary, junior high, high school, college, and adult life (prior to my conscious healing) where in pictures, all looked amazing. But, as soon as I had to trust the members of the group, I would find myself petrified, believing I would be excluded and no one would invite me to their "ice cream party."

The root chakra is one of the major healing agents for your physical healing as well as healing your original programming derived from past-life physical ailments that present themselves in your current body. It is the physical body mastery point. As you will learn, each of our energy centers manages a different part of our physical body and our emotional and energetic body. When this crucial energy center is strong and powerful, our weakness and illness begin to subside. In this chapter, you will learn themes associated with this chakra that will help you begin to feel more safe and secure, and in the next chapter you'll learn many techniques to balance your energy so that you have fewer days that result in forgetfulness or feeling scattered.

The first chakra is the root chakra, the *muladhara* in Sanskrit. It is situated at the base of your spine, pelvic floor, and the perineum, which is the area between the anus and the scrotum or vulva. While the textbook definition of the perineum may mean the outer skin or the deeper structures involved that support your urogenital and gastrointestinal systems, my focal point for you when I reference this area is the inner side of the perineum—the deepest and innermost area at the base of the body's cavity. This energy gathers and can be felt three vertebrae high up from the coccyx.

The main themes of the first chakra are about experiencing a physical body in the physical world, tribal acceptance, safety, and security—being provided for in practical, physical terms, such as food, shelter, and so on. Tribal acceptance is the primal emotional welcoming necessary into a group or family that helps us feel safe, secure, and protected within a group. "Safety in numbers," a theory that in biology allows animals to remain safer in a pack and in humans, dates back to the book of Proverbs from the Bible, which teaches that as we receive collective wisdom from a group, we remain safer and are more successful. As a result, the root chakra is the home of our family of origin issues or security. If we haven't healed our family of origin exclusions or emotional turmoil, physical symptoms begin to arise in this area—emotionally, energetically, and physically.

The antidote to healing our family origin issues around acceptance and safety is by welcoming in the acceptance, safety, and security of a higher power, in whatever terms that means for you. Your higher power can be anything deemed appropriate for you. It can be your version of God, the Universe, or your highest benevolent self. This center is about a higher-powered form of acceptance, safety, and security within this physical world. Knowing you are exactly where you're meant to be right now in this moment and that you are exactly where you are meant to be . . . always.

This is the place of exhale and safety. When this energy center is strong, you will feel provided for. You will feel safe. You will feel secure. You will feel accepted. You will know there is no lack. When we can *be* in this place and sit in this space, feeling the certainty of safety, security, and tribal acceptance, we manifest a safer, more secure, and protected external world. Because these will be the supporting facts our aura will filter through to us. We find the proof in our environment for which we seek and like attracts like. Your internal world defines and corresponds with your external world.

But you have to *feel* it here first, internally. I mean, *really* feel it. Here's how.

Sit in this space and *feel* a higher-powered acceptance, knowing you are the only version of you that exists and God is especially protecting you through the blessings that disguise themselves as challenges. You are exactly who God made you to be, right here, right now. Everything happens in perfect time. Trust 100 percent that you are exactly where you are meant to be. Rest in this acceptance because when you feel it here *first*, inside, you will begin to feel more accepted in your external world.

If you are in a crisis in your life and you are feeling unsafe, bring your attention to the deepest, innermost part of the cavity of your body and rest your focus there until you begin to feel safe. Feelings of safety will ignite here, and as a result, feelings of safety will begin to show up in your external world. Rest in this center in the higher-powered security that exists here, trusting you are always provided for in this life. God is providing for you. If this feels inaccessible to you at first, set intention to feel this type of pure acceptance, and it will come, allowing compassion and forgiveness to flow through you to the people who hurt you.

If you feel you are not being provided for at this moment or are experiencing lack—lack of money, lack of acceptance, lack of safety—focus your attention on your root chakra and perineum area and recount the ways in which you *are* being blessed in your life. You may find you are being provided for only in a certain direction. Perhaps you have money but no true acceptance from family or friends. Or you are experiencing a lack of money but acceptance from friends. Examining where you are feeling abundant can be looked at as bread crumbs that can lead you to your life purpose.

Here is where we can make the most of our energy system.

Energy follows attention. As you begin to recognize some abundance here in one root chakra theme—abundant provision—this will "prime the pump" and allow the energy to flow to the other themes held in this energy center. What resides inside will manifest outside. When you experience the abundance of Divine security here, you will manifest an abundant experience of physical security in your outside world. When you feel Divine safety, follow those bread crumbs to your own secure destiny, and you will begin experiencing a life more grounded, directed, and abundant.

If you are still struggling, you can set an intention to feel safe, secure, and provided for by the Divine. Intention is powerful. As we set our intention, we direct our energy and our energy responds. Do not worry if this feeling is not there yet. You will intend it to be there, and it will manifest in time. Have you ever intended to call a friend and then they called you first before you could call them? Intention is powerful and changes every aspect of our life. We attract what we think about.

When you welcome this higher power into this energy center, and feel it—Divine acceptance, Divine safety, and Divine security—you will have a deep sense of belonging in your life. Over time and with practice, you will begin to feel safer and more secure in all the physical means in your life—acceptance from your loved ones, money, and shelter. You will know, with full certainty, that you are being provided for every moment. As you reach this state, your illness will begin to melt away. The fight-or-flight response in your body will be soothed and you will experience a state of peace and stillness as your body feels safe enough and trusting enough to finally truly exhale and let go.

One of my favorite spiritual leaders is Panache Desai and a phrase of his that I treasure is "Lack is whack!"

Anytime I have a moment of my own worry creeping in and feeling less than provided for, or I worry that there won't be enough of something—money, clients, time—I shout this simple phrase, "Lack is whack!" It instantly shifts my energy and brings me back into my belief system that there is always enough because we attract more of what we focus on. I find myself calm, trusting, and secure that I am on my right path.

Our blessings are not like pie. We don't just get one piece. There is no limit to the blessings we can all receive . . . all at the same time. We always find supporting detail to reinforce the story we tell ourselves, negative or positive. Our aura filters it based on the clarity of our energy center.

Our thoughts trigger emotions, emotions move energy,
and energy manifests physically.
What we do with our energy matters.
If our energy isn't weak, our body doesn't weaken.

We are always provided for, at every moment.

For example, in the process of publishing my book *Angel Birthdays*, I was in search of an illustrator. Many people had offered connections to friends. However, none were the right fit but I knew the right one would come to me at the right time. I hosted an *Angel Birthdays* website launch party to grow an audience.

One of the attendees said, "I need to connect you to my friend."

I had heard this many times before but this time it felt different. The next day, this friend showed me the illustrator's latest book. It was perfect. I connected with the illustrator, discussed the project, and received a quote from her. As much as I was ready to bring this book to life, I did not have that amount of money . . . but I knew not to worry. I knew the Universe would provide. I just wasn't sure how . . . yet.

About a week later, I found a note I had left for myself in a notebook to follow up on an inherited IRA (individual retirement account) from my late brother. I thought to myself, *Yeah, I wonder why I haven't received any account information over the last few months since submitting that rollover paperwork.* I called the company. They had no record of the rollover paperwork, which they said was strange because they never lose paperwork. (It was as if I could see the Universe nudging and winking at me!) So they asked me if I wanted to roll it over or cash it out. Guess how much was in the account?

Yep! The precise amount I needed for the illustrator! Not only did the Universe fund my illustrations but it also provided a wonderful legacy for my brother's IRA.

And that's how it works.

I could tell this story over and over with several different circumstances, from receiving random checks in the mail for amounts precisely matching bills owed down to the cent, to the perfect person showing up at the perfect moment. It's happened so many times. Lack is truly whack! Perhaps it's happened to you, too? I can't wait to hear your stories of provision. Join our community on-line at www.LoveHealThrive.com and share your stories.

The Universe provides, but we never know how or where. We simply must expect it to provide, without question, because it does. If you find yourself anxious and worrying, find a way to keep trusting. Look for small examples—finding a needed item on sale in the store, having a loan repaid you were worried about, or hearing from a friend you wanted to contact. Utilize the above perspective or integrate the techniques explained later in this chapter.

If you don't feel trusting, return to your root chakra and rest there until you feel as though you can trust. In this space, you are being asked to remain in a state of Divine welcoming. Upon welcoming the Divine and accepting the blessings of your life internally, your external world will shift.

First Chakra Description

How do we know if the energy in our root chakra is excessive, deficient, or balanced?

Excessive Root Chakra Energy

Have you ever excluded someone for your own benefit? Have you ever placed material gain over relationships? Have you ever gone to a lunch buffet with someone who piles more and more on their plate and goes back for more . . . just because they can? Have you ever watched someone take more than they need, being thoughtless about what others need?

When the root chakra is excessive, the symptoms of being egotistical, selfish, materialistic, divisive, and greedy arise. Your physical body tends to be more obese. Excessive greed also infers there is a belief in lack that the Universe will not provide when necessary and behavior of being cheap can also arise here.

Deficient Root Chakra Energy

Have you ever had a group of friends where one friend keeps losing their keys, forgets what they're saying, or seems nervous about any plans the group makes? I doubt that friend continues to be invited or maybe the group simply dissolves because no one wants to hurt anyone's feelings by continuing to meet without that person. Perhaps it's even been you. Incorporating a few of these chapter's techniques will help you have an improved group experience and perhaps a repeat invitation for the next night out.

Those with deficient root chakra energy tend to be fearful, underweight, spacey, insecure, procrastinating, and frail with a low sex drive. The adrenal system will be exhausted, and they will find themselves in a state of "fight or flight."

Balanced Root Chakra Energy

Have you ever had a day where everything feels amazing? A day where you feel grounded, present, relaxed, prosperous, stable, and have limitless energy. Your worry begins to fade. You enjoy being in the physical world in a physical body. You know you are safe and provided for, and you feel grounded, calm, and present. You know there is no lack. Or, if thoughts of lack do present themselves, they are quickly remedied with thoughts of abundance and security. It is days like these when you've allowed your root chakra to become your sanctuary, filled with safety, security, and presence. This is what it feels like to have a balanced root chakra.

Location

The location of this energy center is the perineum that expands from the base of the spine and pelvic floor, three vertebrae up the spine in approximate depth across the cavity of the body. For people with cervixes, explore whether the perineum or the underside of your cervix is your preferred focal point. When using the root chakra meditation, choose to focus on your perineum one day and, the following day, choose to focus on the underside of your cervix. Feel the difference for yourself and choose only one area on which to focus your attention. Regardless, the energy depth can be felt as approximately three vertebrae deep.

This is, in part, how the root chakra imbalance contributes to experiencing a miscarriage. When the root chakra energy is full, balanced, and expansive, it supports the underside of the cervix. You can imagine the cervix resting on a lawn or nutrient-dense garden that supports it. When the root chakra energy is stagnant and does not provide a strong foundation for the second chakra, there is not enough energy to keep the fetus held energetically in the body. If you have experienced multiple miscarriages, it might be helpful to take a closer look at the healings offered in chapter 12 and incorporate these techniques. Did you have a traumatic childhood? Were you excluded? Did you feel unsafe between the ages of zero and seven years old? By healing the emotions and the energy in the root chakra, it is possible to transform your body and birthing experience.

The clients that I have worked with who have endured multiple miscarriages all had early childhood trauma. While this might not always be the case, it is something worth investigating.

If you've been worried about maintaining your pregnancy or have lived through a heartbreaking miscarriage or multiple miscarriages, my hope is this wisdom provides some answers and a road map to a worry-free pregnancy and beautiful childbirth. While some focus can be directed toward balancing the second chakra, focus first on the root chakra to nourish and fortify the energy beneath the second chakra to assist with a healthy pregnancy. As you will learn later, focus on the root chakra's counter chakra will be beneficial as well.

Physical Correlations in the Body

The physical correlation section of each chapter details which organs of the body are fed by the energy offered from each chakra. These correlations help you diagnose which chakra may be experiencing an imbalance. If you show physical symptoms in one of the following organs or areas, it would be prudent to study this chapter and its remedies with more in-depth attention. The root chakra's physical correlations include the perineum, spinal column, rectum, pelvic floor, legs, and adrenals.

Color and Clothes

We must build a strong and sturdy foundation for our energy system. The energy in the root chakra is the slowest and deepest frequency of all the energy centers. Our life in the physical world moves slower than our energetic life because we do not have the physical containment to slow us down. This energy center is about us living in our physical world, and our energy needs to match this. This energy center emits a frequency like that emitted by the color red and is measured at approximately 430 hertz, according to "The Visible Spectrum" on Britannica.com. Since we are all at varying degrees of balance, there is a range of root chakra frequencies that hover around this established frequency. Red has the longest wavelength and shortest frequency. In meditation, you can visualize this area to be red to strengthen this center and to strengthen your physical body and your relationship with the physical needs in your life.

Emotions

What happens when you feel excluded from your family or a group of friends? When you worry that you won't have enough money to pay your bills? When you know the Universe is providing for you?

Did you feel hurt, abandoned, lack, or moved with emotion as you read those questions? Each of those stories triggers a different emotion experienced in the root chakra. Here is where we experience our tribal acceptance, safety, security, and being provided for by the Divine and allow our emotions to bring in a physical life that matches it.

Lifetime Development

Most chakras develop during a certain time period in your life. The root chakra develops during the lifetime years of zero to seven. Up to around age seven, most people are in their primal tribe and feel safe and secure. We protect the young to help maintain their feeling of innocence, safety, and security, whether or not we're related to them. This explains why wounding and trauma during this period can have such a lasting effect. If you didn't have a safe and secure experience at this young age, the root chakra is a great starting place. We will cover many effective ways to help you strengthen this center, including journaling and a healing meditation to heal those wounds.

We discover the root cause of first chakra issues by taking note of any emotionally traumatic events that occurred during our first seven years of life. What traumatic childhood event started the energetic imbalance that may or may not have led to your physical illness? Awareness is the first step. In becoming aware of the original situation that triggered your thought pattern, you've already started the healing process. For example, it may have been injustice as a child, such as someone yelling at you for something you hadn't done or showing unfair preference to a sibling. Or maybe it was a traumatic event, such as getting lost, getting separated from a parent in a shopping mall, having a parent go into the hospital, or your parents getting a divorce. Relatively small events can seem enormous to young children, who have a different sense of time than adults. And sadly, of course, there is massive trauma such as abuse, accidents, or bereavement. If you feel your case merits it, you should seek help from a trusted professional counselor as well as doing these exercises.

It's not always a tragic event that causes our energetic disruption. Sometimes it can be as simple as an ice cream sandwich.

This was a tribal rejection my soul has worked hard to heal. After great lengths of healing and pattern recognition, I now help myself stay grounded when presented with a group trust issue. I remind myself I am Divinely accepted, and as I feel Divinely accepted, my external world accepts me, too. I no longer allow my hurt five-year-old emotional self to respond for my adult body. I have shown my five-year-old self how it wasn't personal and have taught her that she is deserving. When she does respond, she responds from a place of acceptance and love. I've reached a place where I know my Divine value and can enjoy my own "ice cream sandwich" with whomever I please.

The greatest part and the hardest part of awakening to your true self is . . . you are not able to become *unaware*. Once you *know* what situation ignited the thoughts that led to the emotions that created the repeated pattern or illness, then you're aware and can't undo this awareness. Painful though it can be, once you are aware of what needs to be healed, the real work begins.

In addition to the safety and security we obtain from this time period in our life, this development period is at the root of any limiting beliefs we may be holding on to as an adult. What absolute truth are you holding on to that may be holding you back from the life of your dreams? Can you also recall an event that happened during this time period that may be connected to this belief? As you begin to heal this energy center, your limiting beliefs will have less power over you as well.

As you begin to heal any emotional pain, notice if it might have been causing an energetic stagnation within the center related to your root chakra. Does the theme of safety, security, and acceptance continue to come into your life? Does this same theme consistently show up throughout the story of your life, just with different faces each chapter? Same problem, different faces? Even sometimes the same faces? If it does, begin to think about what might have happened during the years of zero to seven that may have established the energetic imprint. If needed, pull over into a rest stop and take a restorative break from your journey and this road map to think for a while. This is truly a healing voyage and there is no rush, especially in this very foundational energy. Check it out with family members if possible—sometimes childhood memory plays tricks. Have a notebook handy to jot down any thoughts that arise and keep it for when we come to the section on journaling in chapter 12.

The Everyday Connection: Root Chakra

- Do you lose your keys regularly?
- Have you been wanting more and more of the newest trend?
- Are you double-booking appointments?
- Have you experienced multiple miscarriages?

Our seemingly inconsequential daily habits will direct us to the energy center most disrupted and in need of balance. If you answered "yes" to any of these questions, see how you feel after completing the root chakra meditation found in chapter 10 for a week. You may find you are more focused and less scattered.

CHAPTER 8

The Counter Chakra
to the Root Chakra

EACH ENERGY CENTER pairs with a counter energy center to work in partnership to strengthen and bring balance to the partnership and the collective system. We will explain the counter chakras in much greater detail later, after you have learned about each individual energy center. There's no need to fully grasp and understand the pairings yet. It will make more sense once you've learned about each energy center. (See chapter 39 for a thorough understanding of these energetic partnerships.) Since these pairings play a very significant role in health management, I'll prepare you for how these energy centers integrate.

The root chakra pairs with the heart chakra, which is the fourth chakra, where we hold our self-love and attachment beliefs. These two energy centers work together to bring safety and security to our self and our love relationships. As we feel safe in our root chakra, we feel safer to open our hearts to others and, most importantly, to ourselves. We are more compassionate with ourselves and shower others with love and in turn bask in an overflowing, pure, abundant, and secure love. These themes vacillate until this partnership reaches equilibrium.

The Antidote

The heart chakra energy is the antidote for the root chakra's imbalance. When the root chakra is excessive, it results in greed and being consumed by physical matter and safety. The heart chakra's energy and love for self and others is lacking in this energetic state, and when a focus on self-love and compassion is added, we become more interested in being relationship-rich than material-rich. When a new appreciation and love for people is infused into this materially focused energy, equilibrium is established.

When the root chakra is stagnant, it results in feeling excluded and unsafe. When the heart chakra's healing energy of inclusion and love is focused on inclusion, and love is drawn into the daily experience and equilibrium is established within this partnership.

Counter Chakra Seed Planting

The counter chakra seed planting concept is a fascinating aspect of this holistic partnership. When an idea, concept, or seed is planted during the lifetime experience of the lower three physical, world-based chakras, it may not be realized, expressed, or healed until you are living within the age window of its spiritual counter chakra. A thought or belief planted during the root chakra window heals and expresses itself within the heart chakra window of development.

According to Bruce Lipton, PhD, stem cell biologist, human beings live in a subconscious or theta state of mind from ages zero to seven, and they download many of their subconscious programs during this window of time. This information is found on the YouTube video "Dr. Bruce Lipton Explains How to Reprogram Your Subconscious Mind." Many of the seeds planted during this window heal or express themselves more clearly during the ages of twenty-one to twenty-eight. We may receive the answer or healing to this programming during the counter chakra window. What begins during the root chakra period may be complemented or come to fruition during the heart chakra development period.

CHAPTER 9

The Auric Effect:
The Root Chakra

When our root chakra is imbalanced,
we feel stress and respond with fight, flight,
or freeze in order to survive.

Deficient Root Chakra

During the fight-or-flight state, our aura becomes enlarged and over-sized. This occurs in an effort to energetically assess the danger in the room by expanding several feet away from the body. While this enlarged aura does offer us the intel on whether a situation is dangerous or not, it also takes in all the energy it assesses in the room. This abundant capturing of data and concern for safety often results in taking on too much energy, leaving our heart chakra excessive and our root chakra deficient while trying to overcompensate for the energy inundation from fact-gathering and in effort to help the root chakra feel safe enough to stay. It is important to flee in dangerous situations. However, when the energetic imprint from childhood is established to always be scanning the room, this becomes its established exhaustive state until energetic healing occurs. This person can look like the people-pleaser and over-giver with heart palpitations and high blood pressure and adrenal issues.

Excessive Root Chakra

During the freeze state, our first chakra becomes excessive in the sympathetic state of freeze. As a result, the heart chakra energy floods the root chakra in an effort to balance this partnership, helping the root chakra feel safe enough to connect, leaving the heart chakra depleted and the aura in a minimal state, often merely one-fourth to one-half inch from the body. This person can look materialistic and vain and struggle with heart issues.

The Auric Effect ✧ Root Chakra

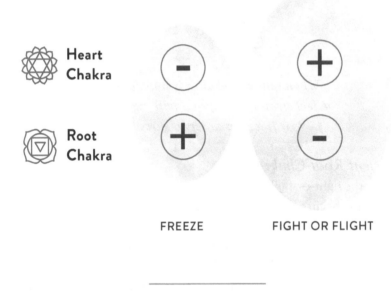

Connecting to Divine safety, Divine security, Divine protection, and Divine acceptance in this space is a highly effective way to heal your root chakra. When you feel safe and secure here, it will begin to be reflected in your external world.

Stay with this thought.

Rest in the calm and protection of this Divine protection. Imagine a golden light pouring down from your higher power and encircling you. You are safe. You are secure. You are accepted. There is no other you than you. There are no Divine errors. Your relationships are perfectly Divine and safe. You are exactly where you are supposed to be and have experienced precisely what you have experienced to be here now.

Go outside and repeat the thought, *I am safe. I am secure. I am protected. I am accepted. I am loved. I am love.* Stand with both feet firmly on the ground—on grass or dirt and barefoot, if possible—and slightly apart. Breathe deeply and enjoy the feeling of security that comes from focusing on these words.

You've just completed your first grounding exercise.

CHAPTER 10

The Importance
of Grounding

WE LIVE IN A WORLD that ungrounds us every moment of every day. We are bombarded by messaging, which may be overly commercial, fear-laden, or toxic, and we are not outside enjoying our world the way we once did. Our children are no longer playing in dirt, climbing trees, or running in the sand, except for short periods usually under parental supervision. We have lost important freedoms. To combat this exile from our rightful inheritance, it is imperative we learn tools to reclaim it. This is why a strong grounding practice is of the utmost importance in living a healthy life.

Health management begins with a practice called grounding. Scientifically, grounding is the exchange of electrons between the earth and our body. The sun releases electrons into the ionosphere, a layer of the atmosphere approximately fifty to four hundred miles away. The sun's rays are so powerful they split the molecules into a negative charge and a positive charge. The positive charge remains in the ionosphere, while from time to time, the negative energy collects, releases, and charges the Earth's surface through lightning.

The negatively charged energy leaves the ionosphere, hits the Earth, and disperses the energy onto the Earth's surface. These free electrons are absorbed into the body and neutralize the free radicals in the body when we stand on the Earth with our bare feet. This process happens so quickly, it's immeasurable. The free radicals built up in the body pair with these negative electrons and are released and neutralized by the negative ions of the Earth's surface. This works the same way the grounding wire works in a building. It is believed this simple act reduces inflammation within the body, improves sleep, and shifts the autonomic nervous system from sympathetic to parasympathetic activation.

Native cultures have used the Earth as its own healing tool. The documentary film *The Earthing Movie* details this process and shares perspectives from the industry's experts, including Clint Ober, the pioneer of this movement.

While the grounding process heals our physical body, there is a spiritual grounding process that heals the subtle body. Spiritually, grounding is bringing presence into the body. It is energetically drawing Mama Earth's energy up through visualization and subtle body energy connection. It is at the core of mindfulness and allows us to be present with ourselves and with whomever we are with at the time. Personally, a grounding practice builds the foundation for your spiritual practice, remaining safe, feeling secure, and being present. In business and everyday life, grounding helps us remember our presentations, present with a stronger energy in everyday meetings and in daily interactions while also forgetting less. In all cases, grounding helps remedy symptoms and helps heal them at the root cause.

My goal for you is to obtain a powerful healing road map with a strong grounding practice at the foundation of that healing. As you create a powerful grounding practice, you will find yourself connected to the Earth and the Divine as you are rocking it as a human on this planet. I want you to experience the best of both worlds. It is possible to be fully connected to the Divine and fully present and powerful here on Earth. Why is this so important?

Our contact with nature is a key factor in maintaining our energy. Children used to play outside in the dirt, roll in the grass, and climb trees. Perhaps you, too, used to spend time outside. Did you take walks, hike, go to the beach, run, ski, or boat? In each of these exercises, did you find yourself surrounded by trees, dirt, and more nature? Take a moment to think about this connection. Did your illness increase as your exposure to nature decreased?

All these activities connect us to the Earth and release disrupted energy from our bodies, meanwhile drawing in healing energy that grounds us. Connection with nature strengthens our energy so we can be resilient to life's struggle.

CHAPTER 11

The Importance of Gratitude: Why It Is Vital

I BELIEVE IT IS IMPERATIVE not just to release what no longer serves us into Mama Earth but to also be grateful for her infinite nourishment and healing. As we fill the Earth with gratitude for all of our resources and thank her for taking what does not serve us first, we create a more balanced relationship for our energy practice. This practice helps us give and receive, not just take from the Earth. Much like you would thank the chef for preparing your meal, or thank someone for having you over for dinner, we thank Mama Earth for the nourishment she gives to us.

As you begin your grounding practice and ground your energy, offer sheer gratitude to Mama Earth for taking from us what does not serve us. Upon bringing attention to your pelvic floor, begin to draw your root down toward the center of the Earth, pausing 90 percent of the way out of respect for Mama Earth. At this moment, we invite Mama Earth to integrate with your root and draw your root down the rest of the way into the center of the Earth. Once connected to the center of the Earth, give gratitude, then release what does not serve you and *then* draw up the Earth's energy from the center of the Earth to ground your energy.

As your first chakra strengthens, you will draw in the healing energy of the Earth. You will learn more about this process in the next section. When you tap into Mama Earth, begin a practice of giving gratitude to her *first* before asking her for *anything*. She will give to us without our gratitude, of course, because she loves us. But in offering gratitude for the flowers, vegetables, resources, the animals, the plants, the sunrises and sunsets, and the oxygen we use every day, we begin our energy connection with gratitude. As we give gratitude to the Earth, we shift our own hearts into a state of gratitude and receiving.

This process is about healing our hearts, our connections, and our earth. It is about using our roots to nourish and give back to the original tree that sourced us and the one we are all connected to. Much like the final scene from *The Giving Tree* by Shel Silverstein, we have left our Divine tree to become a stump. Now it is time for us to connect in gratitude and allow that tree to blossom and come back to life. The beautiful part of this is as we offer gratitude to the core of our Earth, we heal our own hearts simultaneously. The gratitude offered will be the gratitude received. We are all connected.

CHAPTER 12

Tools to Heal Your
Root Chakra Marker

EVERY SPRING, my school's kindergarten class would put on an annual storybook production of a famous fairy tale, offering an incredible opportunity for parents and grandparents alike to swoon and admire all the sweet, darling five- and six-year-olds scream-singing and filling the cafeteria stage with joy. My class performed *Goldilocks and the Three Bears*, and never have I ever wanted to be Goldilocks more than I did as the winter season turned to spring. I behaved so well in class, completed all my homework, raised my hand perfectly, and answered every question with a charming smile to prove I was the best student and natural choice for Goldilocks. Yet, I was cast as Bunny #1 in the fluffle of ten bunnies whose job was to sing and hop around the forest as Goldilocks made her way to Grandmother's house. While this play might not seem as big of a deal now, my five-year-old self was crushed and, ultimately, proba-bly more hurt by what happened next.

I shared my disappointment with my parents, who then told me the teacher had informed them she thought I would be the best Goldilocks, too, but I was too "sure of myself," so she gave the part to another girl. In that painful moment, an energetic imprint was branded into me. The sting of those words impressed upon me the guidance that I should not be too bright and smiley, nor too sad and somber, but to hide my feelings and enthusiasm and act "just right" for the play and for life.

This "don't be too you" lesson would impact me until I reached the age range of twenty-eight to thirty-five, the heart chakra window. Only then did I know I was safe enough and loved enough by others and myself to share my true feelings. I didn't have the tools then to learn how to feel safe and secure with myself when others disapproved of me.

This road map fills this childhood desire for tools and techniques. I am including everything your little (and grown) self needs to learn how to feel safe, secure, and protected in any circumstance. This will be an amazing book of tools and techniques to empower you to be the brightest and happiest imperfect human you know. We are brought here to be joyfully imperfectly perfect. The best part is that by implementing these tools, it will not matter if you get the part. You will live in a state of joy, and that happiness will flood everyone around you and make every day a day where people swoon and adore you because you adore yourself.

We are going to build a tremendous healing plan for you. This plan begins with having a wide array of tools and techniques available for you when necessary. Some tools are recommended to be used daily, to start building up a reservoir of healing, while others are more emergency solutions. Put into practice the tools that feel the best to you first. I encourage you to give each tool a try because you may find yourself needing different tools in different situations. Remembering our themes of safety, security, and thriving as a physical body in the physical world in the root chakra, I've listed the exercises I have found most effective in my work with my students and in my own experience in healing.

Color and Clothes

Our soul knows how to dress itself!

Have you ever gotten dressed to find that your clothes just don't feel right? And it's not that they don't fit. It's possible they don't fit, of course, but the clothes literally don't *feel* right. Well, it's true. They may not be right for you. Or at least, the energy vibration of the color you chose to wear may not match what your energy field needs that day.

Our soul calls us to dress in certain colors to help draw in the energy we need through the frequencies attracted by color. Colors vibrate at different frequencies. When we need to feel more grounded, we feel called to wear red. Clothes that help support your root chakra are red underwear, red shoes and socks, and shirts tucked into your pants. As you wear these clothes, you emit and absorb the slower and lower frequency of red, which will help you feel more grounded and foundationally strong. I have had my toenails painted red for the last decade of my life, so I can stay grounded and present! It doesn't even feel right to have them painted another color.

Trust your intuition. When you feel called to wear a certain color, wear it. This is how Aura-Soma works. Aura-Soma is a color-selective soul-healing tool I use in my practice. I refer to it as spiritual homeopathy. Clients are asked to choose colored bottles, and each color has a different significance. I have found that whatever bottle my client chooses that day, they are typically wearing the same color. It's incredible.

Element

The first five chakras are governed and healed by an element because we are made up of each of these elements. The *element* for the root chakra is earth. Complete one of the following to strengthen this energy center:

- Stand or go for a walk in grass, soil, sand, or mud, preferably barefoot.
- Garden.
- Stand by or sit up against the roots of a tree.
- Imagine your own tree roots.

All these will be so grounding for you. As you have learned, completing these tasks barefoot on the ground is the most healing way for you to ground and heal.

How do you feel during a pleasant day at the beach? You feel calm, centered, grounded. And why is that, do you think? You are walking barefoot through the sand, grounding yourself all day long. Using these grounding techniques, and the meditation that follows, regularly, you can train your own body to feel this peaceful all the time.

Our Five Senses

Have you ever smelled someone's cologne or perfume or smelled food cooking that created a visceral response within you? Perhaps it brought back a childhood memory or reminded you of someone you love. It is because our sense of smell is fed by the energy of our root chakra, and the root chakra feeds our physical body. Our senses are powerful and will bring us back energetically to embodied emotions and events.

Not sure what this sensation feels like? Give this a try. Grab your cinnamon spice and close your eyes and take a deep sniff. Notice where you "feel" this energy experience of smelling in your body. Did you feel it in your root chakra? We do this experiment in class and my students have been amazed by where they actually *feel* the scent.

Smell is our most primal sense and allows us to keep ourselves and our loved ones safe by detecting safe food choices and sometimes even predators. Research has begun to show that our sense of smell can discern the chemical released when experiencing fear. This primal sense is utilized by the body to ensure its safety. Often when people have lost their sense of smell, there is some form of root chakra trauma, either in childhood or tribal rejection as an adult. One of every ten thousand people suffers from anosmia, the loss of the sense of smell. If you are one of them, take a second look at this root chakra chapter and allow yourself to dig a little deeper to see if there is some healing that needs to take place within you to feel safe and accepted.

Organic of Action

As you might imagine, the work organ for the root chakra is the anus. It is through the anus that we release what does not serve us, both physically and energetically. We can squeeze this sphincter to begin to activate our muladhara chakra and bring additional energy to this center. If you are experiencing hemorrhoids, often emotionally caused by anger and fear about the past and financial stress, you may want to revisit both root chakra chapters to shift your energy into a state of security, safety, and abundance.

Food

Have you ever smelled the cooking of someone you adored and felt your entire body pause and experience nourishment down to its core? That "core" is your root chakra being nourished and the inner child who lives there enjoying the tastes and memories associated with that food. The food that supports this chakra includes the following:

- Anything grown in the ground soil has absorbed the healing negative charge of the earth—carrots, potatoes, parsnips, garlic, or sweet potatoes.
- Strawberries, red cherries, red bell peppers— the red-colored food will emit the frequency of this energy center and help strengthen it.
- Eating in general helps you be more grounded because your body has to process the food to nourish the physical body, thus grounding you. Now is not a time for punishing diets or overly severe food restriction. Eat high-vibrational, healthy food and listen to what your body is craving to nourish any vitamin deficiencies.

Essential Oils

The supportive essential oils for this center include the following:

- **CHAMOMILE:** heals discouragement or feeling life has no purpose
- **FRANKINCENSE:** heals abandonment, feeling spiritually disconnected
- **LAVENDER:** calms/heals blocked communication and fear of rejection
- **MYRRH:** heals distrust in others and feeling unsafe in the world
- **SANDALWOOD:** aids in reconnecting with God and spiritual self

These oils are very helpful for your grounding process and can be found at your local health food store or online. If you want to choose only one oil for all of your healing, choose lavender. This oil is the most versatile healing essential oil. Otherwise, as you learned in the chapter 6, muscle-test to decide which oil your body needs.

You can begin with diffusing your oil of choice, smelling it, or placing a drop (combined with coconut oil or another carrier oil like avocado oil) near your nose so you can continue to smell this scent. Take a few drops of this oil and rub it on the bottom of your feet or your perineum to receive the balancing benefits of this practice. If you have sensitive skin, always muscle-test and choose which location is safest for you.

Crystals

The crystals that bring great balance and healing to this center include the following:

- **HEMATITE:** aids in releasing negative energy from your body. This is a powerful stone and can sometimes feel overwhelming for people.

- **SMOKY QUARTZ:** aids in balancing and clearing this center. This is a powerful root chakra crystal.
- **SHUNGITE:** helps you heal your emotions and release what does not serve you, leaving you peaceful and calm.
- **TOURMALINE:** aids in the releasing of negative emotion and helps heal a broken heart, as it disperses grief and emotional pain. You will learn about the important heart connection in this chapter.

You may place these crystals in the back pocket of your pants for the day or tuck them into your sheets at the foot of your bed to help ground your energy. If your sleep becomes disturbed, it is time to remove the crystals from the room. You can also place them inside your bra, within a pouch, or specially designed necklaces for this purpose.

Mantra

LAM, the mantra for this energy center, resonates in keynote C, which is very peaceful and cleansing. The first three notes of the children's song "Old MacDonald Had a Farm" are the note C, so you can begin to think of this note in your head and lower the octave as you are able. As you will learn when we cover meditation, LAM is to be said in the deepest sound possible that your body can create. This mantra will help ground and fortify you. Try saying this mantra ten times while doing household chores or in the shower for an instant grounding technique.

Environmental Shift

What do you have hanging over your bed? Or what do you have stored underneath your bed? Our bed is the conduit for making our body comfortable enough to regenerate and heal itself, and it does so with energy. Energy must be able to easily flow around the bed at night to obtain ideal healing and rest. If there is anything above or below your bed or your bed is placed underneath a window, consider removing the object above your bed or moving your bed away from the window.

Our bodies detoxify, rebalance, and heal while we sleep. Keeping an object or painting overhead while sleeping calls mental attention to that object and does not allow your body to disconnect from this physical world in order to conduct its deep internal healing. A window overhead allows too much energy to release out the window, resulting in disrupted sleep. A painting of water or a fish tank in the room creates too much energy flow in the room to be calming. Water never rests, and you want to create an energetic atmosphere of restfulness in your bedroom.

My daughter once moved the furniture around in her room, which left her extremely busy monthly calendar above her headboard. I warned her to move it, as it would leave her very ungrounded as her mind processed all that was going on in her calendar throughout the night. She decided to let it remain where it had been.

After three weeks, she found herself noticeably jumpy, ungrounded, and filled with anxiety. I reminded her of her calendar's overhead placement, and she removed it. Within weeks, her symptoms vanished.

Our bodies need a secure and peaceful place to rest in order to establish a secure mental, physical, and energetic state. How can you bring more healing to your bedroom?

Yoga

The most helpful yoga pose is the tree pose (*vrksasana*). Ground yourself into the floor, like a tree. When your roots are connected, your tree will bend, but it will not break.

Archangels

Archangel Michael protects us and keeps us safe. He is written about in the Bible, Torah, and Quran as the archangel of protection. He bears a huge sword and shield and arrives with a whole mercy of angels. Archangel Sandalphon assists in the grounding and balancing of our root chakra. We must ask for the assistance of the archangels if we want their help, with the exception of Archangel Michael, who can spontaneously rescue us in life-saving situations. If this resonates with you, begin calling upon Archangel Michael for overall protection and Archangel Sandalphon for grounding assistance and root chakra balance and see what happens in your life. Calling upon an archangel is simply asking for their help by name to assist in a certain way, but if you find you experience fear while driving or walking down a crowded or abandoned street, apply this technique and notice how your energy begins to shift. Calling upon Archangel Michael in moments of fear can be life-altering.

It completely changed my life when I began calling upon Archangel Michael daily, nightly, and during many moments in between. Prior to calling on Archangel Michael for protection, my home would feel less safe, physically and energetically. I would feel spirits in my home, and my daughter and I would often be awakened by them at night. Upon making this shift, I called upon Archangel Michael and his mercy of angels to protect my home every night before going to sleep. This protection meditation is available at www.YouTube.com/ErinGaray: *How to Smudge, Clear and Protect Your Home.* I thanked him for his protection over my home, my family, my car, my business, and anywhere my family would be. Since calling upon Archangel Michael, my daughter and I walk into our home, and it feels protected and safe and we are no longer awakened at night.

The same is true when I am walking down the street at night. The moment I feel nervous because it is late, I thank Archangel Michael for protecting me, and I experience a wave of security and protection flowing over me. If you worry about your safety, I highly recommend you experiment with this practice and watch how your levels of fear reduce. I continue to be protected. If the concept of an archangel does not resonate with you, you may think of this same experience as a wave of high-vibrational energy ensuring your safety. You may see it as gold or indigo light surrounding your path, your car, and the location you are heading toward in that moment. It holds the same function. Intention is powerful.

Ten-Second Rescue

Lying or standing: Envision growing tree roots from your perineum, or down your legs out though the bottoms of your feet, and down through the many layers of the Earth, 90 percent of the way to the inner core. At this moment, invite Mama Earth to grasp and draw your root the rest of the way in, tethering to that innermost core and pulling taut. Invite and bring the energy from the inner core up from the Earth, through your root, to fill and nourish your pelvic floor and perineum.

Seated: See your roots growing directly from your pelvic floor into the Earth. Invite and bring up the energy from the inner core of the Earth to fill in your pelvic floor.

A great way to incorporate this into your day is to do this every time you put on your seat belt. As you click in your seat belt, imagine your roots clicking in. As you pull your seat belt taut, imagine your roots pulling taut as well and drawing the energy up into your pelvic floor.

Homework

Practice grounding from your pelvic floor down your legs, through your feet, and 90 percent of the way into the center of the Earth, inviting Mama Earth to draw it the rest of way, three times in the morning—when you wake up in bed, when stand up out of bed, and when you brush your teeth. If you ground just these three times, you will begin to see a shift in your day and will start feeling more present, less anxious, and more mindful. If you begin with your grounding before going to bed, it will calm your mind and help you fall asleep faster, and you will find, over time, that your body will want to reground first thing in the morning. These key moments will help you build a reservoir of energy balance and healing in your system.

I wish I could tell you that you could complete your homework or ground just once a day, and then you'd be set for the day. But unfortunately, we've become disconnected to what nourishes us, heals us, and helps us thrive. As a result, we are living a life that is *dis*sed—distracted, disrupted, disruptive, and diseased. It's time to build a new reconnecting, healing habit to heal and nourish our bodies and souls. By practicing grounding on a regular basis, you will begin to shift and heal your mindset, body, health, and soul.

Root Chakra Journaling

Each chapter we are going to journal. Please take a few moments to complete this section. We often use this information in meditation, and it's an important part of our healing. I encourage you to utilize this whole experience and get to the root of your challenge by journaling before completing the meditation. Maybe buy yourself a special notebook dedicated to this helpful, therapeutic practice. Points to consider when writing in your journal are the following:

- What experiences around acceptance, safety, and security do you feel might be creating the deficient or excessive energy in your root chakra?
- Did you experience tribal rejection as a child? When? Who? What happened?
- Did you feel unsafe as a child?
- How are you blessed? How are you being provided for by the Universe?

Certainly divorce, abuse, or death can cause a disruption in the energy in our root chakra, but it doesn't have to be tragic to experience a life-long pattern. Being excluded from a group of friends at school lunch, or your family sending you to bed early so they could have dessert without you can bring about feelings and patterns of being excluded. Find those stories and write them all out.

Root Chakra Mantra Review

At the end of each chakra chapter, we will review all the mantras to begin to commit them to memory. This will be vitally important once you have learned about each individual energy center, and we begin to work with this system holistically.

 *Root Chakra Mantra Review*

Chakra	Mantra	How do I remember it?	Keynote
First: ROOT	LAM	L-L-Lowest energy center.	KEYNOTE C: first note in "Old MacDonald Had a Farm"

Root chakra meditation: Join me at www.LoveHealThrive.com to bask in this meditation.

One grounding misconception to cover before meditation: While our roots can grow through our feet while we're standing, the focal point for your grounding is your pelvic floor, your perineum, and the base of your spine, not the bottom of your feet. I once had a client who was in my office who presented with ungrounded energy. I asked her if she was keeping up with her grounding practice.

She said, "Yes, every morning."

I thought to myself, *Hmm, why does she seem so ungrounded then?* Then I asked her, "Where are you grounding from?"

She said, "My feet, of course."

I explained to her how important it was to ground with the focal point in the root chakra and that while we have minor chakras in our feet (and hands—twenty-one minor chakras in total throughout the body), our grounding practice needs to focus on our root chakra first and then can flow through the feet. She came back the next month, and her energetic shift was shocking. She was exponentially more grounded and felt more peaceful about her life. She radiated a peaceful calmness that was felt throughout the room. It was fantastic.

CHAPTER 13

The Emotional Connection to Your Second Chakra Marker: The Sacral Chakra

IT WAS OCTOBER. I was nine years old and in the third grade. Every day, the moment the recess bell would ring, my circle of girlfriends and I raced to the tetherball court where we spent our break spiking the tetherball as hard as we could until it wound tightly around the pole for the imminent champion to claim her victory and move on to her next opponent. Our group was so tight that one day we decided we wanted to turn our group into a club.

We decided we were going to name our club the Rainbow Girls and have shirts made to further establish our cohesiveness.

After weeks of gleeful anticipation, the coveted day had arrived—Shirt Day! These shirts were early-eighties adolescent perfection. The baseball-cut tee with lavender three-quarter sleeves was the perfect frame for our glittery mascot. Upon our chest, we proudly donned the image of a shimmery unicorn, jumping over an even more sparkly rainbow, with purple velvet lettering proudly displaying our name. These shirts shouted connection and sister-hood—every preteen's dream.

We gathered around the tetherball court in a circle for our initiation by the queen, who handed a shirt to each member. Each new Rainbow Girl inhaled the glory of her shirt upon receipt with awe, reverence, and inclusion. Each member anxiously awaited her moment to be gifted the coveted shirt. When the queen arrived in front of me, she had given the last shirt away to the girl before me.

She looked me in the eyes and said, "We didn't have enough for you. Sorry."

These were almost the precise words my grandmother had uttered only five years earlier.

And much like my mom shared her ice cream with me then, the tetherball queen had a shirt made for me weeks after the initiation and carelessly tossed it to me after class one day as an afterthought. That shirt followed the same energetic patterning as the ice cream sandwich had years prior.

This is how energy imprinting works. When we experience trauma, on any level, an energetic imprint is established. In an attempt to clear this imprint that does not serve us, our soul continues to draw in the exact same scenario, often with different faces and names. This is how we will frequently find ourselves saying, "Oh, there it is again. This always happens to me." In actuality, your energetic body is repeating the same singular imprint in an effort to help you respond to scenarios differently and to learn how to overcome this harmful belief. Much like the 1993 film *Groundhog Day*, directed by Harold Ramis, scenario repetition offers our energetic body the same opportunity to respond differently to the same situation until we are no longer triggered by its appearance in our life. Often, we feel frustrated that the same thing happens again and again, but this repetition is our soul's attempt to empower us beyond the injury and allow the energy to no longer stagnate around this topic. Simply by recognizing the pattern of the imprint drawing in the same story over and over, it begins to lessen the intense sting of feeling attacked and victimized because we recognize it is one singular imprint, causing multiple events, not multiple imprints causing many single challenges.

Feeling emotionally empowered is one of the greatest gifts of a healed second chakra. The second chakra is known as the sacral chakra—in Sanskrit, *svadhishthana*. It is located near the sacral region of the spinal cord, between the hips and approximately two inches below your belly button. Our second chakra is the warehouse of our emotions, and it is here our emotional equilibrium resides. It is within this emotional equilibrium that our parasympathetic nervous system is activated, helping us feel calmer and more at peace. This chakra is in a constant process of encouraging our fast-moving emotions to assist and speed up our stuck-in-the-mud emotions. Those slow-moving emotions, in turn, encourage the fast-moving emotions to slow down, so together, an emotional equilibrium of balanced energy and emotion is reached.

This is an intense energy center to heal. We hold many belief systems that run deep and place a lot of energy and significance on our emotions. But when we can rest in the foundation and the strength of the first chakra's power, we can feel safe enough to reach our emotional equilibrium in the second chakra, no longer ruled by our emotions.

Now that you have strengthened your root chakra, and those feelings of acceptance, security, safety, and feeling good about being physical in this physical world, you are ready to honor your emotions. With the root chakra energy in place, we're able to invite our emotions to balance each other and find their own equilibrium.

Have you been doing your homework? Did you find a time to ground three times first thing in the morning? Did you find you felt a little more secure? A little safer? A little more accepted? Did you also happen to notice any little changes in your daily life? This root strength will help you reach emotional equilibrium and balance your emotions.

The main themes of the sacral energy are emotion, connection, desire, and pleasure—sensual pleasure and pleasure from everyday life. It is about creativity and procreation, but while this energy center includes birthing a human, it is not always about a literal baby. What are you being called to bring to life? Where are you called to give life? Ideas, art, a charity? Where can you create something that didn't exist before?

The sacral chakra is the center for true human connection. It is where we connect to ourselves and others. When we do not feel this connection, we can feel alone, lifeless, and full of blame. Our energy gravitates elsewhere in our body, and this imbalance causes more illness. Be loving to that beautiful, perfect self that you are. Enjoy creating. Enjoy connecting. Enjoy feeling connected to others and yourself.

When we don't want to admit that we feel lonely, upset, or hurt, it is often easier to point out in someone else what we're not willing to address in ourselves.

"I know you are, but what am I?"

In grade school, how often did you hear another child blurt this out after being called a taunting name? Actually, children are close to the Divine, and this response is fully accurate. When someone calls you something, comments on your way of life, or criticizes a personality trait, it is actually more telling about what they are not willing to acknowledge within themselves than it is about you. This is the energetic basis of projection. The next time someone's opinion upsets you, acknowledge their pain and their journey (out loud or just mentally) and know it's not about you. Send them a silent blessing and move on. It's not worth lowering your frequency to engage in the banter.

Honor yourself first. Blame goes both ways. We can blame someone else for how we feel, and we can also look at how we are blaming ourselves for the outcome of a circumstance. Blame is the unspoken guilt we feel for not having acted, connected, or communicated in a certain way. You will see how this correlates to your throat chakra later in chapter 25. What have you been blaming yourself over? How have you perhaps blamed someone else for your feelings of inadequacy?

While blame is one of the emotions found in this energy center, there is a myriad of emotions housed in this center, one of which is joy. However, joy is the scariest emotion to feel, according to renowned author Brené Brown. When we are in a state of joy, we anticipate something negative to take it away. Imagine sitting in a truly joyful moment without letting yourself be distracted or worried about something stealing away this feeling. Pay attention the next time you experience joy and allow yourself to pause. Feel it and trust you are deserving of it.

Our thoughts trigger emotions, emotions move energy,
and energy manifests physically.
What we do with our energy matters.
If our energy isn't weak, our body doesn't weaken.

Just as we discussed in the blushing example, our physical body responds to our emotions. Our physical bodies are a representation of our emotions. Here are some real-life examples that support this theory:

- A woman who refused to accept life and distrusted the Universe was diagnosed with Alzheimer's disease.
- A man who spent his life deflecting connection and never sharing his true feelings found he had a heart condition because he never felt safe enough to let his love show.
- A woman with an overbearing husband developed thyroid cancer because she could never speak her truth or feel truly heard.
- A man who felt intensely unsafe in the world and refused to experience life ended up with chronic respiratory problems.
- A widow developed breast cancer over her left breast because her heart was broken and rarely nourished herself. She placed other's needs above her own. She never felt she truly mattered to anyone.
- A man developed testicular cancer after learning his wife had an affair.

I've heard countless stories. While you should in no way blame yourself (remember this is unspoken guilt) or others for any illnesses or life situations you may be experiencing, I encourage you to look at any physical challenges you may have and think about the circumstances that existed just before the physical manifestation presented itself. This may lead you to the emotional accountability and root cause of your illness and offer you a powerful path toward your healing. If energy becomes stagnant, then we can become scattered, unhappy, irritable, and ultimately ill. But the reverse is true, too. Use this information as your guide toward healing.

As we gain awareness of the state of our thoughts and emotions, we can reach a level of health and happiness unparalleled to anything we have experienced previously. Our bodies will not contract something, sustain an injury, or become depressed if the energy is not weak. It is only when the energy body is weakened that we are susceptible to injury or illness. As we strengthen our thoughts, we direct our energy, manage our emotions, and remain healthy. If you are in an accident, often when your energy is vibrant, your healing process is much faster.

Louise Hay, founder of Hay House Publishing, who has published many self-help books including *You Can Heal Your Life*, describes this emotional connection process in her book *Heal Your Body A-Z: The Mental Causes for Physical Illness and the Way to Overcome Them* (Hay House, 2004). This book lists the emotional causes that may lie behind hundreds of ailments and also includes a positive affirmation for each ailment. The positive affirmation will begin to raise your energetic vibration and shift your thought process so that you can ultimately heal your physical body.

The sacral chakra is not only the emotional warehouse of your entire system but also the talisman of wisdom on how to heal your body.

Second Chakra Description

How do we know if the energy in our sacral chakra is excessive, deficient, or balanced?

Excessive Sacral Chakra Energy
You find yourself overreacting, overattached to people, needy in relationships, codependent, obsessive, insatiable, experiencing hoarding behavior and insatiable desires, often in varying degrees and moments throughout your day.

We've all had that friend. The one who after two coffee dates thinks he or she is your very best friend and calls you three times a day and pours on the attention. While at first this is flattering, it can often be the beginning of a needy, codependent relationship that, in my experience, ends in two years, practically to the day! If you are becoming friends with someone who has an excessive second chakra, you will likely notice the above symptoms quickly within your own self or within the other person. This doesn't mean you need to sever the friendship. A relationship with healthy boundaries can always result in a great connected friendship.

Curious what your options are if you're already in the friendship? Should you decide to continue with the friendship, here are a few suggestions:

- Keep clear boundaries, especially on what is important to you.
- Pray for yourself, for the other person, and for the emotional equilibrium of you both.
- Complete this chapter and heal your own second chakra imbalance. Given that we are all connected, it may be that your own imbalanced energy center attracted this friend into your life. As you balance your own energy, the friendship may naturally fall away, or you will help your friend heal their emotional equilibrium along with your own.
- Share *Establishing Equilibrium* with your friend. It will help them balance their own energy.

Deficient Sacral Chakra Energy

You find yourself avoidant of happiness or pleasure, fearing change, lacking creativity, pessimistic, depressed, and experiencing low libido, irregular menstrual cycle, and urinary or bladder infections.

Deep shame about sex can disrupt this center—growing up with a family who wouldn't discuss it, admitting desire, being sexually rejected, being sexually abused, or being the focus of unwanted sexual attention. Keeping quiet about your shame will allow it to creep into every corner or crevice of your life, but there is a solution.

"The antidote to shame is empathy." —Brené Brown, *Atlas of the Heart, 2021*

If you talk about your shame with someone who expresses empathy, the pain cannot survive. Journaling is also effective; being empathetic to yourself is just as powerful. As you write out any feelings of humiliation and distress you felt through these experiences, you will detach from the pain and release it from your physical and emotional body, leaving you more empowered.

Balanced Sacral Chakra Energy

You find yourself feeling life is rich and deeply satisfying. You enjoy life, experience it, and are grateful for all you have. You feel a connection with others, but feel connected to yourself in an intimate way now before you decide to reach out to others. This important personal hierarchy provides a strong sense of emotional authority and is a source for the energy that will nourish you, flowing from your sacral chakra as you connect with others. As you honor yourself first, you don't pass judgment on your desires or on those of others. You bring to life what you are meant to bring to life and do so through your own Divine creativity.

When our emotions are not fully expressed or are expressed indirectly, our sacral chakra becomes imbalanced. Unexpressed emotions turn into desires, and when our desires are not met or satisfied, they can become addictions. We become addicted to patterns that incite certain feelings. We become addicted to the feeling that resides in the sacral chakra. We believe we are addicted to something outside of ourselves when we are actually simply addicted to a certain feeling, or energetic imprint, regardless of whether or not that feeling is beneficial to our lives.

Could you be struggling with any possible addictions? Are they harmless pleasures, or do you really need them to feel "normal"? The glass of wine you drink every night, the social media you peruse, the video games you play, the mindless food you eat at night

. . . what sensation do you receive from such experiences? What experience during the ages seven to fourteen brought you the same sensation or feeling? What happened during that period when your desire was not met? Could that same unmet desire be the source behind your addiction? How is it affecting your relationships?

This is a fundamental part of my concern over the early use of technology. Often, dependence on technology starts during the energy window of seven to fourteen years old, where early addiction begins energetically. Attachment to electronics is beginning even younger now, but this age range is where the true addiction is solidified. If we do not teach our young people boundaries around electronic use, an addiction will be created that will lead to reduced connection, leading to depression. Not only will these young people's social relationships suffer, but also, as they grow older, they will feel the need to trade one addiction for another to satisfy the feeling they are seeking until the root cause is healed. It is so important to set strong boundaries here and learn how to remain connected.

Location

Your second chakra is located above your pubic bone and two to three inches below your navel and approximately two inches in— just above the cervix where applicable.

Physical Correlations in Body

The sacral chakra supports the following organs: reproductive organs, bladder, and kidneys. If you are experiencing any type of illness or pain in these areas, take a closer look at the emotional components associated with this chakra and incorporate some of these tools and techniques in the next chapter to achieve some deep, and very important, emotional healing.

Color

The color red-orange represents this energy center, as the energy and color frequency here vibrates at a frequency of approximately 500 hertz, translating to orange on the visible light spectrum.

Emotions

This chakra is the spring of our emotions. The main emotions that drive this center include pleasure, connection, creativity, blame, and desire, but this is the warehouse of our emotions. It is in the flowing of our emotions from this center where we allow ourselves to connect to another. When our emotions are balanced and we experience this connection with another, we feel alive, connected, and supported. This is also a main focal point for manifesting. When we manifest, we feel into what we desire. Applying this emotional and powerful sacral chakra energy will increase your manifesting abilities.

Lifetime Development

This energy center matures between the ages of seven to fourteen years. Think about that. During this time, our bodies go through puberty and begin to experience more mature emotions. This is often one of the most creative times in our lives because we are full of uninhibited desire and have time to bask in our passions. Most of us have not experienced much rejection at this age, so it is easier to be more courageous, try things out, and express ourselves.

Look back on your interests during this age range if you are feeling lost on your path. There may be significant bread crumbs that could lead you to your life fulfillment. It is often advised that parents watch how their young child plays and note how they show their creativity throughout their day. Their "play" and pleasure is connected to their life purpose.

What brought you joy when you were seven years old? Twelve years old? Fourteen years old? Find it again and watch what happens in your life.

The Everyday Connection— Sacral Chakra

- Have you been withdrawn or feeling a lack of connection to others?
- Have you been struggling with an addiction or obsession?
- Are you struggling to conceive a child?
- Is it always someone else's fault? Do you often blame others directly or unknowingly for your shortcomings and unhappiness? Do you blame others for things that are actually under your control?
- Have you been more codependent lately?
- Have you felt a lack of creativity?
- Are you struggling with a low libido or insatiable libido?
- Have you recently gained more weight or struggled with anorexia?

If you are experiencing any of the above, it may be helpful to take a deeper look at the emotional themes of this section and read the next second chakra section carefully. Choose one or two tools from the toolbox each day so that you've tried each of them within the week. Then you can decide which ones will become daily habits for you.

CHAPTER 14

The Counter Chakra to
the Sacral Chakra

CREATIVITY AND CREATION ARE BORN from the energy of our second chakra, and we bring them to life through our words and expression with our throat chakra, our fifth chakra. The sacral chakra ignites the desires through intense emotion, and the throat chakra speaks the desires into reality. This is how to manifest powerfully.

Between seven and fourteen, we also begin to speak up for ourselves and let our desires be known. When we communicate our emotions, we feel heard. As we feel heard, we feel emotionally connected. This is the result of two balanced energy centers working in great partnership, resulting in healing and balance, creating healthy, balanced relationships.

Dr. John M. Gottman popularized this process in his book *The Relationship Cure,* where he defines this relationship concept as the "emotional bid," where one partner asks for connection and the other partner responds positively to this bid. Repeated successful bid exchanges lead to a satisfying relationship. Failed bids, with no response from the partner, leads to relationship failure.

We can explore this in terms of the chakra system and why this is such a powerful process. The sacral chakra, home of connection and desire, is fueled by an appreciated request made from its counter chakra, the throat chakra. This process links and energizes this energetic partnership. When a bid is made that is not responded to by the partner, the throat chakra becomes stagnant and the sacral chakra becomes excessive with emotions, leading to brooding and energetic distance and separation, making it harder to reestablish this energy connection over time with repeated failed attempts.

When we feel rejected, obsession and addiction can ignite. There becomes an insatiable desire to obtain acceptance or recognition and to feed the unmet craving found in the sacral chakra. I have had several clients who experienced childhood rejection from "mean" girls or boys who continue to struggle with an eating compulsion or addiction, as this behavior is attempting to satiate this longing for connection and acceptance and to be able to speak their truth and to feel truly heard. As the sacral chakra yearns for this connection, the throat chakra becomes deficient, as it is attempting to feed and bring balance to the sacral chakra, leaving the client with thyroid issues, aphonia, or weight challenges.

As you will learn in chapter 16, drinking water can help heal the second chakra. Water is the healing element of the sacral chakra. Interestingly, there is an Ayurvedic recommendation, *ushna udaka*, to boil your water for ten minutes (and sometimes longer depending on your personal body needs) in the morning to transform the property of the water to make it more absorbable for the body. Boiling the water removes the gas from the liquid. This degassed water aids in balancing the sacral chakra but only when the water is effervesced.

You will learn in chapter 28 that ether, also known as gas, balances the throat chakra. Just as water balances the sacral chakra, the element ether balances the throat chakra. The water becomes more efficient in healing the body when its energetic partner element is also reduced. Compromise is required even with these two partner elements.

The boiling and off-gassing water process creates a water structure better absorbed and welcomed into the body because it is balanced physically, elementally, and energetically to offer the maximum healing results upon ingestion. The water reaches a state of elemental balance for the body before consumption. Equilibrium is reached when both chakras are healed by their necessary element. The second chakra is the source of our emotions, and as we balance the energy in this center, we will come to a more harmonious state of being. This center not only helps us process our own emotions but also hear and interpret more accurately the emotions others are feeling as well. The more attuned you are to your own emotions, the more clearly you can discern other people's emotions.

When the energy is not flowing and becomes stuck, we feel disconnected from others and from ourselves. When this happens, we can often feel panic, loneliness, or experience bladder infections or sexual organ issues. The key to healing this center is remaining balanced with our own emotions and recognizing when we have taken on someone else's emotions, which may be triggering our energy or stagnating our energy because we feel erupted or frozen in emotion when the energy becomes too much to handle. This freeze state of emotion causes us to stagnate our energy.

As with all addiction, hoarding behavior may exist in varying degrees. Have you noticed that you can't throw something away "just in case" you might need it? Some preparation is necessary in life, of course, but when you need to hold on to more than one backup, this may be something to ponder. Often, I have seen clients with this condition who had something taken out of their control between the ages of seven to fourteen, which consequently made them believe holding on to things was more important than people. A move, a divorce leading to a division of households, a robbery, a friend taking something without permission, a childhood family without money for food. I have seen these result in the stockpiling of items and excessive food that keeps someone from being organized or living simply.

If you have hoarding tendencies, did one of these occur in your life during the ages of seven to fourteen? Have you found that holding on to things has become a priority over relationships in your life? It's not too late to heal this energy and begin to have meaningful, connected, fulfilling relationships. Begin to notice which is the greater priority—relationships, food, or things.

This is one of the chakras where obsessive-compulsive disorder (OCD) may exist. Obsession is a strong desire, and compulsions are the need to control it. As mentioned earlier, obsession can be triggered by rejection. As the obsession increases, our desire to control it increases. When we do not speak up for ourselves or speak our truth, this can create an imbalance in the sacral chakra that ignites this desire to control because we might have felt powerless in not speaking up. Our second chakra gives us an opportunity to fuel our desires and feel connected to them. As we balance this energy center, OCD obsession begins to calm, and tendencies begin to lessen.

The Antidote

The throat chakra energy is the antidote to the sacral chakra's imbalance.

When the sacral chakra energy is stagnant, a feeling of isolation and detachment exists. This is the moment when someone is talking incessantly but has no emotional connection to their words. The person speaking is seeking connection because there is a lack of connection within but is only able to accomplish long-windedness. When the throat chakra's healing energy of feeling heard and a focus on the emotion of being worthy of feeling heard can be incorporated here, equilibrium is established.

When the sacral chakra is excessive, it is full of blame and feels overemotional. It is lacking the energy from the throat chakra to share its feelings and expression. This is when we feel so emotional, intimidated, or traumatized we can't speak. Once the throat's energy of expression is added, equilibrium is established.

Counter Chakra Seed Planting

The desires ignited between the ages of seven to fourteen may be realized during the window of twenty-eight to thirty-five. On the high side, desire is fulfilled and joy is found. On the low side of this energy, blame for all the reasons why life has not worked out for a person may also present itself if the original desire never manifested.

CHAPTER 15

The Auric Effect:
The Sacral Chakra

Deficient Sacral Chakra
When the sacral chakra is stagnant, the throat chakra is excessive. This creates a forward-reaching aura that attempts to cling to another person, often through excessive talking and grasping for someone to listen. This energy pushes the other person away because the energy is so strong coming at them. As the other person feels this clinging energy, they tend to distance themselves physically, even, without realizing it. The listener may unconsciously take a step back because their energy system wants to stay clear of the clinging auric energy.

This auric energy is sticky and acts like a vacuum in the sacral chakra, looking to cling to connection to fill this energy center. This is the person in the room who will talk for days seeking connection, but no one wants to talk to because their auric energy is full of clinginess, overbearingness, and a lack of true emotional connection. Once this energetic partnership is balanced within, this person has the potential to have great relationships that feel connected and pleasurable and no longer clingy and overbearing.

The Auric Effect ✧ *Sacral Chakra*

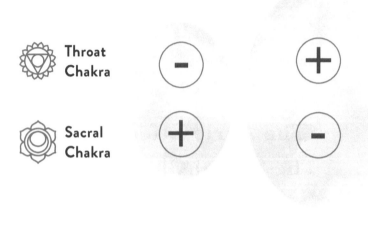

I have seen this aura size to be typically three to four feet around the body. This is the overtalker or liar who is often struggling with sexual organ issues or bladder and kidney issues. If you are experiencing this type of imbalance, shift your mindset to one of knowing your worth and speaking your truth to people who value what you share. This is addressed more in chapters 25 and 28. Attract and magnetize this person of value toward you; never chase. You'll never catch the people you are chasing. Their energy will escape you just like opposing magnets. Become the energy people are drawn to by connecting to yourself first, and you will find life feels more fulfilling and nourishing.

Excessive Sacral Chakra

When the sacral chakra is excessive, the throat chakra is deficient. The person does not feel worthy of speaking or of being heard. Their voice is often diminished either by volume or texture and can sometimes feel nervous about speaking. This auric energy is also sticky because the element of this energy center is imbalanced. There is too much water held within the sacral chakra and as a result there is excessive energy. There is no release of the water through gas by way of speaking. (More on this in chapter 41.) The aura is tighter to the body but has the potential to equally add toxicity to the energetic cords it can create. (More detail on this in chapter 47.) The aura is tighter to the body at less than one inch around the body because there is a belief no one wants to hear their story, so energetically it feels safer not to connect to others' energetic fields. Those who do connect tend to have clingy relationships. This is the quiet talker who is struggling with thyroid, throat, or hearing issues.

CHAPTER 16

Tools to Heal Your Sacral Chakra Marker

TO SAY THIRD GRADE was a tough year for me would be an understatement. My teacher's name was Mrs. Tuttle, although everyone called her Mrs. Turtle. We all loved Mrs. Turtle.

Turtles are revered as one of the most sacred animals, as they represent spirituality, health, and healing. My Universal signs transformed from lightning and thunder to turtles. It makes perfect Divine sense why this year carried with it such transformation.

After tetherball, the next favorite activity of the girls in my class was trading stickers. I was so proud of my curated sticker book. Each page was organized by category and filled with scratch-'n'-sniff, puffy, glitter rainbow and unicorn stickers. I beamed with joy when I carried it around the play yard. Everyone said I had the best sticker book, and, let's be honest, my ego loved that praise.

One morning though, at the sound of the bell, I reached down into my backpack and felt around for it. I began to search faster and faster, as my breath quickened and panic set in. My sticker book was missing! I asked the teacher and everyone in class if they had seen it. No one claimed to know where it was. A few days later, I saw my sticker book in the class bully's backpack, but I was too afraid to ask for it back. A few weeks later, just like the Rainbow

Girls' shirt, it showed up with its original sanctity destroyed. The book was mangled and disassembled. I tried to start a new sticker book, but nothing felt the same. I internally blamed him for ruining this passion of mine rather than owning my lack of standing up to him. I carried that blame for a long time.

If I'm honest, I still feel a little pang and a deep appreciation of a fabulous glitter sticker.

But desire and blame live in the same place in our body, and if we're not aware, we can shift to powerless blame rather than triumphing in powerful desire. When we do not achieve what we desire, it is easier to blame others than hold ourselves accountable for standing up for ourselves, speaking our life into existence, and taking ourselves to the next level. How different would my experience have been if I had stood up for myself and asked for my book back? I would have spoken my truth and basked in my desire and established my own energetic equilibrium here within this partnership.

Where have you allowed your unfulfilled desire to turn into blame?

Our desire can drive us to bring to life the most incredible world-changing ideas and can support us in manifesting our heart's deepest longings. It can also drive us into a dark, lonely place of despair and illness if our energy is not balanced properly. How do we heal this intimate and sacred sanctuary of emotion? How can we go deep enough in our healing to make a difference and emerge from the darkness as an empowered and balanced soul?

Begin to incorporate the following tools and techniques into your everyday life to experience a more emotionally balanced and powerful way of life.

Color and Clothes

How emotional do you get over sports? People scream, cry, and jump up and down! Many people who watch a game experience the full spectrum of emotion. Why do you think teams have certain colors? What do you think happens, energetically, when all of their fans wear the team's colors? Do you think it builds energy for the team?

With what you have learned so far about color attracting energy, I bet you know the answer. The wave of matching color draws in energy to support the team's energy. The same works for each of your energy centers.

When your second chakra is imbalanced, choose to wear orange. This might be easier if you are a San Francisco Giants, Denver Broncos, or Phoenix Suns fan, but I assure you, it is not limited to sports apparel! You can wear orange clothes, jewelry, underwear, PJs, and so on. If you really do not enjoy wearing orange, wrap yourself up in an orange blanket or cuddle up with an orange pillow the next time you feel really upset about something. This will aid in drawing in the orange energy frequency and balancing your energy and emotions.

Element

Water can destroy with its volume, power, and speed. Water can also heal as it cleanses and purifies. It can reach almost every untouchable crevice. What is true for water is also true for the emotions expressed through our words. The water in a racing river jets over rocks and plants, while a still pond grows moss over its surface. Moss grows as a result of the collection of fertilizer and bacteria in the water, often due to runoff collected from somewhere else. Where in your life have you come to an emotional standstill because you've collected too much emotional "fertilizer" from other sources and have found yourself stuck? Or are you just racing so fast there is no time to pay attention to the rocks and plants as you rush by? We experience both—being stuck and rushing. Our energy varies, but it is possible to reach a unified state of emotional equilibrium that helps balance both ends of the emotional spectrum.

What would happen if the rushing water met the still pond? Would the fast water slow and the still water begin to move? The same is true of our emotions. As we put the tools in this chapter into place in our lives, we begin to address our stuck emotions, while also finding control over our overbearing ones. Using the element of water, we find our equilibrium.

Think of your emotions—fast-moving and slow—as flowing back and forth like water. Picture them lapping back and forth, helping each other, in this center, to create overall balance. It's a powerful visualization. When we visualize this energy flowing, it helps the water of our physical body flow as well. Our lymphatic system, blood flow, urine, and digestive fluids find balance when we bring this energy center into equilibrium. If you are struggling with bladder infections or erectile disfunction, take time to feel through this section (and the throat chakra chapters 25 and 28) again and see what emotions may be causing these physical manifestations.

In addition to visualization, you can use physical water to help heal your second chakra. Take a bath or shower. It is not just coincidence that many people "cry it out" in the shower or bath. This element helps release and balance the emotions. Sit by a creek or ocean or listen to water sounds. (YouTube is a good source of natural sounds.) Imagine this water flowing back and forth, cleaning and clearing the heavy, dark, and disrupted emotion that weighs on this space. You may even imagine it as a waterfall descending out of your second chakra. As you become more sensitive to your own energy, this center will feel weighted when you are emotionally upset or stuck. You'll know when it's time for a good rinse.

Water's healing power for this energy center is not limited to visualizing or bathing in it. Our second chakra is also healed by drinking quality water. It is so important to drink a high-quality mineral water not packaged in a plastic bottle. You may also begin a practice of drinking solar water. You can create your own bottle of solar water by placing a glass bottle with a sealed top in the windowsill to absorb the sun's rays. You may write words on the outside of the bottle to infuse the bottle with those frequencies, as in the Dr. Emoto experiment we addressed in chapter 6. As the sun shines into the bottle, it infuses the water with this energy. Or use a colored bottle. Dr. Hew Len, most known for his work with the Ho'oponopono blessing, which helps us acknowledge and heal our reality, advises that a blue bottle will clear subconscious programming and help release unconscious patterning.

Water in all of its forms, both physical and energetic, is deeply healing for this energy center.

Our Five Senses

When we eat, we use a combination of taste (second chakra) and smell (first chakra), and the experience invigorates those two energy centers and heals the inner child within us that was nourished from the ages of seven to fourteen. This is why our favorite family recipes taste so good to us. They not only nourish us physically; they nourish us emotionally and energetically. The movie *Ratatouille* excellently depicts this playback experience as the food critic tastes the food and his mind rewinds on his internal timeline. Internally, he is brought back to himself standing in his grandmother's kitchen smelling the beautiful aroma of the cooking and enjoying her food. This is precisely how powerful food is in healing our energy, body, and spirit because it ignites each one of our senses.

I spent several years writing this book, and as it was nearing the end of my writing process, I found myself saying, "I want it so badly I can taste it." This is second chakra desire and emotion perfectly depicted in terms of our senses. The words we say and the symptoms that arise within us are all connected.

This is also why food is tasteless when we are upset—just like my mom's shared ice cream sandwich. When our second chakra energy is stagnant, so is our sense of taste. The energy is no longer moving, so the juices are not flowing through our mouth. We are working so hard to not feel our emotions that we also do not allow ourselves to taste the deliciousness of life.

This power can also ignite an intense trigger connected to taste. Where could your trigger have been created? Were you told devastating news while eating something as a child? Is there a flavor that brings back the memory of childhood illness that repulses you now? Are you sensitive to tastes and prefer bland food?

The sacral chakra feeds the sense of taste and the sense organ of the tongue. When a trigger disturbance arises in the sense of taste or the tongue, we can look to the themes of this chakra to discover the root cause of this ailment.

Organic of Action

The organ that offers us the opportunity for action in the sacral chakra is the reproductive organ. We give physical experience to our sacral energy through our sexual organs. Our sacral chakra desires are not limited to sexual desires, but it is the organ that offers us the physical experience and provides us with an indicator of imbalance. If you are experiencing sexual organ issues, review chapters 13, 16, 25, and 28 and determine where you can empower yourself more to bring all of your desires and creativity to life.

Food

Foods that support this energy center include oranges, melons, coconuts, honey, and other sweet fruit that will make your mouth water. Of course, continue to drink plenty of high-quality water throughout your day to maintain a high level of water in the body.

Imagine reaching your hand into the pantry and pulling out a bag of dried mangos (or another food on the stated list). You tear off the top, and the aroma of mangos penetrates your nose. You reach into the bag to pull out one mango, orange and perfect, and bite into it, tearing off a delicious bite. You begin to chew the hearty and tough piece of fruit.

What is happening in your mouth? Did you notice that your mouth began to water just at reading about eating a dried mango? Our saliva is part of the waterways of our body, the lymphatic system, and this process opens and heals our sacral chakra. We don't even need to eat physically; our thoughts are that powerful.

Our thoughts trigger emotions, emotions move energy,
and energy manifests physically.
What we do with our energy matters.
If our energy isn't weak, our body doesn't weaken.

Essential Oils

The supportive essential oils for this center include the following:

- **CEDARWOOD:** heals the inability to form emotional bonds and loneliness
- **PATCHOULI:** supports the acceptance of the body and encourages the fluidity of physical body; tempers obsessive traits
- **SANDALWOOD:** heals loneliness and disconnection to others and to the Divine
- **YLANG-YLANG:** aids in healing the inner child and its hurt feelings and traumas.

Use them in your bath, diffuse them, or combine them with a carrier oil such as coconut oil and rub them on your second chakra.

Crystals

The crystals that bring great balance and healing to this center include the following:

- **CARNELIAN:** increases self-esteem and confidence
- **SHUNGITE:** eliminates negative energy and purifies the body
- **TANGERINE QUARTZ:** balances emotions.

You can carry these in your pockets, lie down with these on your second chakra, or use athletic tape and tape them onto your body until you feel your energy frequency has raised appropriately.

Mantra

The seed syllable, or mantra, for this energy center is VAM, reso-nating in keynote D. The first note of the song "Amazing Grace" begins on the note of D, which is why people feel emotional at the start of this moving song. You can find this note and keep this tone in mind during your chanting. We can remember this as the center that feeds our sexual organs and feeds the v-v-vagina. We remember this as *V + Aum = VAM*. Chanting the mantra VAM encourages balance to heal this center.

Environmental Shift

The first and second chakra are tightly intertwined with each other and the bedroom, so this energetic remedy is for the bedroom, too. Do you have a mirror in your bedroom or a television screen that faces the bed or the door's entrance? According to feng shui, the reflection of a mirror or glass reflection can repel or double the energy of that which it is facing. Often, however, we have a mirror facing our bed or in alignment with the doorway. If the mirror is facing the doorway, it reflects all the energy flowing into the room back out, leaving the person sleeping in that room exhausted and potentially depressed because there is no energy flowing to them while their body restores throughout the night. When the mirror faces the bed, it doubles the energy present. If you are single, it will double your single body energetically, so it appears that there are two bodies in the bed. You may find it challenging to find a partner. If you are in relationship with another person, this brings in more than two bodies, so you may find the presence of an affair in your relationship. When you are sick, it can double your illness and it can create mental illness.

Mirrors in the bedroom can cause illness for two reasons. When we have a mirror in alignment with our bed, we can subconscious-ly see another body moving as we roll over at night. This can cause us to startle and remain in a fight-or-flight mental state while we are sleeping, resulting in anxiety rather than falling into a deep, alpha brain state. Secondly (and for some a bit more challenging to accept) at night, your soul travels and returns to its energetic source to rejuvenate and restore. Upon leaving the body, the soul may get startled by seeing its reflection in the mirror, which may cause nightmares. When a mirror is in the bedroom, the soul may see a double set of bodies (the actual body and its reflection) and upon its return to the body, attempt to enter the reflection, leaving the person mentally confused and experiencing depersonalization. Often, this body confusion is at the root of body dysmorphic disorder, a version of OCD, as the soul is confused by which body it is supposed to enter and does not recognize its intended container. Depersonalization may be experienced because the soul is outside the body working to return to its original container. This is also why depersonalization can be a fleeting experience as the soul shifts back and forth between the two body images. When I have a client suffering from body dysmorphic disorder, one of my first questions is whether or not there is a mirror or television set facing the bed. I have found this connection to be very consistent.

If you are struggling with illness or mental unrest, experiment with moving the mirrors out of your room or covering them up with a beautiful scarf or blanket at night and notice how your mental health improves.

Yoga

Sun Salutation (*surya namaskar*) is healing to this center, as it is fluid like water. Child's pose (*balasana*) helps open your hips and connect you with your inner child. Since this energy center heals our seven- to fourteen-year-old, let's begin there.

Archangels

Archangel Raphael is known as the angel of healing. In Hebrew, Raphael means "It is God who heals." Raphael helps us soothe our emotions in this center so that we can obtain a healthy and balanced body and energy system. Say this prayer twice a day, morning and evening, or whenever you think of it: "Archangel Raphael, thank you for helping me heal my body, emotionally, energetically, spiritually, and physically. I am so grateful for your help."

Archangel Raphael's role as the archangel of healing is vital in this chakra, which, as you have learned, is the center of our emotions. He balances and heals our emotions, which ultimately heals our physical bodies.

Our thoughts trigger emotions, emotions move energy,
and energy manifests physically.
What we do with our energy matters.
If our energy isn't weak, our body doesn't weaken.

Ten-Second Rescue

Place the first two fingers of your right hand on your right nostril and breathe in and out of your left nostril for eight to ten breaths. Begin to feel that movement in your sacral area. For this energy center, we breathe only through the left nostril to bring in feelings of calmness and patience. See the next section and chapter 20 for more on how to use nostril breathing.

Homework

Begin a daily practice of chanting VAM during your shower and setting intention for your day. Choose which desire you intend to bring to fruition for the day. Thank the Universe for offering your next step and set intention that you will remain open to how to serve for the day.

As the Bhagavad Gita teaches, "We have a right to the work alone, not to the fruits of our labor." We may never know why we must complete certain tasks, but it is always for our blessing and our good as our soul is developed through our efforts. Trust the next step.

Second Chakra Journaling

What do you really want? What do you long for at night? Describe it in detail.

What addiction are you struggling with right now? Is there an unmet desire from your first answer that is creating this addiction? Was there a childhood experience that set off your longing, typically experienced between ages seven and fourteen?

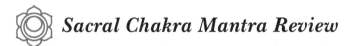 *Sacral Chakra Mantra Review*

Chakra	Mantra	How do I remember it?	Keynote
Second: SACRAL	VAM	V-V-Vagina— connected to sexual organs.	KEYNOTE D: first note in "Amazing Grace"
First: ROOT	LAM	L-L-Lowest energy center.	KEYNOTE C: first note in "Old MacDonald Had a Farm"

Sacral chakra meditation: Join me at www.LoveHealThrive.com for the sacral chakra meditation.

It's safe to connect. It's safe to love. We are more injured by holding back than we are by risking connection. Let yourself bask in connection and watch your life begin to thrive.

CHAPTER 17

The Personal Image Connection to Your Third Chakra Marker: The Solar Plexus Chakra

BY TWELVE YEARS OLD, I had begun to heal from the tetherball queendom trauma and attracted a loving circle of girls who would continue to be a strong ring of trust, love, and certainty for decades to come.

But there was still a part of me that struggled with trust rooted in the childhood seed of exclusion.

So at fourteen, during this energetic window of soul growth, I found a new remedy for the pain I experienced from ages zero to fourteen years old. Tapping into the low-side power of the solar plexus, I decided I would cure this pain by controlling situations instead.

It began in junior high school, innocently enough, when I decided I would run for ASB president. At the time of this story, rap was just beginning to become popular, and I decided I was going to deliver my campaign speech through this new form of communication. What could be cooler?

Election day arrived, and my name was called to address the student body to share my hopes and dreams if elected as their fearless leader. I began my very well-rehearsed rap, and the school auditorium erupted with laughter. I had not anticipated this response, and I had a moment of sheer panic and regret. While my mouth was rapping, my head and heart were trying to decide if I should just finish or run offstage. The strength found within my solar plexus ignited and pushed me through my fear to finish. Upon completion of my rap, the auditorium jumped to their feet and hollered and clapped louder than I have ever heard a group of people applaud. I was so grateful I did not run offstage. Those ten seconds of courage allowed me to become president and also taught me to trust my gut and the Divine outcome. I continued to be class president three out of four years in high school, president of any and every club and organization, culminating in being president of my college sorority.

For what could be safer for my inner child who feared being excluded by a group than controlling the group? Not much. To most, I looked like a powerful, confident overachiever. Only I didn't realize this pattern until I reached adulthood. My subconscious and solar plexus were the only ones who really knew what was going on. I was trying to control my surroundings rather than resting and sitting in a place of allowance and acceptance. Although I didn't lead from this place consciously, I led then, and still lead now, from a place of openhearted love, connection, and service. After decades of spiritual work, I now believe—truly believe to my core—that what needs to leave leaves and what needs to manifest will, all for our blessing. I remain in a state of acceptance and understanding as I welcome life in. I still love old-school rap and have learned to also be a helper within the group who does not have to lead everything. So now when I lead, I lead to inspire, not control.

This state of allowance and acceptance is the bounty we get to reap from a balanced solar plexus.

In this chapter, you are going to learn why the mental push, relentless drive, isolating control, and paralyzing fear can be so unhealthy for you and can lead to digestive illness and mental struggle. You will also learn how there are healthier and more satisfying ways to complete your goals. We are tapping into your third chakra—

your solar plexus or *manipura*. This area is where your ego lives—your personal power as well as your transformation powerhouse that, when activated, will move you forward in your life.

This is also where your fear resides. Once you transform your fear into faith and acceptance in this center, you are able to better discern what is truly a fearful threat so that you no longer live from an overactivated, sympathetic-dominant nervous system. When your solar plexus is balanced and strong, you are able to allow your personal power to surrender to an amazing Divine power that comes through to guide, strengthen, and help you feel fearless—not fearless in an ego sense, but fearless in such a way that you know, with all your soul, that you are being strengthened and guided on the next step of your path by something greater than you. It is in this moment that waves of peace flood your body and you recognize there is typically no need for fear to run our lives.

First, let's go over the lower two chakras, whose strength plays a major role.

You began with your foundation. You strengthened your first (root) chakra to feel safer, more secure, accepted, and provided for in life.

When you feel truly safe and secure, then you are able to balance your emotions in the sanctuary of your emotions, your second (sacral) chakra. You feel safe enough to connect. You feel safe enough to be vulnerable. You feel safe enough to work through your own feelings and help all those emotions reach equilibrium.

When you feel safe, when you feel emotionally balanced, then you are able to *be you*. Unapologetically, joyfully you.

You know who you are. You know what you stand for, and you know your life purpose and have enough energy to move forward toward it on your path.

Your solar plexus is about knowing your self-worth in gold, meaning you understand that just as gold is a precious metal, you are precious and value yourself in the same way you would value gold—a metal that is not only valuable but also does not corrode—just like your true spirit. When you bask in this appreciation for yourself, you will find a genuine confidence to go for what you want in your life and believe and know it will come to fruition. The solar plexus completes the three energy centers that manage your physical world. The first chakra manages your physical needs, your second chakra manages your emotional needs and desires for connection, and the third chakra is about defining you in this physical space and feeling joy in your life. Who are you? What do you stand for? What is important to you? Who are you without a label or identity?

Addiction to pleasure lives in the sacral chakra. Pure joy lives in the solar plexus chakra. To rise above addiction, we can use this feeling of joy as a metaphorical and energetic "carrot" to entice the frequency of desire to elevate, resulting in craving joy more than addiction-seeking pleasure.

The same is true of any relationships that may involve dependence or projection. We can actually support ourselves and dare to be who we are, rather than relying on an addiction to others to do it for us. Often, love affairs (physical and emotional) and codependent relationships of all types occur because we see in someone something that we want in our own life but are not allowing this aspect to shine within ourselves. Sometimes, we may not even feel *worthy* of allowing this trait into our own life. We feel special and unique when this someone, who embodies what we admire, gives us attention. However, in permitting this person to be the reason we feel special and unique, we inadvertently give our own power away. We forget that we are Divinely special and unique. As you find your own worth and cherish your own self-worth in gold and begin to embody the traits you have been longing for yourself, the relationship often falls away.

People who have repeated affairs or repeated codependency issues often have a deep-rooted lack of self-worth or an inability to feel good enough about themselves. They lean on the approval and desire of others to fill this void of self-worth, rather than realizing they can fill it themselves through their own powerful connection with themselves and with the Divine. Learning that you can help yourself feel safe and emotionally secure is empowering. It is the power of the first two chakra centers that supports this third chakra in feeling strong and self-assured.

Our solar plexus is our individual imprint of the Divine and needs no justification or outside endorsement. When we come to know this, we know we are worthy. We know our worth in gold. We know we are special and unique because we are exactly who we are meant to be.

Max Lucado's book *You Are Special* teaches this lesson very powerfully. In this story, a puppet lives in a land where everyone has either gold star stickers or gray dot stickers. Naturally, every puppet wants the gold star stickers. However, there is one puppet with no stickers because neither kind will adhere to her skin. Another puppet, covered in gray stickers, asks her secret. She takes him to the puppet maker who tells him that he is Divinely unique and special and does not need the endorsement of another puppet to know he is loved. With that, his stickers all fall off and he no longer needs anyone else's stickered endorsement.

In these times, those stickers are perfect metaphors for social media likes and comments and the belief that we must obtain others' approval to feel worthy to speak or post something. Post because your soul would not feel complete without spreading that message. Your embodiment alone is worthy of praise regardless of its achievements.

Why Clear the Third Chakra?

Have you ever been so worried about the details of your life that your stomach hurt? Or you were so nervous to give a presentation that you simply weren't hungry? Has a friend ever betrayed you where you felt powerless?

Have you ever experienced one of these examples? What did it feel like? Did it feel like you just got "punched in the gut"? Or that you felt that you were so weak, you couldn't eat or move?

This was the energy of your third chakra feeling diminished. This was the intense moment your energy felt fear from the third chakra, coupled with the emotional turbulence from the second chakra and the lack of safety from the first chakra. But when your third chakra is strong and powerful, and backed up by a strong first and second chakra, like all muscles, it will be more resilient and able to withstand a compromising situation without ever feeling powerless.

In personal terms, a cleared third chakra will help you have a stronger sense of self and a sense of personal power without arrogance or ego. You will experience a state of peace and *knowingness* that will allow you to feel confident in a way that you may not have experienced before. It is a state of inner peace and power wrapped up in one that withstands external challenge.

In business, a cleared third chakra helps alleviate fear over situations and reduces ego-based decisions. A balanced third chakra will encourage collective decision-making in a way that is most beneficial for the team.

Third Chakra Description

How do we know if the energy in our solar plexus chakra is excessive, deficient, or balanced?

Excessive Solar Plexus Chakra Energy

You find yourself feeling angry; struggling with control issues; driven by perfectionism; overreacting to situations; exuding excessive stubbornness; acting overly critical; haunted by eating disorders; and experiencing ulcers or other digestive problems.

Third chakra dominance is easy to spot in your life. It's the person you feel you must speak to cautiously because you just aren't sure when they're going to explode. It's the person who picks on you incessantly and feels that nothing is ever right. Understand that if you are in an entanglement with someone whose third chakra is excessive, they are likely suffering more than you are. They are so unhappy with themselves that it is easier to pick on you than acknowledge their own pain. They simply don't know any other way to treat you yet, nor where to begin healing their own wounds.

If you are the person with the excessive solar plexus, you know how much suffering exists here. Begin to be kinder to yourself and spend a little extra time in this chapter. Remember that like attracts like. We are all connected. If there are people showing up with this in your life, chances are that you are struggling, too.

Deficient Solar Plexus Energy

You are too afraid to make a move because it might be the wrong one, or you might get hurt. This deficiency often involves low self-esteem, difficulty in making decisions, allowing life to pass you by while you do nothing. It is the feeling of retreat when someone overpowers you.

These people allow life to happen to them. They lack a sense of self-worth, or a feeling that they deserve goodness, or they don't believe they are destined to receive blessings. There is a quiet suffering as opposed to the explosive suffering of the excessive solar plexus. Instead of pushing your agenda, this state feels more like you don't even deserve to have an agenda at all due to fear or a feeling of lack of worth. The fear that can build here may cause extreme insecurity and illness, especially when the first and second chakras are weakened. Your energy system will always be trying to bring power back to you; however, the harder your system has to work, the more physical symptoms you may begin to see. Your soul wants its power back and will work exhaustively to help you get it.

Balanced Solar Plexus Chakra Energy

You feel self-confident, have a strong sense of purpose, and are self-motivated, reliable, and able to move forward in life with confidence and power. You can set healthy boundaries.

As we maintain stronger boundaries, we no longer feel compromised emotionally or energetically and this allows our energy center to remain balanced. This vibrant, strong, and balanced energy center leads to less fear, less digestive and mental struggle, and a great deal more faith.

Location

The location of this energy center is below your breastbone and above your navel. It is where we feel sick to our stomach when we experience compromising situations. When you are in a conversation with someone and the person tells you news that feels scary or compromising or that leaves you uncertain, what do you naturally do with your arms? How do you cross them? What area of your body do your arms cover? It tends to be over your solar plexus because your body's energy feels vulnerable and in need of protection—you naturally cross your arms.

The next time you feel unsure or powerless and you cross your arms over your solar plexus, it is time to ground and give your body the love and strength it needs and a reminder of how powerful you actually are.

Physical Correlations in Body

This chakra regulates your digestion, including the stomach, pancreas, gall bladder, and liver. If you struggle with hypoglycemia, diabetes, arthritis, acid reflux, fibromyalgia, nerve pain, organ problems—especially kidneys—or have difficulty gaining or losing weight, dig a little deeper into this chapter and see what past hurts or pain may be causing the disruption before moving on to see if you can heal your condition.

After class one day, a student of mine walked up to me amazed. She could not believe that through her in-class journaling, she was able to precisely pinpoint an intense experience that made her feel powerless at eighteen years old. She was able to connect this to the same year she was diagnosed with diabetes. She identified the root emotional cause of her illness, which triggered her emotions that began her road to healing.

Our thoughts trigger emotions, emotions move energy,
and energy manifests physically.
What we do with our energy matters.
If our energy isn't weak, our body doesn't weaken.

Color

The energy that vibrates in this center can be seen as yellow and gold and vibrates at a frequency of approximately 520 hertz. Do you think it is coincidence that people who are jaundiced have yellow-toned skin and eyes? Jaundice is often a disruption of the gallbladder, pancreas, or liver, all of which are fed by the third chakra energy.

For adults, they can look to their moments of experiencing fear or powerlessness to determine their root cause of their ailment. Illness that occurs before the age of seven tends to be karmic.

For babies with jaundice, any karmic issues may be cleared through prayer, energy clearing, and cord clearing, although, of course, medical advice should be consulted, as well. Again, as always, please check with your doctor for any and all health issues.

Emotions

The solar plexus chakra is the home to our feelings of anger, self-empowerment and disempowerment, frustration, and feelings of powerlessness. It is also where we can exude faith, grace, self-assurance, and a knowingness of security that surpasses any fear.

It is where we can feel "punched in the gut" but is also where we can experience "gut feelings" we can learn to trust as truth over time.

Lifetime Development

This energy center develops between the ages of fourteen and twenty-one. Were you defiant in your teenage years? Looking back, do you think it was defiance or just figuring out life for yourself? What was important to you? It was during this time you began to take a stand for what mattered to you. Where does your personal power come from now? What do you stand for? Who are you? What drives you? These are all the questions that form the strength of this area initially explored during this age period of our lifetime. What ethics did you define for yourself during this time?

The Everyday Connection

- Are you struggling with control?
- Have you felt stuck in your life?
- Have you been riddled with fear?
- Have you felt lost and without a clear idea of who you are?
- Have you been experiencing any digestive issues?

These are all pointers in your everyday life that you may be experiencing solar plexus chakra energy issues. If you said "yes" to any of the above questions, review this chapter and think where you can strengthen yourself in more empowering ways.

CHAPTER 18

The Counter Chakra to the Solar Plexus Chakra

THE SOLAR PLEXUS pairs with our seventh chakra, our crown chakra. It is the connection point we use to connect to the Divine. Much as we connect to Earth through our root chakra, so we connect to the Divine through our crown chakra.

It has been scientifically proven that the central and enteric nervous systems communicate with each other in both directions. The brain communicates with the gut. The gut communicates with the brain. Neurotransmitters have been found in the gut that affect our mood and mental state.

We also know this to be true energetically. The solar plexus feeds the gut and communicates with the brain, which is fed by the crown chakra. Within our third chakra, we transform our fear into faith by leaning on the Divine plan, guidance, and support, the gifts of the crown chakra.

It is important to understand that as you clean the physical gut from candida and parasites, it clears the energy in the solar plexus center, which allows the crown chakra to clear as well. Many reports have suggested that as you clean up the gut, brain fog disappears. The clearing of the gut gets the energetic seesaw moving again between the energy centers. Our gut is often referred to as our second brain, and we understand why this is true through this partnership.

One client suffered from both diabetes and dyslexia. This can result from a deficient solar plexus and an excessive crown chakra. These two conditions are linked, as the crown chakra becomes excessive while it is attempting to feed and balance the solar plexus's energetic deficiency, often caused by overcriticism and fear. The opposite energetic partnership can present itself as well. In TCM, the gall bladder reflects one's state of courage and decisiveness. Here, the solar plexus is showing symptoms due to overthinking and analysis and leaning less on Divine trust.

When an injury or tragedy strikes, we find ourselves predicting what *could* happen and the ways the situation could get worse. This is a function of an excessive solar plexus and diminished crown chakra. We are creating stories or hallucinations because we are fear-driven, and as a result this vast amount of fear depletes our crown chakra energy. Have you ever been in an accident or someone was injured? My daughter injured herself and I found myself saying the wrong words for things all day long. I caught myself telling predictive stories and realized my crown chakra was depleted and my solar plexus was fearful and igniting this energy imbalance. I paused and flowed golden light into my crown chakra and, almost instantly, began to think clearer, speak more accurately, and feel less fear by welcoming in the faith of the Divine plan. All was and is well.

The Antidote

The antidote to the solar plexus imbalance is the crown chakra's healing energy. Which aspects of your crown chakra need to be added to your solar plexus to establish equilibrium?

When the solar plexus is excessive, it results in fear and an intense need for control. Life becomes riddled with fear and control because this energy center is lacking the faith and trust offered by the belief and trust in a Divine plan that is always blessing us.

When the crown chakra's energy of the Divine plan and the perfect next step can be focused on, equilibrium is established.

When the third chakra is deficient, the result is a life without structure or motivation. One may feel confused, unmotivated, or lost while the crown chakra is left to wonder and wander without the clear defining structure and healthy organization offered by a balanced solar plexus. Once the structure of third chakra is added to this partnership, a perfect plan blended with order and Divine intuition is established.

Counter Chakra Seed Planting

The fears we create or believe are soothed by the strengthening of our crown chakra. As you will learn in chapters 33 and 36, the crown chakra helps us know that all things happen for a reason and there is nothing to fear. Everything is for our blessing and allows us to relinquish control and fear. What belief seed is planted from ages fourteen to twenty-one blossoms upon spiritual awakening. The crown chakra energy opens once the chakras leading up to it are opened and balanced.

CHAPTER 19

The Auric Effect:
The Solar Plexus Chakra

Deficient Solar Plexus
When the solar plexus chakra is stagnant and the crown chakra is excessive, the individual's aura is too widely dispersed, and the person often overthinks, overtrusts, and struggles with digestive, eye, and feet issues.

Excessive Solar Plexus
When the solar plexus chakra is excessive and the crown chakra is deficient, the aura is too tight, as it is trying to control everything within its reach. The energy feels structured, hard, and tight in an attempt to fiercely control everything that enters its field. This tends to look like exhaustive focus coupled with a desire for intense control. Headaches and digestive, eye, and feet issues often occur.

If you are experiencing either auric effect, add your antidote, ground your energy, and complete the meditation at www.LoveHealThrive.com for the solar plexus.

The Auric Effect ✧ Solar Plexus Chakra

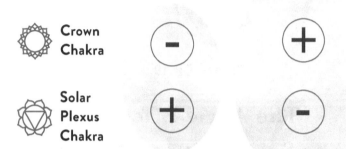

CHAPTER 20

Tools to Heal Your
Solar Plexus Chakra Marker

MY YOUNG DAUGHTERS couldn't wait to go to Girl Scout camp. Part of the prerequisite for attending this camp was that a parent needed to work at the camp. As a result, I found myself at Girl Scout camp every summer for several summers. I helped girls learn how to cook with a Dutch oven over an open fire and we made aluminum foil box ovens and baked cookies with them, but every parent fled and hid when the directors asked for helpers for the knot station.

For life skills, every Girl Scout had to learn how to tie knots, such as the bowline and clover hitch. If you know the bowline knots, you know how confusing it can be to have the bunny wrap around the tree and back down the hole. My bunny was always lost, and I remain challenged by knots to this day—and not just all the confusing knots the camp director frustratingly kept showing me. I struggle with knots of resentment, a result of an imbalanced solar plexus.

Do you also struggle with holding on to resentment, too? Do you also struggle with acid reflux?

My bet is . . . if you have one of these conditions, you probably have the other.

I struggled with both of these for years and have used the following process to heal my body and my heart. I hope this brings you incredible healing, too.

Knots of resentment are energetic binds that collect underneath your rib cage and create stagnant energy. It ultimately opens the emotional window for acid reflux to enter in physically.

First, what is a knot? Knots are complicated. They are layered, intricate, and detailed. To unravel them takes just as much finesse as it does to tie them. If you pull one end, it can tighten the knot, but you can also pull another end and the knot magically unravels.

The same is true of our knots of resentment. Why do we hold on to resentment? Resentment clings to the belief that there was only one way, typically our way, for something to unfold, and when it does not unfold the way we wanted, blame and resentment quickly follow.

Clearly, if we had acted differently, the situation would have been different.

While this may be true, perhaps the process of healing from that experience serves a greater purpose in your life. Our resentment remains because our feelings were hurt and something important to us was not as important to someone else. We were left disempowered and hurt by their actions. We felt devalued and less important than whatever it was the other person chose to accomplish than your desired outcome.

Our ego leads us to believe we have a right to be mad at this person, but that person probably does not even remember the event and the only "upset" remaining is within you.

It's simply not worth it. This resentment is causing physical and emotional harm. How do we remedy these knots?

Just like your shoestrings, we pull these knots apart, string by string, inch by inch. Forgiveness is the remedy for resentment. Forgiveness is a process—an ABC process.

The ABCs of Forgiveness

It begins with awareness.

A. Awareness. We must be aware of what we feel resentful about and also realize the other person made a different choice than the one we wanted them to make.

A choice. That's it. It wasn't personal although I know it feels very, very personal. Sometimes it's hard to recognize that our partners, friends, and family have their hang-ups, too. The faster you allow them to have hang-ups and release your expectations for them, the faster you will heal.

Their action of not choosing you does not take away from your value. Not being valued is at the root of resentment. You didn't value me the way I wanted to be valued and now I'm mad. As I have previously written, feeling mad is our way of covering up our hurt.

I cannot stress this lesson enough that your value is infinite. Holding on to this resentment hands your power over to this person, believing their actions matter more than your actions.

I can tell you, that resentment of them choosing something else instead is only hurting you. It is time to let them make their choice and for you to know you are infinitely valued and loved by something greater than this person's priorities.

B. Believability. If they have apologized, believe them. They are sorry, and depending on how long you've been hurt over this, they may be really sorry. Do both of you a favor—believe them and their apology.

At the same time, I encourage you to bask in your infinite value, knowing that apologies are a desire of one's ego rather than a conduit for relationship healing. You are whole and complete without an apology. Requiring your healing to be dependent on another's words or actions gives your power away and devalues your worth, leading to even more acid reflux.

This helps remove the knots of resentment and control within you. You are whole and complete and filled with Divine perfection. Apologies are a human requirement.

Think bigger. Believe bigger. Believe in yourself.

C. Compassion. Looking at this person whom you allowed to create this knot of resentment within you and realizing they are a human being brings in peace and healing.

They may have made an insensitive choice. This is true but allow yourself to get into an energetic state that surpasses the ability for their choice—or any choice—to affect you or to tie a knot within you.

Compassion helps you move into a state of forgiveness and helps loosen your knots.

When you can feel yourself move through all three of these stages, forgiveness and healing are imminent. This ABCs of Forgiveness process has healed my acid reflux in ways I never expected as I came to value myself in greater and more powerful ways.

The solar plexus imbalance can also present itself as an internal pressure that drives you to push harder. Drink more coffee, stay up later, and force completion because you *must* finish or feel unvalued and ashamed. You continue to push what feels like the square peg into the round hole because you don't feel good enough about yourself . . . this completion should make you feel whole and complete. You keep trying to move forward and keep being met with challenge after challenge, yet you push your way forward, which leads you down the path to illness. Some call this grit and determination. I call this an imbalanced third chakra. While grit and determination can be applauded, there is a tipping point when it becomes too much and reaches a state of unhealthiness. The opposite is true too. When the solar plexus is deficient, you are unmotivated and don't have the impetus to try or feel too afraid to take the first step.

There is a healthy, powerful place in between these two mental extremes. Imagine being able to complete your goal with ease, joy, and grace. When we allow the Divine to guide and strengthen us as an individual in this energy center, we are "power-full." When we allow this center to be driven by our entitled ego, we become a "power-fool." The solar plexus chakra is your unique infusion of Divine power and is designed specifically for you. When you work against this, life feels harder. When you follow your passion and what lights you up, life falls into place effortlessly.

There is a difference between force and effort. Force requires you to push against an opposing element. Effort asks you to do *something*, but it is completed without resistance because it is Divinely guided and inspired. When your solar plexus is balanced, life flows. It all feels supported and power-full.

Because of the nature of this chakra, you may need to take a little longer than you did with the first two chakras to immerse yourself in these techniques and work through them. Return to this chapter as needed. If you do not feel ready to address this energy center yet, I invite you to revisit chakras 1 and 2 to incorporate more of those techniques into your daily routine. (See chapters 7 and 13.) This system is foundational, and as you strengthen the energy centers supporting your solar plexus, you will feel more prepared to continue.

Color and Clothes

The energy of this chakra would be visible on the color spectrum as yellow. Invite in self-worth, confidence, and power! Don your yellow! Wear yellow clothes and gold jewelry. Go for gold! Know your worth in gold! If yellow isn't a flattering color for you, you may wear a yellow tank top under your clothes, wear yellow pajamas, or wrap yourself up in a yellow or shimmery gold blanket with the intention of transforming your fear into faith and to know you are powerful, strong, and worthy.

Element

The element that governs and heals this center is fire. It is no coincidence that we refer to honoring our solar plexus by doing things that light us up.

When we are living in a state of joy, the fire within us is burning at a perfect size. We may be "on fire" with a creative project. However, our fire can burn too hot or not brightly enough. To strengthen this area, light a candle, sit by a fire and stare into it, or, if you do not have live flames, listen to audio tracks of campfire crackling and envision the fire.

When I experience control issues, illness, fear, feeling overwhelmed, or thinking life is coming at me too intensely, my favorite solution is to imagine creating a fire in the space between my breastbone and navel, so big that it burns up whatever is coming at me. Whatever it is—an experience, a person, a decision, a to-do list—it will no longer hold its power over me.

With this visualization, you can "burn off" the emotional velocity of the external factor and sit in a place of confidence and self-power, much like the Christian faith associates the Holy Spirit with fire—defining it as passion and a means for purification. When you feel that this worry has burned to ashes and no longer holds power over your mind, you can see the purified energy in this center grow bigger than whatever threatened you. You can allow your energy to grow as large as necessary so you no longer feel overwhelmed. This is Divine energy and protection aiding in helping you overcome your overwhelm, not the energy of personal ego.

Our Five Senses

Have you been having eye problems such as blurry vision, floaters, or even a torn retina? I have several clients with third chakra issues who have serious eye issues. It is not just coincidence. The sense fed by our solar plexus is our eyesight. Referring back to our jaundice example, isn't it interesting that when the pancreas, or another third chakra organ, is imbalanced, the yellow coloring appears in the eyes? It is incredible to witness the many signs our bodies give us.

The good news is these symptoms can offer us the road map to our healing.

Organ of Action

When we know who we are and what we want, we move forward. We are able to move forward through our feet and legs. If you are experiencing numbness in your legs and feet, toe fungus, or pulled muscles, notice which side of the body it is on (and consult a doctor for persistent numbness). If it is on the right side of your body, are you struggling with a man in your life? If you are a man and your right leg is having trouble, are you not standing up for yourself? Are you too afraid to move forward? If it is the left side of the body, are you afraid to move forward with a woman? If you are a woman, are you too afraid to move forward?

Our feet and legs tell a valuable story about the balance of our third chakra, the *manipura*. Every client I have seen who has stomach problems also has eye problems and either leg or feet issues. These are all connected and offer you incredible guidance.

Collect the evidence and determine how you can move forward more powerfully in your own life.

Food

This energy center fuels your digestion system, so food and the process of its digestion are very important for this chakra and your energetic state. Food that is yellow in color and warming is supportive including yellow and orange peppers, lemons, corn, sweet potatoes, ginger, turmeric, and chamomile tea.

Agni means fire in Sanskrit. In Ayurvedic medicine, it is recommended to eat in a way that supports this fire in your belly at the source of your digestion. Here are a few recommendations to keep your *agni* burning:

- Drink warm or room-temperature water. Avoid ice unless you are in hot temperatures and your *agni* has become too hot and needs immediate cooling. You may even add ginger to your boiled water.
- Refrain from drinking water approximately twenty minutes before or after your meals. Drinking dilutes stomach acid and douses the *agni* in your stomach.
- Do not snack in between meals. Snacking does not allow your fire to replenish and be prepared to process the next meal. If you are finding yourself hungry, consider adding a bit more fat to your meals to sustain your energy and satisfy your appetite longer.

Essential Oils

The supportive essential oils for this center include the following:

- **FRANKINCENSE:** heals father issues, abandonment fears, and spiritual disconnect
- **MYRRH:** heals mother issues, distrust of others, feeling fearful of the world
- **ROMAN CHAMOMILE:** assists in determining life purpose

Rub these oils, mixed with a carrier oil such as fractionated coconut oil, on your solar plexus and around that area, front and back. Remember our solar plexus releases in the front and back of our body, so we want to ensure we are aiding both energy points. Burning incense of these oils is beneficial, too, as it incorporates the healing power of fire into these oils.

Crystals

Manipura means "lustrous gem or city of jewels," so crystals are very helpful for this energy center. The crystals that bring great balance and healing to this center include the following:

- **TIGER'S EYE:** balances your ego and willpower
- **CITRINE:** brings abundance as it attracts happiness and joy into your life
- **PYRITE:** offers great protection and encourages self-reflection

You may lie down with one crystal at the front and one at the back side of your body, or tape them onto your body with athletic tape until you feel that your energy is strengthened enough to reach a state of thriving.

Mantra

The healing mantra for this chakra is RAM, in the keynote of E. We can find this note by remembering the children's song, "Mary had a Little Lamb." The first note of this song begins on the note of E. When you are feeling controlling, angry, or apathetic, take a deep breath and begin to chant the word "RAM" in the tone of E, and allow your solar plexus to fill up with purpose, self-worth, and wisdom. It really will lift you out of a slump quickly. You can remember this mantra by imaging a powerful animal—the ram—the animal that carries in this seed sound and is the vehicle of the fire god, Agni. No one questions the power, strength, and assuredness of a ram; this animal is power-embodied. The mantra RAM is pronounced differently than the animal pronunciation. It is pronounced *r-aum* but the image is the same—strong, powerful, and sure of self.

Environmental Shift

For our environmental shift, we are going to cleanse and clear your crystals and set them with your best intention so they can invigorate your energy and the energy of your home. You can clear your crystals in a number of ways:

1. You may place your crystals on a slab of selenite to clear and cleanse. Leave them overnight or until you feel that it is time to remove them.
2. If you are looking to heal your first chakra with your crystals, use earth to cleanse them because, as you have learned, the root chakra is balanced by earth. Bury them in the ground until you remember them. When you remember them, it will be time for them to come out. You will forget about them and remember them at the perfect moment. It's a fun surprise to rediscover them.
3. If you are intending to use your crystals to strengthen your second chakra, place your crystals out in the new moon or the full moon for a deep cleanse and lunar charge. New moon energy supports new beginnings and setting intention, while full moon energy holds the energy for completion and release. Both are powerful and necessary energies for different times in our lives.

    Cleanse and charge your crystals based on what you need in your life in this moment. Leave them out overnight or for at least eight hours. Our second chakra, the sacral chakra, is fueled by lunar energy, and allowing your crystals to absorb this energy will be beneficial to your sacral chakra. Additionally, you can cleanse some of your crystals in natural waters or saltwater by giving them a bath. Be sure that your crystals are water-safe. For example, selenite will melt in water.
4. If you are intending to heal your third chakra with your crystals, place them in direct sunlight. The solar plexus is fed by solar energy and will be balanced by solar-infused

crystals. I leave my crystals on a sunny windowsill in my office where they are constantly absorbing the sun and the moon every day. Sun can fade your crystals' color over time, so it is important to pay attention when they may need a break from the direct light. Additionally, you can use burning sage to clear your crystals.

5. If you are looking to heal your heart chakra with crystals, bring yourself into a place of intention, through meditation or being quiet with precise crystal clearing intention for a few minutes. When you feel ready, blow your cleansing intention onto your crystals.

6. If you are looking to heal your fifth chakra with your crystals, use sound to clear your crystals. Use singing bowls, tuning forks, loud music, or your own song or chant to clear your crystals and set intention for them. Bathe your crystals in sound by allowing the sound to reach all sides of the crystal until the sound bath feels complete.

With each of the above forms of crystal clearing, intention is the most powerful tool you can use. Set precise and powerful intention when clearing and charging your crystals, and clear them once you feel called to clear them. They are calling out to you to cleanse them. Once these crystals are cleared, you may place them around you or your home where you feel called or you can consult a feng shui practitioner or bagua map.

Yoga

Anything that brings heat to the solar plexus is good here, such as the boat pose (*navasana*), seated spinal twist (*marichyasana*), or the warrior (*virabhadrasana*.) Consult one of the many excellent yoga channels on YouTube.

Core exercises are also fantastic for strengthening the third chakra. Consult your local gym or look online for a suitable workout. Make sure you speak to an accredited physical trainer to ensure exercises are right for your health and fitness levels.

Do not overextend yourself. This energy center is about knowing yourself and honoring yourself. Check out some stretches and warm-up exercises before launching into poses, and remember to contact your health care provider if in any doubt about your health or fitness.

Archangels

Archangel Haniel is the healing archangel for the third chakra, traditionally associated with joy and intuition. When we surrender our fear, we find joy. When we listen to our gut instincts, we are listening to our intuition. Haniel aids in helping you do both.

Here is a beautiful prayer for letting go: "Thank you, Archangel Haniel, for helping me transform my personal power into this great Divine power by surrendering my way. I know that I am not powerless, I am actually an infusion of Divine power."

Ten-Second Rescue

Ground. (See the grounding practice in chapter 10.) Hold your hand over your third chakra and repeat RAM until you begin to calm down.

Now let's complete our nostril breathing we began in the last chapter. As you might remember, you breathed through the left nostril to let go and bring calm to the body. When you breathe through your right nostril only, you energize your energy and alleviate the irritation and pride that can be found in this center.

Begin by blocking the left nostril with the left thumb. Now breathe long deep breaths only though the right nostril.

The solar plexus chakra is an area that benefits from this type of focused, intensive breathwork because it strengthens the diaphragm in a significant way. In our meditation, you will learn three powerful breathing techniques that will empower you and give you the opportunity to control your energy and your response to life.

Homework

Use one breathing technique (detailed in meditation found online) for one minute to assist in a moment of discontent. Notice how you feel afterward.

Solar Plexus Chakra Journaling

What experiences do you feel might be creating the deficient or excessive energy in your solar plexus? Was there a disempowering or fearful experience that took place during the ages of fourteen and twenty-one? What experience made you begin to doubt yourself? When did you not "listen to your gut"? What do you regret and wish you could release? When did you experience a moment where you felt powerless? When did you feel truly powerful? Describe how feeling powerful felt.

 ## *Solar Plexus Chakra Mantra Review*

Chakra	Mantra	How do I remember it?	Keynote
Third: SOLAR PLEXUS	RAM	I stand in my power like a strong ram.	KEYNOTE E: first note in "Mary Had a Little Lamb"
Second: SACRAL	VAM	V-V-Vagina— connected to sexual organs.	KEYNOTE D: first note in "Amazing Grace"
First: ROOT	LAM	L-L-Lowest energy center.	KEYNOTE C: first note in "Old MacDonald Had a Farm"

Solar plexus meditation: Before this meditation begins, we will go through several breathing techniques and in which circumstances to apply them before and after meditation. You are going to clear what does not serve you and step into the certainty of who you are and what you are meant to do here on this Earth. You are about to become Divinely power-full.

Join me at www.LoveHealThrive.com for the breathing and solar plexus meditation.

CHAPTER 21

The Self-Worth Connection to Your Fourth Chakra Marker: The Heart Chakra

AT TWENTY-ONE, I fell in love, like the real kind of love. At first, I didn't even want a boyfriend, as I was so preoccupied with being the perfect friend. I didn't have time for a boyfriend. But one night while studying for accounting, this young man called me out on my personal accounting and my mask of cheery Goldilocks-seeking perfection.

He said, "You know, you don't have to be happy all the time. In fact, I would prefer it if you just let your emotions be your emotions. If you're sad, be sad. If you're mad, be mad. That way, I know if you're happy, you're really happy."

Growing up fulfilling the role of hero and mascot in an alcoholic dysfunctional family, no one had ever told me I could share my true feelings. I was always on the cover up—pretending all is well to ensure I wasn't the one causing the problems. It was in this pivotal moment when I began to realize my feelings had value and my voice mattered to someone else. Most importantly, though, I realized it mattered to me. I no longer had to be the perfect shell of myself to be Goldilocks. I was finally "just right" being simple authentic me.

The heart chakra is called the self-worth marker for a reason. It is the moment when we realize our worth and identity do not belong in someone else's hands. Rather we define our worth and set up standards for how people honor and treat us. We also learn to love ourselves for our true selves.

In this chapter and the next, you will learn how to reach a place that exudes openhearted contentment, happiness, and gratitude. In Sanskrit, the heart chakra is called *anahata*, which means "unhurt, unstruck, unbeaten."

Reflect back to a time when you were visiting with your best friend or hosting a party. Can you remember how your heart felt? Did it feel soft and overflowing with love? Did you offer many big, warm hugs? When we hug, our heart center often lines up with and connects with the person we are hugging. When we really love someone, we give them extra-long hugs so our bodies can exchange heart energy on a deep level. This is also why we give the one-armed side hug to someone when we're upset with them or don't really like them. We protect our own heart from them and don't allow their energy into our hearts. Think back to your big hugs and your side arm hugs and see how this truth aligns.

Our bodies always know what we need
and will always protect us.

Our heart chakra is the home of love—self-love, friendship love, and romantic love. This Divine love is at the root of all healing, and it begins with self-love. The core purpose of this chakra is to love yourself first, so you have generous love to share with others. In this chakra, we also learn how to release the attachments that may be keeping us in our current heart space.

Resentments stem from unhealthy attachments to the heart, also recognized as expectations. Sometimes we can find ourselves believing outcomes are supposed to be a certain way or thinking someone was supposed to act or respond a certain way to a situation. When they don't respond, or the situation does not turn out the way we had hoped, resentment creeps in. It is empowering and important to understand this resentment is created by *your* expectations. As long as you remain attached to your outcome, you may be closed off to the blessings that are trying to find their way to you. When we can let go of our expectations of others and of circumstances, we not only have less resentment, but we are also blessed more than we could ever have imagined.

Could you refrain from believing that love has to be given or received in a certain way? Love is limitless, and the more sacred the love, the greater its effect. Let go of your attachments of how it should be. When you place attached expectations on people, places, things, and outcomes, you can block the many ways God wants to bless you. I can assure you: the Universe's way is much better than our way. When you release attachments to the way you think it's supposed to be or the way it's supposed to happen, you open the door to countless adjacent possibilities that will enrich you in a way you would never have thought possible and is much better than what you could have envisioned.

When we are unable to open our heart's door and we continue to feed our resentments and expectations instead, we often find ourselves in a state of depression and illness. We believe life is supposed to be a certain way, and when it is not, we get anxious. When people continue to disappoint us (by not meeting our expectations), we withdraw our energy, leaving ourselves isolated, disconnected, and depressed. The heart center's balance is critical in maintaining a healthy life. Once you reach a state of balance, your life will be overflowing with love and connectedness, which is the focus of this chapter.

Before we go any further into the heart chakra, let's review our chakras again to show you how this is all beginning to piece together. As you will see, the heart chakra forms a bridge between the three upper and three lower chakras—powerfully located in the middle.

First chakra. Our first chakra is located near our pelvic floor, the base of our spine, and perineum. (It can also be the underside of the cervix.) It is in this energy center where you can settle in and just *be*. Settled into this space, you feel safe, secure, and provided for by the Universe. You are in your sanctuary.

Second chakra. When you feel safe, secure, and provided for, *then* you are able to delve into the emotions of the second chakra and balance them. When this sanctuary of emotions is in balance, you find a passion for life, your creativity is ignited, and you experience a rich feeling of connection to the people in your life.

Third chakra. When you feel safe, connected, and emotionally balanced, then you can stand strong in your third chakra, the solar plexus. You know who you are and what you're here to do. You feel sure enough to move forward with your life purpose.

These three chakras are referred to as the physical chakras because they manage everything about our energy on Earth—it's about all of our physical needs.

Fourth chakra. Now we reach the heart chakra. The heart chakra is the astral bridge that connects our three physical chakras to our three spiritual chakras located above the heart chakra. (The word *astral* refers to nonphysical experiences that invoke the use of psychic experiences. The astral bridge connects our physical experiences to their psychic counterparts through this blending of energy through the heart chakra. Thus, the term *astral bridge* is applied here.)

From here, we are able to give from a place that is selfless, open-hearted, and filled with Divine love.

When all four of these chakras are balanced:

- You love from a place that feels safe, secure, and accepted.
- You love from a place that feels connected and emotionally balanced.

- You love from a place that is uniquely you.
  No one loves the way you do, and you feel safe and
  connected enough to love those in your life freely.

It's a love that is nourishing and bountiful, feels connected to others, and can forgive and let go. Here is where the balanced heart chakra exists.

Have you experienced that magical feeling of connection when you've had an amazing talk with a friend or a loved one or held a puppy or a baby and looked into its eyes? When something really moves you, what gesture do you make with your body? You often cover your heart with your hand. This is not a coincidence. Our heart can feel vulnerable and as if it needs extra protection when we're moved, so our body protects it.

Our bodies always know what we need
and will always protect us.

Not only is this where we are connected to others—remember, it's where we are connected to ourselves—this is where our self-love resides. Imagine you have a self-love bucket nestled in the middle of your heart space. Is your bucket overflowing, full, or empty? We're all born with an overflowing bucket that is being continually replenished by our Divine connection. Over time, we may slowly disconnect from our pure Divine connection and continue to give and give until we are depleted, exhausted, overwhelmed, and depressed. Until we learn how to refill it, it continues to empty. Many continue to give from this empty state because they believe it is righteous to do so. The martyr has not yet learned how to fill up their own bucket. Martyrdom and people-pleasing are not a Divine mission. The Divine wants us to give from overflow. It is up to us to learn how to refill our bucket and maintain our state of energy overflow. It is intended that we give only from a bucket that is overflowing.

As I mentioned earlier, at twenty-one, I was the perfect friend—the friend who organized all the birthday events for all the friends. I loved organizing, but I am sure on some unconscious level it was also done to ensure someone would want to organize a dinner for my birthday, too. I was the planner, the helper, the one who always called friends on their birthday and the one who remembered all the details. I prided myself on this whole being-the-perfect-friend thing.

I was the perfect friend to everyone except to one person . . . myself.

I still pride myself on being a good friend but now make sure that those thoughtful actions come from a place of Divine over-flow. I make sure that I nourish myself and give from a place that is connected and full of Divine presence. Otherwise, what I give isn't very pretty. Have you experienced a moment when someone gives to you when they are not in a state of overflow? You both know it and it doesn't feel good for either one of you. It doesn't feel good for them to give to you from this space because they're emptying their bucket, and no one is fooling anyone. It doesn't feel good to receive from this place either.

Energy is felt and people-pleasing martyr energy ranks up there with some of the subtlest painful experiences to be felt by all. People pleasing stems from a lack of self-love. We believe we must please everyone around us to be loved. The secret here though is that as you begin to love yourself more and allow this beautiful Divine love in, your desire to people-please reduces because you know that others simply need to reach this same energetic state for themselves as well. You cannot do it for them.

I used to cast the net out wide to be the perfect friend to everyone, which left me exhausted and with surface-level friendships that were unfulfilling. This was also the same relationship I had with myself. Over the last several decades, I've established a deeper, more connected, and authentic relationship with myself, and this energetic state has, in turn, attracted the same type of friendships in my life. Those that are not the match to this authentic energy have fallen away, leaving me with even more energy to nourish the relationships I desire to invest in.

One of the goals for this chakra is to reestablish your energy flow to obtain this overflowing bucket so you are always giving from surplus. If you are giving from an empty bucket, what kind of love are you giving, anyway? Probably not the kind of love you'd like to receive. Because we're all connected, people feel this.

I imagine you've probably experienced a time when someone was helping you, but they didn't really want to be helping. Could you tell? I bet you could. However, you can also feel the difference when you are giving from overflow and receiving from overflow. It feels wonderful for everyone involved. In this chapter, you will begin to love yourself first, so that you have unlimited love to give. When you have your bucket filled and overflowing with unconditional love, you are able to tap into Divine love that is never-ending and always available to support.

Fourth Chakra Description

How do we know if the energy in our heart chakra is excessive, deficient, or balanced?

Excessive Heart Chakra Energy

There can be an unhealthy surge of energy that flows from your heart center when it is excessive. In attempting to love someone or something so passionately, you abandon yourself and forget how to caretake and love yourself. Do you recognize yourself in any of the following?

- People pleaser
- Codependent
- Overgiver
- Person unable to say "no"
- Victim
- Martyr
- Person without boundaries
- Drama queen ruled by emotions

- Person who is friends with everyone because there is no discernment or discrimination for the well-matched friend
- Someone stuck in their story or in the pain of their past
- Bossy friend/parent/coworker who is overly demanding of others

Deficient Heart Chakra Energy

As you can imagine, if there is a surge of energy in the excessive state of this energy center, there is a withdrawal of energy in its deficient state.

Signs here include the following:

- Feeling withdrawn
- Avoiding socializing
- Overly critical of self and others
- Overwhelming grief
- Loneliness
- Isolation
- Anger
- Jealousy
- Fear of betrayal
- Manipulative behaviors
- Inability to trust yourself

Balanced Heart Chakra Energy

When your heart energy is balanced, you are flowing with love and compassion. You are quick to forgive. You accept others and yourself. People feel loved and accepted unconditionally around you. People feel at peace around you, as you exude more compassion than judgment. You find yourself loving others and, most importantly, loving yourself. A balanced heart space feels blissful. We are able to rest in connected stillness with another. Before we can achieve this state, we have to learn some important lessons to balance our heart chakra.

Lessons of the Heart

The first lesson of the heart is that we must first love ourselves before we can love others.

For almost a year after my mom died, I had pink eye (conjunctivitis). I would shy away from having my photo taken. I couldn't wear makeup. I was constantly explaining my condition because people would take one look at my eye and cringe in pain. My days were spent bouncing between the acupuncturist's office and the Western doctor to get more eye drops. In Chinese medicine, pink eye is diagnosed as "liver fire," where the liver is too hot from anger, resentment, and emotion. In addition to a very pink eye, my liver did physically hurt during that year even though I continued to see doctors weekly. Nothing healed me.

At this time of extreme loss and grief over my mom's death, I wasn't being very nice to myself. I would put myself down for my grief, internally ridiculing myself for my reaction and telling myself that I should be handling life better. I shouldn't be so tired, so sad, so exhausted, so so so. I put myself down for everything, even including how I was grieving. I wanted the gripping pain to stop, and it bewildered me how I could hurt so much when I couldn't *see* my pain. I believed my lack was to blame.

About two years into my grief, I tried Aura-Soma, a system of color, plant, and crystal energies. It used small bottles of pretty colored oils, which could be applied to the body to promote health and healing. My particular bottle was for healing self-criticism and lack of self-love. Every day, I rubbed this oil on my arms and my heart and told myself, *I am worthy of giving and receiving love. I am enough.*

Throughout the next nine months, I cried and wept and healed. Life presented me with challenges to help me discern just how well I was doing on my self-love path—a test I would often fail. After nine months—the same amount of time it takes to gestate a new life (hardly a coincidence)—I rubbed the last bit of oil on my body, and the very next day, my pink eye disappeared. I would not have believed it myself if it had not happened to me, but it is remarkably true.

I experienced a palpable shift. My eye was not the only thing that had cleared in me. When a situation arose where my "old self" might have put me down, I would catch my internal voice and say, *Nope! You don't talk to yourself that way anymore.* If I was slow to catch the negative self-talk and I said something cruel to myself, I would feel a twinge in my liver that reminded me once again, *Nope! You don't talk to yourself that way anymore.* As I've said before, it's remarkable how accurately the body mirrors our thoughts and emotions.

We just celebrated my mom's fifteenth Angel Birthday, and to this day, my pink eye has not returned. I don't speak to myself that way anymore. And neither should you.

Our thoughts trigger emotions, emotions move energy,
and energy manifests physically.
What we do with our energy matters.
If our energy isn't weak, our body doesn't weaken.

What are your thoughts and emotions creating in your body? How can you redirect the voice in your head to bring about a healthy, happy, and powerful body fueled by love, light, and passion for your day? It all begins with a simple thought. Make sure the thought that greets you each day is one of love and appreciation, morning, noon, and night.

Loving yourself first is not selfish. Self-care can look like many healthy behaviors—going to sleep early, meditating, eating healthy, exercising, going to acupuncture, enjoying lunch with a friend, painting, journaling, playing music, drinking a cup of tea, or any other activity that fills your bucket. As you choose to spend time with yourself, you are filling your own bucket and you are subconsciously telling yourself that you are worthy of your own time and attention. This feeds your inner child. In an incredible parenting book entitled *Buddha Never Raised Kids & Jesus Didn't Drive Carpool: Seven Principles for Parenting with Soul,* author Vickie Falcone advises that every child needs to feel PHIL'd (powerful, heard, important, loved) every day. Once

PHIL'd, the child behaves better because their primal needs have been nourished. I believe everyone needs to feel PHIL'd, not just children. We each have an inner child that needs this kind of love and attention, and when we offer this to ourselves first, we feel better and behave better because we also feel powerful, heard, important, and loved.

The second lesson of the heart is nonattachment to people, circumstances, results, or things.

When we can let go of the thoughts that things . . .

- should be a certain way
- could be a certain way if . . .
- would be a certain way if we only . . .

. . . we welcome a life of possibilities waiting to bless us.

When we release these expectations, God blesses us in ways greater than we would ever imagine being blessed. As we addressed earlier, it is when we cling to these expectations that we find ourselves riddled with resentment. It is through awareness of our expectation that we purify ourselves from it.

Our demands and expectations of others are often rooted in our love language, and our love language is often created by the love we did not receive as a child. Once we recognize the expectations we are holding for others, we can begin to fulfill our own needs and no longer give our power away to others to fulfill those needs.

It is all about the journey.

When you work through a project, big or small, you grow, you expand, you learn new skills, you create relationships, you become more patient and wiser. Could this be enough for you? Could your personal growth and expansion be sufficient, recognizing that all these internal gifts are gifts enough?

However, the great little secret behind this teaching is that as we appreciate the wisdom and growth we obtain through the process, we are often blessed in even bigger ways upon completion of the project. But the important nuance of this perspective is your focus throughout the project. Is your focus on the millions of dollars you will earn upon completion or is it upon the learning, growth, and personal shift you will experience through the process? Will you adhere to your attachment to the outcome or recognize through the process you became the person the Universe had always intended for you to be? This also applies to the growth we experience in relationships. If someone irritates you, can you appreciate that your growth in learning how to become resilient to the situation is blessing enough?

Our growth is truly our greatest gift.

Location

The location of this chakra is in the center of the chest at the heart level. It resides at the center of the seven chakras, with three chakras below that manage our physical desires of the world and three chakras above the heart that support our spiritual needs. This is the chakra where our physical and spiritual needs meet and offer an astral bridge to connect the two sets of chakras.

Physical Correlations in Body

Have you ever noticed when someone is grieving or feels insecure, they stand in a concave position with their shoulders slightly forward and their chest rounded inward? Interesting that this state, when your heart is not only emotionally depressed but also physically (and energetically) depressed, is called depression. This is also what deficient heart energy looks like. When this happens, we know, based on what you've learned, that a person with this posture may not have a lot of love for themselves. They may be struggling with envy or a state of extreme attachment to ideas in their life. Notice those in your life who hold this posture and see how this truth measures up. This discovery may help you hold more compassion for them.

Conversely, when someone embodies great self-love and feels balanced in their heart chakra, what does their body look like? Their shoulders are back, and their chin and chest are up and ready to allow their heart energy to flow and bless others.

When the heart energy is excessive, we see an overexaggerated chin up, chest up, and shoulders back, although it often feels false. While the chest may be forward, it lacks a softness that exists when the heart is balanced. It is too afraid to be soft and vulnerable.

Remember we are doing this work for our own journey and healing and not to point out to others all the issues they might be having. If they are in your life and they are having the issue, you are, too. Your internal world defines your external world, and like attracts like. So, if you are seeing these symptoms in others, begin with compassion for them and for you.

The symptomatic physical correlations in the body include the cardiovascular system, blood, immune system, thymus gland, lungs, ribs, breasts, lymphatic system, arms, and hands. The ailments that can exist here are high blood pressure, heart palpitations, heart attack, lung issues, and bronchitis. If you are experiencing any of these symptoms, review this chapter and the next chapter and decide how you can soften your heart and allow your bucket to be filled.

Color

The energy frequency that emanates from this chakra is approximately 550 hertz and is visible as the color green. It is no coincidence that jealousy is referred to as the "green-eyed monster"— someone can be "green with envy" or we believe the "grass is greener" somewhere else. The truth remains: energy flows where attention goes, and the grass is greenest where you water it with your attention.

Emotions

Our shoulders and heart rise and fall with every breath, sigh and sob when we truly release the grief and sadness held in this center. When we are grieving, we want things to go back to the way they were. We don't want things to change. Grief is a powerful change agent, but the truth is grief never wanted to change your environment, it wants to change your heart. As you release your sadness and your attachment to the way things were, can you begin to seek out how this grief is preparing you and readying you for your next step?

We can fill our heart with gratitude, true love, self-love, compassion, and happiness. The heart chakra is about allowing this pure love to flow generously and unobstructed from your heart energy center to another. Whether you are in conversation, hugging, or sitting still with someone, it is in the moment when you feel connected and that you are one, where you are in a shared balanced heart space and allowing this beautiful energy to flow out to bless everyone. While this energy blesses everyone it reaches, in offering this heart energy to all, it blesses you the most.

Lifetime Development

The lessons learned here on releasing our expectations of people and letting go of the "have" replay of our mind—"should have, would have, could have"—are so infinitely important here that, if not learned, these barriers will block us from proceeding further on our spiritual development. Passing through this roadblock of your spiritual development is imperative to your development and healing. As we let go of our expectations and welcome in more love, we will find we feel happier and are healthier. The increased flow of energy in this center feeds the root chakra energy and allows the root of your healing to be nourished.

Have you experienced that blissful moment of first falling in love? What did that love look like? Was it balanced or did you lose yourself? Did your heart remain open throughout the relationship or did it close down once it asked you to give more? This chakra develops between the ages of twenty-one and twenty-eight. During this time, many of us fall in love for the first time, get married, and begin to appreciate our own selves and love ourselves more. We learn to set boundaries. This can also be a time when we can feel isolated and lonely in our heart chakra if we have abandoned ourselves in relationships or have felt completely undeserving of a relationship.

Regardless of which path you experienced, this is the time period where you begin to awaken again to journey back to your soul and usher on your next phase of spiritual and energetic healing.

The Everyday Connection

- Have you been feeling distant from your loved ones?
- Are you struggling with, "It should be like this . . ." or, "It's supposed to be *this* way . . ."?
- Do you feel that the grass is greener elsewhere?
- Have you been struggling with eczema or high blood pressure?

If you answered "yes" to any of the above questions, it may benefit you to review this chapter and the next and incorporate a few of these techniques. See how you feel in a week or so. Our excessive or diminished heart chakra energy shows up in many differing ways. It is important when you recognize a symptom to pause, reflect on the teachings of this chapter, and choose at least one of the tools to incorporate in the following chapter until your symptom dissipates.

CHAPTER 22

The Counter Chakra to the Heart Chakra

WHEN DO YOU OPEN UP emotionally to a new friend or partner in a new relationship? When do you start to tell your deepest, truest stories? Many of us begin to share our most intimate stories once we feel safe and secure with someone. This is true because the heart chakra pairs with the root chakra. The strength of the root chakra makes it safe enough for our heart chakra to open and share more fully. This partnership brings safety and security into our love relationships and helps us release expectations and resentment in a safe and accepted manner. The same is true when we feel nervous and our heart feels fluttery. We need to remind our heart that we are safe and secure. We can invite the *bija* mantra LAM (the root chakra mantra) and the healing element of the root chakra's earth energy into your fluttery heart chakra, and they will soothe and calm your nervous heart.

The next time you feel nervous, imagine Mama Earth calming your heart as you chant, out loud or to yourself, "LAM, LAM, LAM." I complete this exercise every time I give a talk. During a talk, I get passionate, and my energy moves from my root chakra into my heart and throat as I am sharing my teachings. As part of my "pregame warm-up," I strengthen my root chakra and calm my heart with the root chakra strength so that I remain calm, present, connected, and grounded throughout my presentations. A friend of mine who is very anxious to fly uses this technique whenever she has moments of panic in the air, and it has made her a calmer passenger.

The Antidote

What aspects of the root chakra need to be added to the heart chakra to establish energetic equilibrium here? The antidote to the imbalanced heart chakra energy is the root chakra's healing energy.

When the heart chakra's energy is excessive, people pleasing and boundaryless love results. When we add the antidote of the root chakra's safety and security into this energy, knowing we are safe regardless of peoples' opinions of us, equilibrium is established and love looks balanced and healthy.

When the heart chakra's energy is stagnant, isolation and depression result and there is a strong desire to make your own safety and security yourself, believing no one will be there for you and the Universe will not provide. When we add the antidote of the root chakra's feeling of tribal inclusion and Divine provision in both material and emotional abundance, equilibrium is established, depression lifts, and a love for self and others appears.

Counter Chakra Seed Planting

It is fascinating how my own counter chakra seed expression clearly defines the counter chakra seed principle. My bet is that you will begin to discover your expressions too. Between the ages of twenty-one and twenty-eight, I worked at an entertainment marketing agency that ran all the national marketing partnerships for a famous ice cream franchise. What could be more healing for my root chakra and little self who didn't get her own ice cream sandwich than for me to, decades later, sit in business meetings creating new ice creams and sundaes themed to entertainment properties? Our pitch meetings where we all ate our way through the many products we invented were a dream come true for me on such a deep level. I was not only invited to the ice cream party, but I helped create the ice cream. Aside from learning the importance of a tactical protein and healthy, fat-laden pre-meal to these meetings, I learned acceptance began with me. I learned how to honor myself and love myself and that I was whole and complete with or without being invited to the ice cream party. As a result, I basked in both strong root chakra and heart chakra energy together during this time of powerhouse partnership where a little ice cream went a long way.

CHAPTER 23

The Auric Effect:
The Heart Chakra

Deficient Heart Chakra

When the heart chakra is stagnant, the root chakra is excessive, leading to anger, irritability, and caring more about money and material goods than people. The aura is minimally sized to not allow anyone's energy to interact with this energy. This person often is greedy, materialistic, and vain and struggles with heart challenges.

Excessive Heart Chakra

When the root chakra is deficient, this leads to an excessive heart chakra. The root chakra becomes more protective because it feels unsafe due to its energetic stagnation and needs to take in as much data as it can from its surroundings. It does this by extending its aura out many feet in order to "read the room" and discern how safe the body is in its surroundings. This aura size can be in excess of five feet or more. This person often is the people pleaser struggling with adrenal fatigue.

Grounding your energy will remedy both of these auric states, allowing you to feel safe and secure and provided for within your environment.

The Auric Effect ✧ Heart Chakra

CHAPTER 24

Tools to Heal Your
Heart Chakra Marker

PRIOR TO MANAGING the marketing for the ice cream franchise, I planned premieres for a renowned feature film studio. From afar, it was one of the most coveted jobs in Hollywood. I attended the hottest premieres, which also meant I also attended to the needs of everyone who went to those premieres. I was the girl with the clipboard at the door and learned quickly how to read people—those who were honest and those who were trying to lie their way in.

As keeper of the attendee lair, I truly came to know and recognize a broad range of consciousness and moral standards in people. Strangers would call me and say, "Don't you know who I am? I deserve more tickets," without any regard to the other actors involved in making the film or anyone else. They wanted what they wanted. I was yelled at, lied to, and berated on a daily basis. But one gentleman will forever remain in my memory. He was a lovely writer from London.

If you can believe it at the time, writers—the people who made the entire movie possible through their imagination—were contracted for only two tickets. For every film, each writer only received a "plus one" to the viewing of their work of art. It was only a few weeks before the premiere of his movie and my phone rang.

Everything about this conversation was different from the rest, beginning with him acknowledging me by name. He said he knew writers were contracted for only two tickets but that his parents were flying over from London in case there was anything I could do to get them in.

No berating.

No yelling.

Just a connected heartfelt request.

He wanted his parents at his premiere.

And while the main theater was completely booked, there was an overflow theater next door, so I was able to get him tickets there and gave him two extra tickets so they could all attend the after-party together. He was so grateful and appreciative. I will never forget this encounter because every other conversation was always filled with such venom that I remained shocked that people believed this type of treatment would get them what they wanted.

While certainly this was a sign of the times and courtesy has improved, I imagine this still happens quite a bit. When we approach people with kindness, we receive kindness. It might not always be just like the kindness you offer, but it is their version of kindness.

When we approach people with love, we receive love.

How are you approaching people these days? Are you complaining to people all the time? Does your life resemble this conversation? Or are you being kind toward others? Is that showing up, too? How are you interacting with those you love, with those you work with, and with those you bump into every day?

As you become this beacon of light and gratitude, gratitude will find you, too. As we bask in gratitude, we shift our energetic state into a state of receiving in order to receive the life of our dreams.

When we are in a state of receiving, we draw our blessings toward us rather than having to chase after them. We can live in a state of empowerment and joy rather than feeling depleted and exhausted trying to capture our dreams. I often think about how I might have been able to shift that work experience if I could go back and work through it with all that I know now about energy attraction and manifesting. We draw in the corresponding energy we emit.

Life can be about breathless, meaningful moments that allow our heart chakra to overflow with happiness, love, and connection. Or life can be full of chasing, envy, jealousy, isolation, and illness. You get to choose. It begins with you choosing you. In this chapter you will find many powerful ways to balance your heart and bring in a life full of connection and love.

Color and Clothes

Wearing green attracts the energy that balances your heart chakra. When you are feeling anxious or envious or would like to feel greater connection with others, choose to wear the color green, perhaps even flowing, airy clothes that are emerald green. Wearing an emerald-green pendant attracts direct healing energy to your heart chakra.

Many years ago, shortly after my mom passed away, I dressed for my day and chose a shirt to wear that just did not feel right. The shirt fit fine and matched my outfit, but I was so uncomfortable. What I didn't know was the shirt was not attracting the energy I needed for the day. Luckily, I switched my shirt to a green shirt, and my body let out the biggest exhale I'd ever experienced. I thought it was so curious to have had that physical reaction, even back then, because it felt like true somatic relief. It was as if I had finally found the proper shirt to wear for the day. Turns out this happened because my heart chakra was finally receiving the energy support necessary to heal my grief through the energy attraction of the green shirt.

Looking back on that experience, I didn't realize then how deeply I exhaled and the instantaneous healing I'd received from this seemingly simple choice. My lungs could finally release some of the grief they were carrying because there was reinforcement from the heart energy attracted by my green shirt.

Weighted pillows and blankets are sometimes recommended for anxiety healing, to be strapped on to or held to the chest, where it is claimed the main anxiety points reside. Weighted blankets also bring soothing to all the energy on the skin, the sensory organ for the heart chakra as it calms the surrounding energy. Experiment with an additional green pillowcase to see how the color therapy increases your healing.

While these tools are recommended to ease anxiety by applying them to the heart chakra and the skin, we now know that the partner to the heart chakra and the true anxiety trigger begins in the root chakra. These tools are attempting to heal anxiety by soothing the excessive heart chakra, which is a great approach. By supporting the heart chakra, the root chakra will be balanced as well within this energetic partnership.

Element

When we embrace our loved ones, we often breathe them in. We breathe in their essence, their scent, and their energy. Why do they smell so good to us? There are two reasons. The element that heals our heart chakra is air. As we breathe our loved one in, we are filling our lungs with air that has also been filled with their energy. As you learned in the aura section, energy releases into the aura, and during an embrace, your energetic fields and auras are layered together. Not only are the air's elemental healing properties healing your lungs, but also the scent of your loved one begins to heal your root chakra's connection to the sense of smell, which strengthens your experience of feeling safe and secure as this energetic partnership is nourished.

Remember your root chakra and your heart chakra are partner chakras. Breathing in your loved one's essence is one of the most healing modalities you can experience because it heals the entire energetic partnership. According to Virginia Satir, author and therapist, we need four hugs a day to survive, eight hugs a day to maintain, and twelve hugs to move forward. Begin your hugging practice and begin to heal your body and this powerful energetic partnership.

Hugging is not our only healing modality for this energy center, although it's a very good one. Breathing techniques, such as the Ujjayi breath you learned online in the chapter 20 meditation video found at www.LoveHealThrive.com, are incredible healing agents, too. Going for a hike through the trees helps you to heal both your heart chakra, by breathing in the fresh air, and your root chakra, via the scent and grounding energy of the trees. Walking along the beach and taking in the fresh clean ocean air also accomplishes this healing.

Have you been waking up between the hours of 3:00 a.m. and 5:00 a.m.? In Traditional Chinese Medicine (TCM), it is believed the lung channel balances and heals itself during these hours of the night. This is why we often find ourselves sighing in an attempt to draw in balancing air to shift the grief energy away from our lungs. If you are waking up consistently during these hours of the night, review all the ways you can strengthen and heal your heart chakra that feeds your lungs. You may also see an acupuncturist. Our body tells us everything we need to know to heal itself.

Our Five Senses

Remember the time you held someone's hand for the first time and felt your heart flutter? According to research by the University of North Carolina Chapel Hill, hugging and holding hands for ten minutes is associated with lower blood pressure and a lower heart rate, as compared to those who do not hold hands. In our previous hugging example, the shared energy balances the heart chakra, allowing the heart to be more efficient, while the touch of the hands activates the skin's energy, helping lower blood pressure.

Have you ever noticed how relaxing it is to take a nap near an open window with a gentle warm breeze flowing through it caressing your skin? The combination of the balancing element of air with your skin allow your heart chakra to begin to be balanced, leaving you relaxed and happy.

Touch is the sense that aids in healing of the heart chakra, and the balance of this chakra shows up through our skin. If you are struggling with skin conditions, eczema, or rashes (especially on the hands), it is important to take a closer look at this chakra's teachings and see what might be lying below the surface that you may need to heal. I had a chakra series student who came down with a head-to-toe poison oak rash after processing the heart chakra week. He came to class on the throat chakra week and had not drawn the connection to the heart work he had begun the week prior. His rash indicated that he had begun to bring to the surface some grief and unpeaceful feelings during his heart chakra week's work but still had more healing to bring into his heart and root chakra to find true balance, along with happiness and clearer skin.

We can walk through poison oak and develop a rash. However, if the energy isn't weak, the body won't weaken. If our energy is strong, it will withstand external circumstances and maintain a strong physical body from the inside out if the energetic and emotional body is balanced and strong. This is true of every external encounter from poison oak to frustrating people. When our chakra energy is vibrant, our auric layer is strong and prevents external triggers from causing us harm. This is true of allergies, too.

TCM claims that allergies are caused by a weakening of the protective force around you. This is called Wei Qi in this system and it is understood that the lungs help provide the energy to help keep this energy fortified. When this protective energy is not strong, pathogens are able to enter the mouth and nose. When a body gets sick in this way, it is termed *catching wind*. Interestingly, the balancing element for the lungs is air. When the lung air is powerful, you do not catch wind.

We can use our elements to remain healthy and strong. Breathwork and fresh air are powerful tools to maintain this energetic protection.

This TCM shield functions much like the aura. It's the same energetic experience described applying system-specific terminology.

When someone experiences a physically abusive relationship, i.e. being pushed and hit, it can hinder the heart chakra energy as it tries to ignite the root chakra energy as a way to feel (and be) protected and safe. Allowing this type of abuse to continue can result in stagnation of the heart energy founded on self-love. If you are in this situation and find yourself ungrounded and closed off from others, know that you are loved and you are worthy. You are filled with and are Divine love. As you fill your self-love bucket, you will come to know you are protected and deserve to be loved. Choose to love yourself first and watch your emotional and physical body and surroundings begin to shift as you fill your own bucket up first.

Abuse, of any kind, or any unwanted touching can also create an energetic stagnation in this energy center. As you find your strength energetically, you will find the power and determination to change your physical circumstances. You deserve to be loved unconditionally.

My husband's love language, based on the book and system *The 5 Love Languages,* written by Gary Chapman, is physical touch. I, however, am an empath who struggles with physical touch because when I touch someone, I feel their emotions, their energy state, and their disposition. Does this sound familiar? For me, it is so much more than holding hands. At the end of a long day, when we are sitting on the couch watching a show, it takes dedication and intention on my part to remember to cuddle or hold his hand because I love him and want him to feel loved.

How can we increase the healing of your heart through your skin? Wear your most comfortable clothes, day and night. If you are looking to get new sheets, investigate their softness before purchasing. I recently bought a silk pillowcase, and I can feel the difference in my heart chakra as I lay my head down every night, enjoying the softness.

Massage is an important tool in this energy center. You may get a massage, have someone you love massage you, or use a foam roller and self-massage. You may also rub coconut oil or another carrier oil combined with the appropriate essential oil onto your skin after showering with the simple intention of *I love you.* Incorporate that love into your skin and watch how it heals your heart. By invigorating the skin through each of these four types of massages, we invigorate and balance the heart chakra.

A fantastic way to draw in the counter chakra system for assessment here is to refer to the TCM Face Mapping system and see which organ the blemishes on your face correlate with according to the map. Once you know which organ is connected to your blemish, locate which chakra that organ is connected to and then begin to heal its counter chakra to establish equilibrium here.

Organ of Action

How can we show our feelings to another person? We can shake hands, hold hands, hug, massage one another, or write letters and journal. We pet our beloved animals with our hands to show them our adoration. The organ of action of the heart chakra is the hand. From heart to hand, our deepest feelings are expressed. Are you struggling with dry, itchy hands? Do you constantly need to reapply lotion? If so, do you feel you are giving yourself enough space to be you? Are you itching to get out of a situation? Have you been grieving? Have you been loving to yourself? We can look at which hand is causing you problems, much as we did in the solar plexus work organ of the legs and feet. Are you struggling with your right hand? Is there a male in your life whom you are struggling to hold on to or itching to leave? If your left hand has a rash, are you looking for more attention from a woman? Have you received enough sustenance, emotionally and physically? Take notice and reflect a little deeper to see how your emotions may be showing up in your hands.

Our body tells us everything we need to know.

If you've been struggling with the skin on your hands, reflect back on these two heart chakra chapters and determine how full your self-love bucket is, and choose how you are going to refill it so it reaches the necessary state of overflow.

Food

The recommendations for your heart energy health do not depart very far from the physical heart-health diet generally prescribed by nutritionists. A diet high in vitamin K has been scientifically proven to protect against heart disease. Does vitamin K feed the physical heart or does the high-vibrating energy from all those beautiful green vegetables feed the heart chakra energy? Either way, it is time to consume delicious, fresh, green vegetables such as broccoli, spinach, kale, cucumber, parsley, basil, and thyme. Juice and drink them or eat them. If you are feeling jealous, envious, or sad, be sure to consume plenty of these healing greens. Feeling sad and would rather eat chocolate? Chocolate can soothe your taste buds and your nutrition, too. Just 1 ounce of raw cacao dark chocolate contains 2.3 micrograms of vitamin K. While sugar will lower your vibration, the vitamin K in the bar can offer some healing.

Essential Oils

The supportive essential oils for this center include the following:

- **DOTERRA BREATHE*** (combination of eucalyptus and peppermint): heals despair, attachments, and depression
- **ROSE:** heals a broken heart
- **YLANG YLANG:** heals grief and sadness

You may diffuse your essential oils or breathe in their scent directly from the bottle (without touching your skin) several times a day. As we discussed in the Element section of this chapter, breathing in these scents will heal your heart chakra through the air you inhale and your root chakra via your smelling of it. This will result in a strengthened energetic partnership. You may also rub one to three drops of this oil onto your heart chakra, along with a carrier oil, into the front and back of your heart chakra (the release points), making sure you rub around your entire body at the level of your heart.

---

*Young Living and Revive are other great essential oils as well. Oils may also be purchased from your local health food store or farmers' market and online.

Crystals

The crystals that bring great balance and healing to this center include the following:

- **EMERALD:** encourages loyalty and friendship and maintains relationship balance
- **PINK OPAL:** helps heal emotional trauma and offers balance between the feminine and masculine heart needs
- **ROSE QUARTZ:** softens the heart to be open to self-love, friendship love, and romantic love
- **MALACHITE:** aids in relations breakthrough and balancing the heart

These are fantastic stones to wear as necklaces to balance the energy closest to your heart chakra. If you wear a bra, they can be placed inside your bra or taped onto your body with athletic tape. It is also very effective to lie down with them, or set them next to your bedside table, perhaps even next to a picture of a loved one. You can program your crystal to be for healing or for the attraction of abundance into your relationship.

Mantra

The mantra for this energy center that we can call upon to chant when we are feeling envious, jealous, lonely, or sad is the word YAM (YUM), keynote F. We can remember it because being in love feels yummy! The Beatles' song, "Come Together" is played in the key F major, so as we find our note F for our mantra, we can keep this song in our heads, which is perfect. The heart chakra is all about each of us coming together and meeting in our heart chakras, connected and full of love to share. You may also join me on www. LoveHealThrive.com, and I will chant with you.

Upon reaching the heart chakra, you leave the land of physical chakras to take the astral bridge to the spiritual chakras. There is a physical lightness supported by the black antelope or gazelle energy embodied within this mantra.

Environmental Shift

Knowing that the strengthening element for this chakra is air, take a moment to clear the air in your home.

- Clear your home with white sage, also called smudging. Smudging may make your home smokier at first but will ultimately clean and clear up to 94 percent of the bacteria in the air within your home (see chapter 48 for a detailed description of smudging).
- Diffuse essential oils and help raise the vibration of your home.
- Add a few plants known for cleaning the air and releasing more oxygen. These plants include the following:
  Areca palm. This plant has the ability to purify the room by removing dangerous chemicals.
  Gerbera daisies. These are not only beautiful flowers, but they also produce a high level of oxygen.
  Chinese evergreen. This plant emits a high oxygen content while purifying the air of your indoor spaces.

Listen to your intuition on where to place these plants. Often where you feel they should go is where the house needs them the most. It is important that each room (or area in the bagua map) have a balance of each element—earth, fire, water, metal, and wood—to keep each room balanced. You can also consult a bagua map or work with a feng shui practitioner to assess where these plants may best fit, but I have found intuition often knows best.

In addition to the plants helping clear the air, the soil that they live in helps bring in a grounding component to balance out its energetic partner, creating a strengthened, balanced energetic partnership.

Yoga

How can we open and balance the heart through yoga? There are many incredible heart-opening poses in yoga. Cobra pose and cat-cow pose are both great positions for opening your heart center.

If you are pregnant or have back injuries, consult your doctor first. It is likely you should perform only the cow pose.

Archangels

Chamuel is the archangel who aids in the healing of the heart chakra, the angel of peaceful relationships, and who helps make all things beautiful—relationships, homes, and art. Chamuel is often depicted with a heart representing love. Not only does Archangel Chamuel assist in balancing our heart, Chamuel works on the same frequency as St. Anthony and can help find lost items for you.

Here is a handy prayer: "Angel of love, dear Archangel Chamuel, thank you for guiding me to find what I'm looking for, which includes . . ." [give specific details about your search]. And of course, "Dear St. Anthony, please gather 'round, something's lost that must be found."

Often the energy we call upon for a certain intention is sourced from the same energy but called by a different name. Intention is powerful and is not differentiated by a name. It is felt and summoned by intention. So whether you call upon Chamuel or St. Anthony or any other name, set the intention for asking for Divine help, and it will be received.

We can certainly ask for Chamuel's assistance to help us find our keys (which after your root chakra grounding practice you may not lose as often), but how else can we ask for this powerful archangel's assistance? We can ask for Chamuel's help in finding ourselves. How often are you searching for love? It could be that you are looking for someone to love, or it could be that you are looking for the love in your relationship to fill you in a different way. Either way, we can ask for Archangel Chamuel to help us find the love we seek that will balance and nourish our hearts and make our life beautiful.

Ten-Second Rescue

Place your hand over your heart and repeat the mantra *YAM* to feel more loving and less jealous, envious, or insecure.

When you feel balanced and centered, you are in a better place to respond to situations, create, and make decisions. Use this technique the next time you are faced with a big decision. Place your hands on your heart chakra and repeat your heart mantra of choice. Think about one side of your decision, exclusively. Notice how you feel. Where do you feel it most, above or below the heart? Now, repeat the mantra and think about the other choice and notice where you feel it the most in your body. If you felt it mostly below your heart, it may serve only your physical needs. If you felt it above your heart, it may also serve your spiritual needs. This may be the better choice, since it serves both.

Homework

Take a moment to self-massage every night and offer gratitude for each part of your body you are touching. There are many wonderful massage videos on YouTube that allow you to nourish your energy and skin, which ultimately rejuvenates your heart chakra.

Heart Chakra Journaling

What experiences do you feel might be creating the deficient or excessive energy in your heart chakra? From ages twenty-one to twenty-eight, what experiences left you feeling you needed to be a people pleaser? Did it benefit you in some way to take care for others first? What experience taught you it was unsafe to love? Or that you couldn't trust others? Did you lose yourself in friendships or a relationship during this time?

I grew up with an alcoholic father. People pleasing was my survival mechanism. Between twenty-one and twenty-eight years old,

I oversacrificed and planned all the events for my friends and family—gave, gave, gave—until I reached depletion, depression, and exhaustion and I then learned to take care of myself.

Have you learned how to take care of yourself and make yourself a priority? If so, how do you take care of yourself now? What do you love most about yourself? What attachments (to people, places, outcome) do you have right now that are keeping you from receiving more blessings in your life?

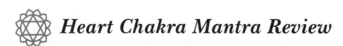 ## *Heart Chakra Mantra Review*

Chakra	Mantra	How do I remember it?	Keynote
Fourth: HEART	YAM	Being in love is yummy!	KEYNOTE F: first note in "Come Together"
Third: SOLAR PLEXUS	RAM	I stand in my power like a strong ram.	KEYNOTE E: first note in "Mary Had a Little Lamb"
Second: SACRAL	VAM	V-V-Vagina— connected to sexual organs.	KEYNOTE D: first note in "Amazing Grace"
First: ROOT	LAM	L-L-Lowest energy center.	KEYNOTE C: first note in "Old MacDonald Had a Farm"

Heart chakra meditation: Love heals all. There is no more important meditation than one of self-love and compassion to draw in the healthiest life. Join me for my heart meditation at www.Love HealThrive.com.

CHAPTER 25

The "Speaking Your Truth" Connection to Your Fifth Chakra Marker: The Throat Chakra

AT TWENTY-NINE, I became a mother. The words you speak as a mother mold and nurture another human being. You try your best but sometimes your heart's message isn't communicated properly. And sometimes your words do reflect your emotional state when you wish they didn't because what you said hurt someone else. This is work of the throat chakra.

My mom, my best friend, died when I was thirty-three. I had two children who were under four years old at the time. We had just moved to a new city, and I was trying my best to keep it together. My husband worked late most nights, but in an effort to create the illusion of family dinner, we called Daddy on the phone every night on speakerphone and placed the phone in the middle of the kitchen table. He would talk to us throughout dinner.

One night, we called and left a message because he wasn't in his office, and my daughter, in an attempt to get my closer attention, threw her plate of food on the floor. Reflecting back on it now, she was probably mad he didn't answer the phone. Exhausted, grieving, and frustrated, I yelled at her for breaking a plate, making a mess, and wasting all that food. As it turns out though, I never hung up the phone.

Later that evening, my husband replayed the voicemail that greeted him upon returning to his desk. I was embarrassed and horrified at how hurt and angry I sounded as I yelled, and I also reminded him I was doing the best I could, given every circumstance.

I am not proud of this moment, but it was a pivotal moment in my parenting and throat chakra journey. I had the unique opportunity to experience the impact my voice was making on my children by hearing it myself. It was a moment that changed me forever.

I have taken into account the impact I make on the ones I love and communicate my truth very differently now. I proudly giggle to myself when my teenage daughter says that I am using my "She's in trouble voice," when I am quiet, controlled, and stoic. Oh, how life changes us.

I learned how to speak my truth in a way that was better received, and I learned, most importantly, what and who I needed to stand up for, especially if that person was me, and how to communicate it in a loving and welcoming manner.

Our throat chakra has many aspects that reveal to us where we need to speak up, discern our own truth, and draw stronger boundaries.

These are significant ways this imbalance shows up in our life:

- Have you recently been feeling unheard no matter how much you talk?
- Have you felt so depleted that you don't even try and share your opinion?
- Have you been manifesting things quickly into your life?

What happens when you truly share your hopes, dreams, and ideas? You feel vibrant, alive, and connected to life and to others. It is an invigorating experience, and it feels fantastic.

What happens when you are so afraid to speak that you freeze or worry so much about what you are going to say that you never even make an attempt to speak? Or when you do speak, it comes out frightened and weak. Social anxiety can feel debilitating, and the more you think about it, the worse it seems to get. When we are riddled with this type of worry and fear, we may not feel we are serving our purpose on Earth. We are here to be seen and heard. Throughout this chapter, you will learn how to bring power and strength to this center, so you begin to not only speak your truth but do so compassionately and lovingly. You will master three techniques in this chapter.

1. Know your truth.
2. Speak your truth.
3. Hear another's truth.

Know Your Truth

This is the hardest energy center for people to work on because it is where we speak our truth and feel heard. It's where we convey what we really want to say. However, the tricky thing about conveying our message is that we must be clear about what we want to say before we say it.

I have taught the Chakra Series Course for years. It is an eight-week intensive on the chakra system and how to incorporate its healing into your life. I would have near-perfect attendance from my students every week. Consistently though, every time we arrived to the throat chakra, half of the class would go missing. At first, I thought it was a big game on that night that all the super fans wanted to attend. But this began to happen every single session. So at one point I mentioned it to the class and took a poll and they all agreed the topic itself was what was keeping everyone away. As a result, I began to warn people that they may begin to feel this way and suggested to love themselves enough to be brave together and show up. From that point on, people began to take the risk to dive into their truth and began to live a more empowered and authentic life.

We must listen to our own self first. It can sometimes take time to know what we want to convey and what we truly believe. What do you believe in? What do you stand for?

When our fifth chakra is clear, we are able to speak our truth and manifest what we want in our lives. Have you ever desired something only to see it show up in your life by the next day? We speak our dreams into existence. This is why vision boards are so powerful. They help us refine our desire so we are clear on what we want to manifest. In the creation of the board, we set the intention for our dream to come to fruition. Intention is powerful and attracts the energy that will bring our physical manifestation to life. Knowing what we want creates a whole new life.

But what if you don't know what you want? When you have struggled with low throat chakra energy, your primal truth may be clouded. You may not know what you truly want any more because, in the past, you may have weighed the consequence of asking for what you want and decided it was never worth it. Perhaps you were ridiculed for asking for what you wanted. It may even have been this that led to your illness. Perhaps you were never listened to, so you believed there was no value to your truth.

When the time comes for someone to ask you for your opinion, you freeze or shy away from the interaction, rather than standing in your power and allowing your great ideas, thoughts, and opinions to be heard. In this chapter, you will come to know your truth. In knowing your truth, your truth becomes intention. Intention is powerful. When you know your intention, manifestation quickly follows.

Speak Your Truth

Speaking your truth can look like being honest—bet you guessed this one—and most of us achieve this one daily, thankfully!

Speaking your truth can also look like believing what you say. This one can get a little trickier. In work and in life, we often feel like we're supposed to say "the right thing" to make others happy or to excel in a certain way, leaving life feeling a bit scripted and inauthentic.

The truth is people may hear your words, but if your heart isn't into what you are saying, people will notice. This is true whether you are comforting a friend or pitching a business idea. Only pitch what you believe in because people will feel it.

It's energetic.

Our energy always tells the truth, so make sure your words do too. Your audience, whether it be to your kids or to a room of twenty or a thousand people, will feel the dissonance or the congruence of whatever it is you are saying. If your words match your energy, people will resonate with you. They will believe you and feel inspired by you. They will embrace your passion and trust you.

But if you don't believe in what you're selling, whether it is a business idea or parental wisdom, this dissonance is also felt. It's that moment when you leave the meeting and have your immediate reaction and find yourself saying one of two things: "I can't put my finger on it, but I just don't feel like I can trust that person" or "I don't know why, but I just have a good feeling about this."

The congruency of words matching energy is the magic ingredient that creates that good feeling. What we say matters and how we say it matters even more. Our vibe speaks louder than words. Choose your words and passions wisely. They help you create a life that you love and one that others believe you love too.

Speaking our truth is where we speak our desire into life. Manifestation occurs in the sacred space that lies between intention and allowance. Once you know what you want, intention builds. As intention builds, energy attracts. As energy attracts, physical manifestation materializes. You speak your life into existence with the strength of your energy foundation. If you've been working your way through all the chakras as I suggested in the preceding chapters, strengthening the energy of each center, your foundation may look something like this:

- By strengthening your first root chakra, you felt safe, secure, and provided for by the Divine.
- Because you felt safe, you were able to strengthen the second chakra, reach a state of emotional equilibrium, and ignite your passion.
- Because your emotions were balanced and you felt safe, you were able to turn your fear into faith and surrender

personal power to a Divine or higher power to guide and direct you.

- Once all of your physical body needs were strengthened, you were able to cross the astral bridge over to the heart chakra, where you were able to fill up your self-love bucket, release attachments to all outcomes, and tap into that place within the heart where everyone is connected.

For this energy center, the throat chakra, you are going to take your security, emotional equilibrium, and Divinely powered self who is unattached to outcome and verbalize your needs and desires so you can manifest the life of your dreams.

Throat chakra blockage can contribute to other blockages because we don't allow the body to purify the stuck energy within. Our mouth is a powerful conduit for purification, not only for our throat chakra but also for all the chakras below it. Feelings of guilt can easily "clog" this chakra. It is vital to clear this energy by speaking both your internal truth to yourself and your outward truth to others. In doing so, these energy centers remain strong and continue to build a powerful foundation upon each other. When you feel safe, balanced, and fearless, it will be easier for you to say what you need to say, compassionately, lovingly, and without attachment.

This chakra is about speaking your truth and being true to your word. Being true to your word does not just mean refraining from lying. It means that if you casually suggest lunch to someone, for example, you make sure you follow up with definite plans for a date. Otherwise, don't offer the casual "Oh, let's get together for . . ." if you have no intention of fulfilling the offer. Unfulfilled intentions will clutter this energy center up much as guilt does. Our word choices are full of intention. I've recently paid attention to how I use the word *unfortunately*. Often, we use that word to make another person feel better when we can't attend something. "Unfortunately, I can't go because . . ." Is it really unfortunate, though? Surely whatever follows *unfortunately* is merely a better, more necessary match for you. There's nothing unfortunate about it, and there is no need to dampen the energy of this preferred choice. You don't have to hide your light to make others feel better. It's okay not to attend something. If you are speaking your truth and walking your path, what you do instead will be where you are meant to be and will always be filled with fortunate blessings both for you and for others. Begin to watch that word or any other word that might stick out for you in your vocabulary. All words, including small ones (and especially small ones, like *no* or *yes*), can be powerful life-changers.

Striking the right balance between speaking your truth and being tactful and loving is one of the greatest challenges of this energy center. Fear of not being accepted may hinder your truthful verbal expression. Or you may fear being truthful and harming someone. Remember we are all connected. Speak your truth in a way you'd like to receive it. Loving yourself enough to ask for what you need or want is the ultimate lesson here.

Many years ago, I was asked to be room mom for my child's class. I am brilliant at many things, but keeping track of emails is not one of them. I knew this about myself, and I knew this role would not fulfill me. Upon being asked, I politely said, "No, thank you. I have many other talents and am happy to help in lots of other ways. This is not the right fit for me or for the class." And that was it. I did not say any more. I said it lovingly and with so much joy I caught the woman who asked me by surprise because I was just so pleasantly matter-of-fact about it. I knew my truth, and I wasn't afraid to speak it. I think this lesson is important no matter what environment you are in.

Know your truth. Know what will make you happy. Know that you have nothing to prove, and if you're saying "yes" with an empty bucket, no one wins. Everyone would be happier if they used this system and spoke only their truth. They would be fulfilled in ways that truly fed them.

Gossip is also quite prevalent. However, gossip multiplies negative energy. If you find yourself surrounded by negative energy and experiences, it may be time to examine what energy is being released from your manifestation center and begin to shift your energy, and your conversations, accordingly.

We bring in more of what we focus on. Energy flows where attention goes. We can begin to change the way we view people, focusing on their positive aspects rather than their negative ones or what's "wrong" with them. We can learn to appreciate people for what they bring to our reality rather than what they lack or do wrong. Compassion for others can begin only when we have compassion for ourselves first.

Hear Another's Truth

Just as you are true to your word, allow others to own the truth in their words, without personalizing it. When someone declares something, it is spoken from their perspective and from the clarity of their energy. Find compassion for them if you disagree, accept where they are, and allow their energy and words to roll off your energy. Regardless of how it might have triggered you, it has nothing to do with you. It has everything to do with them and their personal experience.

The Ring of Truth

Have you ever heard a speaker say something or have you ever read a theory and felt its truth in your body? You may have felt chills up your spine, a depth of power in your gut, a flutter in your heart, or goose bumps on your skin. This physical response to truth is termed the *ring of truth*, since truth resonates deeply with our vibration. The frequency of those words experienced feels in sync with our own frequency.

This Universal confirmation occurs when we hear truth or lessons that feel accurate, receive a message from an angel, or discover new insight revealing the intuition we felt was correct. We can also feel it simultaneously upon receipt of our intuitive guidance.

Scientifically, goose bumps are a natural nerve response from the sympathetic nervous system—the nerves responsible for our unconscious fight-or-flight response. Our sympathetic nervous system mounts a response to fear, but it has also been proven that goose bumps also respond to awe, excitement, and pride according to research from Harvard Medical School.

Deep truth vibrates at a similar frequency to awe. Our soul contains its own record of knowledge, called the Akashic records, and when truth is heard, it rings true with this soul knowledge and is also felt deeply by physical symptoms. Truth is felt mentally, emotionally, energetically, and physically.

However, have you ever felt the energy in the air of someone lying? It feels heavy on your spine, an apprehension in your gut, a protection over your heart, and you may even find yourself stepping backward away from the person who is lying. Your energetic body does not want to integrate with the low vibration of lies.

This is how "actions speak louder than words." It should really state, "energy speaks louder than words." We feel the energy of the message being delivered—truth or lie. The vibration of a message is either in sync with our soul or it is discordant. This is not limited to lies. If our heart is not into what we are saying, others feel that the words coming out of your mouth do not match the energy flowing from your throat chakra. The opposite is true too. When someone is passionate and speaking their truth, you feel it. You can feel the resonance of their words and throat chakra energy being congruent. This is why we will often say, "Wow, I resonated with what that speaker said so much." You were on the same energetic frequency as the speaker but first the speaker needed to be in resonance with their own self first. Their words matched their energy, offering you the opportunity to resonate with their words.

I give an entire talk on how our vibe speaks louder than words, and this is one of the concepts we cover.

Basking in the ring of truth invites our energetic body to resonate at its highest level and attract more truth tellers into our lives. We attract at the level of vibration where we are.

The Uncompliment

This used to come up with my daughters a lot when they were younger until we invented this term, the *uncompliment*. When I would give one a compliment, the other would get offended or say, "What about me?" I taught them that my complimenting one was not an "uncompliment" to the other—the initial compliment didn't denigrate the other or detract from her goodness. This was an important shift in understanding for them, which they were able to take and translate to school, friends, and coaches. The compliment of one does not take away from the richness of the other. Both can be amazing without the need for external praise. It also teaches that people are allowed to shine by themselves without having to share in the light and that "your turn" will come, too. Doesn't it feel better to receive an authentic compliment anyway rather than the inclusive compliment? It's been such a powerful recognition of self-esteem, self-love, and humbleness. How many times have you fallen victim to the "uncompliment"?

Hearing another's truth does not mean giving permission for someone to dump on you. As you raise your vibration, you will attract fewer of these friends, anyway, but if you have a childhood friend who continues to dump on you, it is important to set proper boundaries and help them find theirs. Give them a copy of *Establishing Equilibrium* and let them establish their own source of happiness as they come to hear their own story first. Once you've set proper boundaries, here is a great three-step process to listening:

1. Maintaining eye contact
2. Remaining present, also known as holding space
3. Listening with ultimate compassion

It is important to incorporate all three of these traits into your active listening. Maintaining eye contact allows you to connect with the window to their soul that houses their shen (as you learned in chapter 2) and feel seen as well as heard. Maintaining presence subconsciously tells the other person they are worthy of your undivided attention. If you are distracted, these actions energetically send the message this person is unimportant to you. The beloved Thich Nhat Hanh calls it "listening with ultimate compassion and allowing another to empty their hearts." This means we remain quiet and allow the other person to share without judgment or criticism. Offering this state of listening reciprocates the same energy back to you as you feel connected and heard, too.

However, the opposite can be true as well. Irritation toward others and voicing that irritation can cause an imbalance within the throat chakra. Our mothers were right when they said, "If you have nothing nice to say, say nothing at all." Ultimately, we often become irritated at another because something feels weak or less than within our own system, and we are holding that person to the attachments of our heart chakra—to people, places, things, and outcomes. Complaining about the person is not going to make it or them better. If you find this happening, head on back to the heart chakra (chapters 21 and 24) to review and nourish your heart a little deeper.

Feeling heard can take many forms: verbal, written, and even artistic expression can all help us feel heard and powerful. We can express and bring great clarity to this energy center through writing. Sometimes, we are able to discern our own thoughts in a more meaningful way when we write them down, for example if we feel our verbal inhibitions are blocking our truth. Since our goal with this energy center is to bring clarity, we want to achieve it in a way we are best served. So write out your truth if that is what feels best for you.

As we write, we begin to detach from the intensity we feel around certain subjects. And as we detach, our perspective begins to shift. Journaling is one of the most effective means of discerning and conveying your truth. Feeling heard in every capacity brings peace to this center.

Do you journal? If not, do you play an instrument? Do you create art? Do you make vision boards? How does your truth long to be heard?

Fifth Chakra Description

How do we know if the energy in our throat chakra is excessive, deficient, or balanced?

Excessive Throat Chakra Energy

How many times have you experienced that person who continues to talk and talk and seems to not pick up on any social cues they've overtalked? They continue talking because they *want* to feel heard but don't *feel* heard. Despite excessive talking, they cannot find their true expression. We all know this person. I tend to find my head begins to circle and spin while listening to excessive throat chakra people, as my sensing is trying to find the core meaning to what they are saying while trying to follow their disconnected sporadic energy. Have you ever noticed this? This is why it is called "talking in circles." The energy never moves forward. It just circles.

Sadly, excessive throat chakra sufferers are often very lonely because they do not ever feel heard. However, it is their lesson to learn how to connect to and listen to themselves first but to understand they are worthy of their own time, energy, and perspective without needing external validation from another. Upon learning this crucial lesson, they will finally feel satisfied. People with excessive throat chakra energy tend to be over-opinionated and very critical of others and how they are performing in life. They may be verbally abusive to those around them, sometimes yelling more than necessary. They don't allow others to "talk back" or voice opinions about certain situations—it's their way or no way. But they're also their own worst critics. Other unpleasant traits include speaking rudely or out of turn, gossiping, nonstop talking, arrogance, condescension, manipulativeness, and lying. When we can recognize this in another, we can hold compassion for them, knowing how miserable their perspective of their world must be. When you are able to achieve this level of compassion, another person's bad mood will no longer affect you.

Deficient Throat Chakra Energy

Have you ever had to encourage someone to talk who felt so nervous they couldn't speak? Have you ever experienced a relationship where you just couldn't maintain a conversation or where it seemed the conversation felt forced? People with deficient throat energy may be unable to express themselves and will often be misinterpreted or misunderstood by others. They're considered wishy-washy or unreliable. Telling the truth and being honest with themselves is challenging for them. They may be fearful of being judged and rejected, leading to social anxiety and diminished self-esteem. People with deficient energy in this area long to realize their dreams but can never bring them into fruition. There is a great deal of apathy in not even attempting to share their thoughts or opinions. There is no desire to speak up for themselves because they do not love themselves enough (fourth chakra), feel worthy enough (third chakra), have any desire to speak up (second chakra), or feel safe enough to speak up (first chakra).

Apathy is more dangerous than anger. Anger shows that the person still cares enough to express themselves, where apathy presents itself with no energy left to care or fight. If you are in a relationship and decide it's not worth dealing with someone else's excessive throat chakra energy, choose to powerfully decide their validation no longer matters. You choose to speak to those who honor, respect, and appreciate you. As you hold this power for yourself, often this will reflect in your partner, and they will begin to appreciate and respect you, too.

Balanced Throat Chakra Energy

Have you ever been amazed by someone who knew just what they wanted and asked for what they wanted, eloquently and with grace? People with a balanced throat chakra know how to convey their truth! They have the balance of true expression, comprised of both silence and speech. They offer thoughtful, clear, and helpful advice. They know what they want out of life, and they are not afraid to ask for it—it often manifests quickly. They are not afraid to express their weaknesses, and people respect them for this. There is a feeling of grace, connection, and clarity that exudes from a person with a balanced throat chakra as they bless others with their kind, helpful, and direct words.

I used to be petrified of the Q&A time after giving talks. Now, I've come to realize this is the most joyous part of my time with a group. It offers an opportunity for us to connect and for people to integrate their learning into their lives. One reason I think I used to be so afraid was being "caught" about not knowing something. Over time, I've learned to authentically say, "That is a great question. Let me research and get back to you." This honest and real response lends itself to even more connection with my group and helps them feel even closer to me. Our authentic vibe speaks louder than our words. It is important to be transparent in your words and intention.

Location

The throat chakra is located within and just above the V created by your collar bones. Think about the recommended position for public speaking—shoulders back, chest up, chin slightly raised, and straight spine. How does this position your throat chakra? It opens and clears it to share its energy. Your energy flows out of this center while you are speaking words from your mouth. This is how your vibe speaks louder than your words. People can hear the words spoken from your mouth, but they energetically *feel* what you are saying as energy releases from your throat chakra. What has your vibe been saying recently?

Can you recall a time when you knew someone was lying to you because you could *feel* it was a lie? Almost everyone can. The question was never *if* they lied, the only question was how big the lie was. We can all feel a lie because it is never about the words spoken. It is energetic. The energy that releases from the throat chakra always tells the truth. If the words you are speaking are not truthful, a dissonance is felt between the words and the throat chakra energy. This is how we *feel* the lie. We feel the mismatched energy to the spoken word. This also occurs when someone's heart is not into what they are saying. Apathy creates this dissonance as well. The real magic happens though when someone is telling the truth and speaking their truth with passion. When the words and energy match, this congruence is felt and inspires people because they also feel the resonance and profound experience of this heart-felt truth being expressed and are emotionally and energetically moved by the words and energy shared.

Truth and lies are told for a myriad of reasons. While your impulsive response might be to get disgusted or angry at someone who lies, what if you could look at them with eyes of compassion? What if the source of lying does not stem from an actual intention to lie? Do you think it could be possible it is a deep desire for acceptance? Typically, if someone habitually lies, there was often a lack of acceptance as a child from their mother and/or father. The person finds themselves going through their life with a deep longing for this primal acceptance of and connection with their inner child. When faced with a situation where they must admit something others might not approve of, their fear of not being accepted and the threat of more disconnection is so great they choose to lie to achieve what they believe is acceptance and connection rather than disappointing someone. This perspective does not condone their lying. It simply inspires compassion for the liar in your life. When you can begin to have more compassion in your own heart for this person, your heart softens and heals, and as a result, your personal vibration rises. As you raise your vibration, you remain healthier and happier, and perhaps the liar feels safer and more able to tell the truth with you as a result.

Physical Correlations in Body

Have you noticed that when you attempt to speak about something upsetting, it catches in your throat? Or if you're upset with someone, your throat becomes sore? This is the physical manifestation within our body. It is your body attempting to find its truth and to find enough strength to share it. It's no coincidence when we talk about feeling upset, we say we're "feeling choked up" or have a "lump in my throat." Due to the tightening of the larynx and vocal muscles, our voice can be affected, sometimes severely. Psychogenic voice loss can affect some people after trauma or acute stress. Even when there's no obvious organic cause, it becomes impossible for them to speak (aphonia).

If you are suffering from these conditions, be sure to reread this chapter and the second chakra chapters (chapters 13 and 16) and take note of what emotions penetrate these areas. Begin to journal or talk to a friend or counselor about how these themes are affecting your life to bring balance and a feeling of being heard into this space.

The following are also conditions that show up when the throat chakra energy is imbalanced: throat lumps, laryngitis, sore throat, tonsillitis, teeth problems, thrush, jaw problems, earaches, ear problems, sinus infections, thyroid problems, sore shoulders, arms, neck, and mouth sores.

Our thoughts trigger emotions, emotions move energy,
and energy manifests physically.
What we do with our energy matters.
If our energy isn't weak, our body doesn't weaken.

Does it make sense now, understanding where this energy center is located, how someone who does not speak up for themselves might end up with a thyroid condition? If you have hypothyroidism, have you been speaking up for yourself or was there a significant event in your life where you did not speak up for yourself between the ages of seven and fourteen? If you have hyperthyroidism, do you find yourself continually talking or gossiping? Where in your life have you not felt heard and continue to talk? Do you still hold on to that deep longing to be heard? It is not only the thyroid that is affected by our imbalanced energy in this center. Remember, this is about listening as well so this energy center can feed every part in this region of our body.

Can you think back to the last time you had laryngitis? Can you remember what happened right before you got sick? Did something happen where you did not speak your truth? Or were you so mad that you could not speak? By strengthening your throat chakra, you will be able to bring balance to your relationships, your health, and with yourself.

Color

The vibration of this energy on the visible color spectrum is sky blue, resonating at approximately 600 hertz—the color of truth, loyalty, wisdom, and peaceful communication. I often wear blue while recording or giving presentations to support my energy in offering the purest and most helpful energetic information and vibe possible.

Emotions

In Louise Hay's book mentioned earlier, *Heal Your Body A-Z*, which describes the emotional causes of ailments, a throat problem is described as "the inability to speak for oneself. Swallowed anger. Stifled creativity. Refusal to change."

Think back to the times in your life when you had laryngitis or other throat problems and see if it correlates to what was going on emotionally with your life. It is powerful to gain the awareness that our emotional bodies and physical bodies are so interconnected. In this energy center, we feel heard or unheard. We are passionate about what we are saying or we are stoic. We feel our connection through our communication.

Lifetime Development

The developmental years for this chakra are twenty-eight to thirty-five. How did you speak up for yourself from these ages? Often this is the time when we begin to find our truth and our voice. We begin to speak up for ourselves. Typically, we may begin to have awareness and heal past childhood trauma and come to terms with past issues on a personal level. (Some of us may engage in therapy. This can be a wonderful way of speaking our truth and listening with intent.) Professionally, this is often a time when we are pursuing our careers, giving work presentations, and manifesting a great deal of success in our lives. Being heard professionally is not limited to giving presentations but can also be in the creation of art, editing of videos, or writing a book. Do you feel worthy of feeling heard by others in your everyday life or simply heard by yourself? How is your truth being presented to the world?

The Everyday Connection

- Have you been stewing about something but refuse to talk about it?
- Do you feel you keep getting cut off in conversation?
- Have you been experiencing feelings of guilt?
- Have you had thyroid issues?
- Have you had trouble manifesting what you want in your life?

If you've experienced any of the above, take another look at this chapter and choose one or two tools from the next chapter to add to your week. Watch how that struggle begins to shift as you begin to know your truth, speak your truth, and hold other's truths. It is empowering to know and speak your truth and to live from this state every day.

CHAPTER 26

The Counter Chakra to
the Throat Chakra

HAVE YOU EVER been so overwhelmingly emotional that you were speechless? We can begin to put the pieces together here. As has been already connected, the throat chakra is paired with the sacral chakra, the sanctuary of the emotions. The strength and balance of the sacral chakra determines the strength of the throat chakra. When the sacral chakra has a stronger draw of emotion when you feel deeply about something, the throat chakra sends its energy to the sacral chakra in an attempt to reach equilibrium within the joint partnership. This is how you can find yourself speechless or unable to speak when you feel very emotional. The opposite is true too. Often those who are overtalkers tend not to be connected to their emotions and seem to drone on and on, typically about apathetic nonsense or details. This is the result of the sacral chakra sending its energy to the throat chakra to keep up with the incessant energy output in an attempt for connection, leaving the sacral chakra lacking in energetic and emotional access. The output of words without the connection energy offered by the sacral chakra creates a challenge for everyone involved in the conversation. The garrulous speaker gets exhausted from talking so much and feels frustrated at the lack of connection, and the listener feels bored and tired from trying to hold space for a conversation that is full of facts and details but lacks intimacy and emotion.

Lying requires continued energy and effort. Think about when you've told a lie, even a small one. You have to continue to tell more and more lies to cover it up. It requires excessive throat energy. Applying the counter chakra partnership here, we can see it map out that the constant energy draw of the throat chakra will cause the sacral chakra energy to be deficient, attempting to feed the need of the throat chakra. Individuals who are suffering from erectile dysfunction and bladder infections might want to take a closer look at how their truth telling, or lack thereof, may be manifesting physically in their deficient sacral chakra energy. I have also seen this present itself when couples are in an argument. Often, one person refuses to talk and creates stagnant throat chakra energy, holding back words and backing up emotions in the sacral chakra, resulting in excessive emotion and energy in the sacral chakra, presenting as a bladder infection. How does this partnership show up in your life? Do you need to talk a little less or be more truthful with your words to increase the energy in the sacral chakra to establish equilibrium here within this partnership?

––––––––––

"You are only as sick as your secrets" is a slogan that has been shared in recovery programs for years and is attributed to Orval Hobart Mowrer, American psychologist and professor of psychology at the University of Illinois from 1948 to 1975 known for his research on behavior therapy. To hold back truth, or to keep a secret, in your throat chakra would require you to hold back your energy, causing the energy in this center to become stagnant. While the throat chakra and sacral chakra establish equilibrium in partnership together, the throat chakra also aids in the emotional and energetic release for all the chakras below it when the mantras are chanted. When the mantra is chanted, stagnant energy or harmful emotion is drawn up from the associated chakra and then is ultimately released out of the mouth, the work organ of the throat chakra. If the throat chakra energy is stagnant, because it needs to hold on to lies or secrets, then this energetic release conduit becomes stagnant too, causing a backup of energy in all the lower chakras. Eventually, this systemic stagnation leads to illness because the energy does not flow through the organs and has no clear exit through the throat chakra.

There is great and necessary healing available in this energetic pairing of the throat and sacral chakras. Journaling, talking to someone who listens compassionately, as well as learning to listen compassionately will bring incredible balance to this center.

One final example of this powerful partnership and the healing it can bring into your life is with break-ups, either with a love or a friendship. After a breakup, our second chakra is experiencing so much emotion, it calls upon the throat chakra to balance it. Our sacral chakra is experiencing so many emotions that the throat chakra energy is diminished, as it is flooding the sacral chakra with energy. As a result, our thyroid can slow down, resulting in additional weight gain, often experienced after a break-up or loss of a loved one.

We need each other to survive. If you are feeling too afraid to speak or to begin to convey your truth, I hope you will dive in deeper into this chapter and the root chakra chapters (which work very closely with the second chakra) to find your healing and the connection you are seeking. The world needs to hear what you have to say. You are worthy of being heard and of feeling heard, by one person or by many. And as you find your balance, you will manifest the life you desire where you feel connected to the people in your life and safe enough to speak your truth.

Compulsive eating or drinking stems from an excessive sacral chakra and a deficient throat chakra. There is so much deficiency in the throat chakra that the sacral chakra becomes excessive. This sacral chakra deficiency can be caused by childhood rejection, childhood traumas, and the abuse listed in the Counter Chakra section but with a different coping mechanism. Rather than talking incessantly, the throat chakra sufferer is attempting to fill and satisfy the throat chakra through excess food and drink. This is where the concept of comfort food is applied. There are healthy, balanced versions of comfort food, of course—enjoying our grand-mother's bread recipe or our grandfather's waffles. Why do these bring in so much comfort? They are connected to the emotions and love experienced with these people during a specific time. As we eat these foods, the emotions in our second chakra are invigorated as well. However, when we turn to food for comfort that is not beneficial to our body or mind, it can create a severe imbalance. Compulsive eaters and drinkers believe food or drink will soothe the throat chakra craving, but this center is not seeking physical nourishment. It is longing for energetic and emotional nourishment and connection.

This same concept applies to addiction. As you may recall from chapters 13 and 16 on the sacral chakra, addiction lives in this center. The emotions so deeply traumatized here in the second chakra ignited this addiction, based on a need to bring balance to a traumatic event from the ages of seven to fourteen. Many addicts describe feeling empty inside. Their addiction is longing to fill the deficient energy in the sacral chakra, caused by a powerful event in their childhood, by drinking, eating, or doing drugs to satiate the thirst or hunger of the addiction.

The Antidote

The sacral chakra energy is the antidote to an imbalanced throat chakra. What aspects of the sacral chakra need to be added to the throat chakra to establish equilibrium within the partnership?

When the throat chakra is excessive, it talks constantly but feels heard by no one. When the antidote of the sacral chakra's connection and emotional energy is added to the words being expressed, emotions are felt by all, connection and energetic equilibrium is established. Ultimately, healing needs to be brought to the sacral chakra first to bring enough energy there to connect these two energy centers for connected, authentic conversation.

When the throat chakra's energy is stagnant, there is an inability to express oneself and one's feelings because there is an excessive amount of emotion in the sacral chakra and no energy in the throat to express it because it has flooded its energy into the sacral chakra to bring healing to the unsettled emotions. This looks like the over-emotional person who is too upset to speak or feels unworthy to speak. When the antidote of the sacral chakra's connection energy is added to the throat energy, the juice of emotion and worthiness of expression is felt and balance is restored.

Counter Chakra Seed Planting

Where we failed to materialize our desires from ages seven to fourteen, we bring them to life from twenty-eight to thirty-five. The blame we learned as a child can emerge as a powerful desire that comes to fruition as an adult, especially when we learn at an early age to own our life and blaming is a lack of accountability and deflection from our own empowerment. When we learn to believe in ourselves and speak truth to ourselves and others, we draw in the manifestations of our desires. This is how and why we cry along with the Olympians crying on the podium. The inception point of that desire to become a champion often occurred during the sacral chakra window of development and materialized in the throat chakra window. This is why it is felt so *deeply* . . . the emotions planted during this powerful window of creation express themselves in this spiritual counter chakra.

CHAPTER 27

The Auric Effect:
The Throat Chakra

Deficient Throat Chakra

When the throat chakra is stagnant, the sacral chakra is excessive. This is the incredibly emotional individual who cannot speak because they are too angry, guilty, or emotional. This leads to a small aura because the person may not feel worthy of feeling heard or not know how to express themselves in a way that will be heard as a result of excessive emotion or intimidation. When the aura is smaller around us, we are more sensitive. We feel more and experience more because we have less auric energy surrounding us to pad and encapsulate our primary energy system. This energetic state is often less than six inches around the body. This is the person who is soft-spoken but feels edgy or emotional and who is often suffering from throat, thyroid, or hearing issues.

Excessive Throat Chakra

When the throat chakra is excessive, the energy is incessant but unconnected. This person speaks to everyone and no one at the same time because there is no connective sacral energy infused into the message. Without the sacral energy of connection, the words and message are lost, and the individual feels alone. The aura is wide and capturing, trying to stick to whomever will listen. This is the loud overtalker in the room who is often struggling with sexual organ, bladder, or kidney issues.

The Auric Effect ✦ *Throat Chakra*

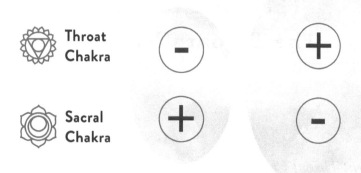

CHAPTER 28

Tools to Heal Your
Throat Chakra Marker

WHEN WE FIRST MOVED to our current hometown, I decided to try to make some mom friends through a club. This particular group requested any potential new member to send an email to the group with a background introduction. I thought this a bit extreme but assumed it was how things were done in this area. There was only one woman who responded to my email. She had grown up in the same area I had just moved from. I couldn't wait to meet her and talk about my previous hometown.

My introduction was approved, and I was invited to the next meeting although it was clear these women were set in their friend group and had no interest in talking to me from the moment I walked in the door. They were on one side of the room, and I awkwardly played with my daughter on the steps opposite them by myself until my email buddy walked in and the energy in the room completely shifted. She still maintains this superpower to this very day. We had the best time talking, and after the meeting, I sent her a reply email asking her to hang out separately.

Even today, we joke that I hit on her. I did enjoy her company and I wanted her to know. It was the beginning of speaking my truth with this amazing soul. I had no idea the ways she was going to help me heal.

After that meeting, we continued to run into each other everywhere—at church, at Santa's helicopter arrival, at the store. It was clear the Universe was nudging me toward this incredible person. After countless run-ins, we decided to bump into each other on purpose and began meeting at the park weekly, alternating who would pick up coffees for each other, and we spent hours talking and bonding over life, motherhood, and incredible coffee.

This friend continues to hold space for me to speak and listens wholeheartedly. She offers amazing advice and has included me in her groups for every family tradition from annual candy apple making to holiday cookie decorating.

She single-handedly healed that feeling of exclusion as she not only included me but also created a lifelong bond and cherished traditions for my entire family over tasty food and drink. All had never tasted so good, since my sacral chakra energy flowed with the feeling of inclusion and connection.

My experience is an incredible example of speaking your truth and listening whole-heartedly—both aspects of a balanced throat chakra. But if you haven't balanced your throat chakra yet, you will experience mounting frustration as you use more words, energy, and time to get your point across, while people *never* seem to get what you're saying. Whether it is the worry about being tripped up and humiliated by your own words or the fear of speaking to a packed auditorium, a group of friends, or just one single person, it can be so worrisome you choose to remain quiet instead.

Whatever the issue, if you feel you can't express your essence, read through this chapter carefully. Start using the techniques, one by one, until they are assimilated into your everyday experience. As you incorporate these tools, you will find yourself knowing your truth, speaking your truth, and the ability to hear another's truth without feeling slighted or threatened.

Color and Clothes

Sky-blue scarves, collared shirts, necklaces, and earrings help bring more energy to this center. Reflecting back on the recommended speaking posture and keeping your throat chakra and the V of your collar bones open, how safe does this feel for you? Do you feel more powerful keeping this area clear and free while allowing your message and vibe to be clearly felt by those you are communicating with? Or would you prefer to wear a sky-blue necklace or scarf and allow this supportive energy to be felt? Both choices are great. Sometimes we don't feel strong enough to go "bare" and have our energy seen and felt unfiltered.

Remember this energy is experienced in both the sacral chakra and the throat chakra. When we are approaching an emotionally charged situation that may invigorate your sacral chakra, wearing sky-blue may assist in expressing your emotions in an emotionally balanced way. Thankfully, we have this tool to bring more energy into your throat chakra and help you live your most empowered life.

Element

When you are compassionately listening, it is often called holding "space" for another. You may hold space for the other person so they can express their truth and vice versa. It's a beautiful release and acknowledgment of mutual truth. What is this "space" made of that we hold for each other?

This space is described as ether or, in Sanskrit, *akasha* or the presence of emptiness. This ether becomes the welcoming home for all the other elements to fill. How can we understand how this looks in our body? What holds your lungs open during your exhale? The ether holds the lungs open so that they can be filled with the element of air on the inhale. What holds your veins open for the blood to flow through? Ether holds your veins open so they can be filled with the element of water (blood). We also hold space for someone to fill when they need to share their stories.

We can make this experience of ether more tangible through this following exercise. Hold your palms up in front of your face, creating a curved dome covering your nose and mouth. Take a big inhale and hold your breath for a moment. Notice what is left inside your palms. This is space. This is ether. This is the pause and the presence we bring to another when we listen compassionately. As you hold space for others, people will begin to hold space for you. How much space have you given to yourself to listen to yourself and to come to know your own truth? How much space have you held for yourself?

Our Five Senses

Have you ever been the recipient of someone listening compassionately to you? It's an incredible feeling. You feel heard and your soul feels seen. You feel safe, connected, valued, and loved. (Notice that those adjectives align as follows: *safe* = root chakra; *connected* = sacral chakra; *valued* = solar plexus chakra; and *loved* = heart chakra.)

Hearing is the main sense. This is where we feel truly heard—and feeling heard isn't always about words. We can feel heard in silence and in people's attentiveness. Striking a beautiful balance between listening and speaking is a key attribute to the health of this energy center—listening with presence. Putting down your electronic device, walking away from your work when your loved one is speaking to you, or listening to yourself when your intuition or your body even whispers to you, *It's time to stop.*

Listening to ourselves—not just replayed voicemails but our thoughts, intuition, and inner voice—is one of the most transformative ways we can strengthen this energy center. We must know our truth before we can speak our truth. Your body and soul know what they need from you. They will guide you toward what you have been seeking. Get quiet and listen.

It is also important to understand what you hear affects this energy center, too, and creates its own trigger. Have you been listening to the news too much? Have you been around toxic friends or family members? In *The Monk Who Sold His Ferrari*, profanity is described as verbal assaults to the soul. Boundaries are the greatest form of self-love, and choosing to limit your exposure to this type of energy will help you raise your energy state.

Organ of Action

Once you know your truth, how do you share it? Usually, we feel most known by speaking our truth through our mouth, this energy center's organ of action. This organ can tell us many things about our health. If you are experiencing canker sores, for example, are you holding back words of anger or blame? If you are struggling with tooth problems, have you been in analysis paralysis and need to decide on something? Choosing to not make a decision is a decision. If you are experiencing mouth problems, review these chapters on the throat chakra and the sacral chakra and begin to clear what is standing in your way to speaking your truth.

We can also use this organ of action to help purify each of the energy centers below the throat chakra. The throat chakra is the purification center for each of the energy centers. We can draw up stagnant energy from the energy centers and release it out the mouth through mantra chanting.

Many years ago, early on in my chakra-clearing practice, I completed the meditation you will learn in the following chapter and experienced what felt and looked like in my mind's eye a black energetic "furball." I felt it coming up from the other chakras and had to cough it up, just like a cat would cough up a furball. It was crazy! Once cleared, I noticed my energy connection became much clearer throughout my entire body.

It is worth doing this work to clear and cleanse your energy.

Food

When you have a sore throat, sometimes the only thing you can consume is liquid, water, soup, or a popsicle. This energy center is paired with the sacral chakra rejuvenated by water. While the healing element for the throat chakra is ether or space, it is important to give yourself time and space to heal. Water rinses your body of viruses and bacteria and brings more balance to the emotions that caused you to get ill.

It is important to drink lots of nourishing water, along with high-quality foods such as soups, bone broths, sauces, or juices that lubricate the mouth and throat and bring balance to the sacral chakra. Fruits high in water and juicing fruits are beneficial.

If you are overeating, is it nutritional nourishment that you need? Or would you be more satisfied by spiritual and energetic nourishment?

Essential Oils

The supportive essential oils for this center include the following:

- **FRANKINCENSE:** heals father wounds and abandonment fears
- **LAVENDER:** heals blocked communication and fear of rejection
- **SANDALWOOD:** helps you feel connected to God or spiritual self
- **YLANG YLANG:** heals disconnection from inner child and joylessness

You can add these to a fractionated coconut oil or another carrier oil and rub them on your throat chakra, beginning with the *V* notch in your collar bone and then circling around your neck. If you are finding more of the imbalance stems from the sacral chakra, you can rub these oils, in the same fashion, around your sacral chakra or take a bath with a few drops of these oils in the water.

Crystals

The crystals that bring great balance and healing to this center include the following:

- **AQUAMARINE:** brings closure, helps in major life changes, and protects the psyche from taking on negative vibrations and behaviors
- **TURQUOISE:** master healing stone that brings healing to your body, mind, and spirit

Aquamarine and turquoise both reflect this chakra's color of blue, helping activate the throat area and boosting communication skills both in speaking and in listening. A necklace made of these crystals will strengthen the energy but keeping them in your pocket assists your energy as well.

Mantra

Have you ever noticed when you've just finished journaling, writing a report, or typing a lengthy email, you take a deep breath and make a humming sound or sigh? As energy rises up the central energy line (*sushumna nadi*), it can release from the throat, the purification center for this chakra. Each of the chakras below the throat chakra can be purified through the throat chakra as the energy rises up from the root chakra. We clear the energy we were using as we reach completion to make room for new, intended energy.

We can assist the energy in this center by humming and singing. Humming increases the energy in this center, while singing releases energy from the center. Appropriately, the *bija* mantra here is HAM, chanted like HUM. You can remember this mantra because this is where you hum. The keynote of this mantra is G, which is the first note in the children's song "Itsy Bitsy Spider." The vehicle for this mantra is carried in on an elephant, an animal known for its gentleness, wisdom, power, and strength—the traits and embodiment of someone speaking with a balanced throat chakra.

Environmental Shift

We absorb what we hear, as I shared in chapter 6 when I described Dr. Emoto's study on water. Just as we want to avoid toxic friends and news, so we also want to avoid disruptive sounds in the home. Eliminate any sounds that are irritating, such as squeaky doorknobs and doors, floorboards or dripping taps. If you are struggling with misophonia, you may find that these simple shifts offer great healing.

Taking some olive oil and nourishing the hinges and doorknobs on the doors and cabinets should eliminate the noise. Recently, I had several doors and hinges squeaking upon opening, and it was beginning to irritate me. Since this was irritating me, I was attracting more irritation into my life because we attract in the same vibrational frequency we resonate at in that moment. I applied the oil and now bask in the silence and attract only peace into my life.

The peace generated in the house without these startling repetitive noises is unbelievable. This simple shift will bring about great peace into your life, offering a calming to your emotions through this improved silence.

Yoga

Lion's breath is a very powerful cleansing agent for this energy center. In lion's breath, you take a large inhale through your nose and open your mouth as wide as you can, bringing your tongue down until practically touching (or touching if possible) your chin and exhaling with the sound of *haahhh*, releasing with intent what does not serve you.

Bridge pose (*setu bandha sarvangasana*) is a beneficial pose to bring energy to the throat chakra. Take this position slowly and do not strain.

Archangels

Viewed as a messenger from God, Archangel Gabriel is associated with communication and is often portrayed holding a trumpet to get everyone's attention so he is heard. In Luke 1:19, Archangel Gabriel says, "I am Gabriel, who stands in the presence of God, and I have been sent to speak to you and bring you this good news."

I feel this is how powerful we should all feel when we speak our truth. To know we are each Divine beings who stand in the presence of God as we speak our truth. If you need assistance in conveying your truth, you can call upon Archangel Gabriel for assistance by saying, "Gabriel, thank you for helping me convey my truth and feel truly heard."

Ten-Second Rescue

Sounds are critical for this energy center, so we benefit from singing, humming, chanting, and screaming, if necessary. Hum to grow energy or sing or chant to release energy and tone the vagus nerve to create a parasympathetic dominant state within your body. Envision whatever is holding you back as you release it out of your mouth and transform it into a beautiful fire in front of you, while filling this newfound space with manifestation, intention, and truth.

Homework

Know your truth. Keep a journal next to your bed and write down the first thing you think of upon awakening. This is the moment when you are closest to the Divine. If you are looking for your truth, let the Divine begin to guide you to it.

Speak your truth. We are what we speak. Offer one authentic compliment to yourself in the mirror and to another person, every day for one week. Begin to seek things of beauty and of joy in your life. As you seek out compliments for yourself, you will attract more things that you love into your life and have more joy to share in speaking your truth.

Hear another's truth. Decide what type of boundaries you need to set with friends or family members to have healthier conversations. Do you need to limit your time in talking to them? Do you outwardly need to speak your truth and place stronger boundaries? Or is it enough internally to decide on how you will listen? Once you have your boundaries clarified, have a conversation and practice your compassionate listening skills—eye contact, presence, and listening only with your eyes.

Throat Chakra Journaling

When was the first time you remember not speaking your truth? Or when was the most significant time for you that you did not speak your truth? When did you speak up for yourself? What did you say? How good did it feel? If you could say anything to someone or do anything you ever dreamed of, what would you say or what would you do? Describe what that is and how that would *feel* to you. If you had no obligations or rules, what would you want to do tomorrow and who would you want to be there?

Throat Chakra Mantra Review

Chakra	Mantra	How do I remember it?	Keynote
Fifth: **THROAT**	HAM	This is the area where we hum.	KEYNOTE G: first note in "Itsy Bitsy Spider"
Fourth: **HEART**	YAM	Being in love is yummy!	KEYNOTE F: first note in "Come Together"
Third: **SOLAR PLEXUS**	RAM	I stand in my power like a strong ram.	KEYNOTE E: first note in "Mary Had a Little Lamb"
Second: **SACRAL**	VAM	V-V-Vagina—connected to sexual organs.	KEYNOTE D: first note in "Amazing Grace"
First: **ROOT**	LAM	L-L-Lowest energy center.	KEYNOTE C: first note in "Old MacDonald Had a Farm"

Throat chakra meditation: Feeling safe enough to speak your truth is at the beginning of sharing your truth. Join me for this throat chakra meditation at www.LoveHealThrive.com.

Throat Clearing Partner Work

This exercise produces a poignant experience in speaking your truth and feeling truly heard. Find a partner who feels safe and approachable. Your life partner may be a great choice but please honor yourself first for this exercise and choose someone else if he or she is not the right choice. If the person you choose is not on this healing journey along with you, teach them the basics of active listening and journaling from this chapter.

Each of you will then take a two-minute turn. One person will share their journaling—what is keeping them from speaking their truth and what they want to manifest in their life. The listener will use everything they learned in this section about listening, such as holding space, and will maintain eye contact, but use zero words—not one. Not even a *hmm* or an *uh-huh*. The listener is to let their eyes *only* do the talking for two minutes and watch what happens. It's amazing.

The speaker will feel truly heard, and the listener will be amazed how much they can communicate with only their eyes. If emotions arise during the sharing and someone, or both of you, feel they need to respond to what you have just shared, complete another round of sharing and allow it to be a response round. Continue to hold space for the other one at a time and complete as many rounds as necessary until your time together feels complete.

Often we put so much pressure on ourselves to *say* the right thing that we end up not really listening. This activity gives you proof that your presence is the best support. Please be sure to try this one out!

If you'd like to begin by yourself, you can start by completing this exercise in front of a mirror, perhaps even spending two minutes complimenting yourself to begin to ignite feelings of self-love and healing.

CHAPTER 29

The Connection Between Your Intuition and Your Sixth Chakra Marker: The Third Eye Chakra

IN MY TWENTIES, I would trip, drop my keys, and forget what I was saying. I was an energetic hot mess. Born a medium and psychic and not understanding yet how to manage my superpower skills left me looking clumsy and oversensitive. I was so clumsy I earned the beloved nickname "Grace" by my closest group of friends.

Now, I barely recognize that girl anymore.

I certainly still drop glasses. However, I know now that glass breaking clears energy in a space, so rather than passing judgment on myself, I honor the experience and reflect on what I was just thinking about right before the glass broke.

It has always brought confirmation that the energy in this space needed to be cleared regarding this specific topic. The shattering of the glass has always redirected my thoughts in the best way possible. I now not only have a new outlook on glasses breaking but also have an entire toolbox of techniques I apply to my life every day, many of which you are learning on this road map.

Over the last two decades, I've learned how to ground my energy, live in the present moment, and allow the future to take care of itself by maintaining my focus on what I can control. I maintain a positive mindset and give myself compassion and love when I get too far ahead of today by reminding myself I am always being blessed.

Big hugs from my hubby also helps! Those hugs, along with meditation, actually do the same thing. They cause me to be still and focus only on the present moment.

When we can draw in our focus from our past trauma rumination and our future worry and live in the here-and-now moment, magic happens. We give space to the present moment blessings that are waiting to be bestowed upon us. We breathe. We take in the moment. We trip less and keep track of our keys. We use our sixth sense to determine and hear the Universe's nudge in the right direction.

When we attempt to imagine and anticipate the many avenues the future can take, we expend unnecessary energy. When we use our energy this way, it lowers our frequency and we attract lower-vibe people and experiences into our lives. When we can use our energy to appreciate every moment of the day—the sun rising, the bees pollinating the fruit trees, the smile shining on our loved one's face—we elevate our energetic frequency with this gratitude and bring in its high-vibe frequency match into our life.

How do you spend your energy? Do you worry about the past or future or appreciate the now? There are certainly a lot of things that we could worry about right now . . . or we can sit in a place of security, faith, and trust knowing we will always be blessed. Our greatest signs, guidance, and blessings often show up in the most bizarre forms at first. What we perceive as struggle often results in our character being strengthened and expanded. What begins in hardships results in blessings.

As you shift your energy, the world shifts its energy.

We are all connected.

You want to make a difference in all the chaos of this world right now? Begin with bringing peace, faith, and love into your own mind and heart and watch how fast your world begins to shift.

Have you ever felt you just knew something but couldn't explain why? Have you ever experienced creativity and weren't sure where the ideas were coming from? Have you ever believed something that couldn't have been further from the truth?

These are all signs that our sixth chakra energy, known as the third eye or *ajna* center, is imbalanced. Our sixth chakra connects us to our mind's eye, imagination, psychic ability, intuition, and our innermost self. From this place, we receive Divine guidance and tap into our deepest wisdom.

When we feel safe and secure, our emotions are balanced, we know who we are, we *love* who we are, and we can speak our truth. *Then* we can tap into the boundless energy source that will take all of our personalized and individual understanding, energy, and strength, and direct it with Universal Divine guidance and wisdom.

Because the chakras below the sixth chakra are now strengthened and balanced, the third eye feels safe to connect and to open up to this amazing Divine guidance. Parents would not teach a baby how to drive a car. There must be much growth and many skills mastered before learning how to drive. The same is true of your energetic and spiritual development. While there are many classes and books on opening the third eye, and many people are very motivated to experience this coveted state, it is imperative to strengthen the foundation of your system first so this center can bless your life. Taken too soon and too impetuously, this path risks wreaking havoc in the form of sleepless nights, moodiness, and misconceptions about their surrounding experiences.

How often have you felt the urge to call a friend because you felt they needed you, only to find out they really did need you? That is your intuition. If you don't feel you're quite ready to start growing your intuition, feel free to reread the previous chapters and work through them again, focusing first on the root chakra. Once the underlying chakras are balanced, you will find you naturally gravitate upward to the third eye and the inner vision and guidance it can access.

When this center is flowing and strong, we are able to see via our mind's eye. This is the place in our mind that can see beyond the physical and integrates all levels of understanding—the physical, emotional, spiritual, and energetic. The third eye balances all the elements of the chakras located below it. We see the past and the present with our physical eyes, and we see the illumination of the future with our third eye through the Universal intelligence received through this energy center. This is the central command center both in receiving information from the Divine and in applying this information to your individual self. You will receive continual information through this center, and it may surprise you. You may get to a place where you just "know" things, and then research the subject or hear news to find you knew it already!

When we tune into our inner silence and truly get quiet, a greater peace and wisdom will rise up within us to guide us in the most profound way. By admitting we don't know the answer to something, we soften our solar plexus and ego. As we quiet our mind, we become still enough to allow this energy center to do what it does best—guide us, lead us, and direct us.

Conversely, when this energy center is imbalanced, great struggle can be felt. Hallucinations, believing stories that are not true, making up stories in your head, or experiencing depersonalization, where one no longer feels connected to the body, are all results of this energy center being imbalanced. Since the third eye is the command center and balances all the energy centers beneath it, when it is imbalanced, it can cause all the energy centers to be imbalanced, resulting in feelings of detachment. Completing these exercises and building a very strong foundation is important so that when you reach this energy center, you feel safe, secure, supported, and empowered.

Sixth Chakra Description

How do we know if the energy in our third eye is excessive, deficient, or balanced?

Excessive Third Eye Chakra Energy
When your third eye produces too much energy, it can be difficult to concentrate and can even lead to hallucinations or challenges with concentration. This is where it's so important to do the work

and build a very strong foundation! This is the reason why I review the preceding chakras in every chapter, and why you should review your energy system each chapter, too. It is vital to continue to strengthen and build the foundation of each chakra, especially your physical chakras, before reaching this energy center.

As previously stated, when people open their third eye too quickly without the proper foundation, they can run into trouble and find themselves moody, unable to sleep, and experience hallucinations. But if you do your work and build your energetic foundation, you will find this energy center to be a powerful source of guidance and wisdom and will not need to worry about undesirable side effects. Please go back to previous chapters if you need to strengthen your own foundation. Bookmark this page and come back to it when you're ready. Be honest with yourself and recognize where you need to be working.

Deficient Third Eye Chakra Energy

Have you had times when you found yourself simply unable to come to a conclusion on a topic? Or experienced feelings so intense they felt unmanageable when trying to make a decision? If energy is deficient in the third eye chakra center, it can be hard to focus, process and remember information, and make decisions. When you are thinking about something or trying to figure something out while sitting at your desk, you may have automatically rested your right palm on your forehead with your elbow on the table while trying to quiet your mind. This is the physical body's way of supporting your energetic body. Energy is released through a minor chakra in your right palm to your third eye so it can figure something out.

It is also hard to dream or recall your dreams when your third eye is deficient. Our dreams are the conduit by which our subconscious mind and the Divine communicate with us. As you strengthen this energy, this guidance will become clearer too.

Balanced Third Eye Chakra Energy

Have you ever just "known" the truth? Known what was true in a situation or the actual true facts without understanding why or how you know it? This is a state of higher consciousness, in which you are receiving Divine guidance. You experience definitive wisdom and strong intuitive abilities. This center activates your clairvoyance and telepathy, which creates a state of intuitive intelligence.

This energy center, when balanced, supports you in honoring your integrity and taking responsibility for your actions. It helps you understand, on a deeper level and with more intricate detail, why you should make a certain choice, because you have the Divine insight to inform you.

In my experience, reaching this higher state of consciousness entails a real expansion in awareness, including astral travel, out-of-body experiences, and receiving messages from spirit guides and guardian angels. It means being spiritually aware. These are all very natural results of this increased intuitive awareness.

As mentioned, Divine guidance can also occur while you're sleeping, whether or not you are aware of it. Some people have experienced waking up to the sound of wind chimes, bells, or nature sounds when there is no apparent source for them. It's also common at this stage to experience a dream with someone, especially someone who has died, that feels "so real" the person wakes up in tears. Many people believe they receive comforting messages in this way from those who have passed on. However, waking up bawling can also be a function of energetic release because the connection with the Divine in such events is so intense, the physical body is unable to handle it and needs to release some of the intensity of the experience.

As you continue to strengthen your system, your physical body's frequency will rise and you will experience less need to release these types of experiences, but at first, it's similar to attempting to drink water from a fire hose when you're only ready to drink from a straw. Like all muscles, as you strengthen this energy center and the energy centers that support it, you will be able to handle more and more.

If this sounds far-fetched to you, that's okay. Reaching this level of connection is often a process. In addition, many people do not have an interest in strengthening these muscles to utilize these capabilities. However, I want you to know that you have them as a possibility, and they are there if you would like to refine them. It may also offer some explanation if you have encountered such experiences already and did not know what was happening.

Remote Viewing and Real-Life Connection to Intuition

Acceptance of such abilities is becoming more mainstream. The military is known to have hired people who are highly intuitive and gifted in remote viewing to help find missing soldiers. The police are also known to employ those with psychic vision sometimes. Remote viewing is a long-distance form of sensing used to gather impressions, which might be useful in terms of information and intelligence. This occurs through a balanced third eye chakra center and can be a powerful tool to use for this type of work.

Anyone can "see" what is happening with a loved one. Ask any mother if they knew their child was in danger or sick before they found out and they will tell you they most certainly did know. My daughter was once in a location with an active shooter. From the moment she had left the house that night with her friends, my instincts were not at peace. I couldn't shake this awful feeling but tried because she was already out for the night. I checked my phone intensely for about five minutes before my daughter called me to tell me she was running out of the area and would call back when she was safely in another location. My instincts had known all along. Thankfully when I talked to her, I also *knew* she would be okay, too. Our third eye not only gives us incredible guidance and foresight, it also blesses us with peace and deep knowing that all will be well.

We are all connected. When you think of someone and they call or text, it is not a coincidence. This is why our thoughts are so incredibly powerful. This is how your thoughts can heal relationships without long, drawn-out conversations. As you think about someone, an energetic connection is established with your third eye and theirs. If you are in a disagreement, you can utilize all you have learned so far about your own themes and healing and see how you might be contributing to or filtering the disagreement. As you begin to work through your stories and layers, the relationship will begin to mend because the energy that draws you two together will shift as you alter your side of the energetic connection.

When you reach a place of healing within your own heart, you can begin to send love, compassion, and forgiveness to the other person. By sending these high-vibe thoughts, emotions, and energy, it will shift the relationship. You are not mind-controlling or shifting another person. By healing your energy and sending high-vibe energy to another, you are raising the energy that *connects* you. You are simply changing *your* contribution to the energy connection. This is one of the greatest ways to heal a relationship—knowing you have the power to do so on your own.

Remember, your thoughts create your life and the state of your emotional and physical health.

Our thoughts trigger emotions, emotions move energy,
and energy manifests physically.
What we do with our energy matters.
If our energy isn't weak, our body doesn't weaken.

Along with such powerful intuition comes great responsibility. It is essential we choose to use our intuition for our own guidance and clarification. We are not meant to use astral travel or remote viewing with malicious intent or to interfere with others' lives. This type of usage would create great karmic debt. Highest intention and permission from another are recommended before using your intuition to view their energy or situation or to offer guidance. Integrity is of the utmost significance here. Strong integrity is one of the greatest blessings received with a balanced *ajna* (third eye chakra). As you begin to become more sensitive to your energy, you will begin to sense when something feels right and when something doesn't. You will be able to choose the path of integrity based on noticing what feels like a high vibration and what feels like a low vibration. Your body and your intuition will be more powerfully integrated, and discerning truth will become a different experience for you. You prefer to be feeling good surrounded by high vibration.

This principle also applies to the assessment of the chakras. While you are assessing your own chakra system, it is common to recognize symptoms in others. We are all connected, so if it is showing up in their life, chances are it is in your system, too. Such synchronicity can be helpful, as it means you can explain this system to them to help them heal, too. This system is not intended for you to judge them or attempt to separate yourself in a position of superiority. Its beauty is in the self-awareness and healing it offers you, and as you heal, others will heal around you.

Location

Have you ever felt a tingling between your eyebrows when meditating? Or an ache in between your eyebrows when you were trying to discern the truth about a situation? This was your third eye chakra utilizing its energy to help you clarify a choice or bring more peace into your day. Your third eye chakra is located about a half an inch above and between the eyebrows, just above your brow line.

Pause for a moment, close your eyes and imagine your favorite place. Maybe it's a vacation spot or the comfort of your own bed. What do you see? How do you feel? What do you hear? What do you smell? Bask in this place, soaking in all you love about this space. The location in your mind where you created this wonderful image is your mind's eye, the neural correlates of consciousness within your mind. You've probably been using this center your entire life without recognition of it. Now you can know it and use it powerfully.

Energetically, the *pingala* and *ida nadis* reside in the root chakra, along with the *sushumna nadi*. From this place, the *sushumna nadi* runs up the central line, or spine. The *pingala* begins with flowing out to the right and the *ida* flows out to the left. These two energy lines crisscross through the body, meeting up at each chakra point until it reaches *ajna*. All three energy lines meet here to gather and connect before flowing into Divine consciousness through the crown chakra, which you will learn about in chapter 33. This movement is important to understand as we move forward on your journey.

Physical Correlations in Body

Light sensitivity and migraines can be a result of stuck energy in the third eye. I once had a student who developed a migraine the day after one of my meditation classes. We discussed her experience of the class, and she had followed the class guidance up until the third eye directions. She wanted to remain in the third eye center rather than release the energy as was directed in class. As a result of not releasing the stuck energy into the Divine, she developed her migraine.

If you are struggling with migraines, review this chapter and be sure to drink lots of mineral water. Intuitive energy work depletes our physical bodies of a significant amount of minerals, and as you learned in chapter 12, earth balances our root chakra. This happens because we need to remain powerfully grounded to have balanced intuition. If we do not remain connected to Mama Earth and her continual flow of minerals as we ground and intuit, our minerals become deficient. As you are learning and strengthening your grounding practice, you can supplement these minerals through mineral water.

I used to suffer from migraines all the time. Once I switched my water choice over to a high mineral water (in non-plastic bottles), I no longer experienced migraines. I have certainly also improved my grounding techniques over the years as well, but I've always found this mineral water insurance to be helpful in keeping my migraines away. If I start to feel one coming on, I drink a few bottles of mineral water and it dissipates.

The areas that are affected by the energy flow of the third eye include the lower part of the brain and pituitary gland. Physical ailments resulting from an imbalanced third eye can include brain cysts, tumors, seizures, strokes, insomnia, depression, migraines, panic, hormonal imbalances, and dizziness. If you are struggling with any of these conditions, review each of your energy centers to strengthen them and review the third eye suggestions in these two chapters. The pituitary gland is responsible for maintaining homeostasis throughout the body through the release of hormones that affect the organs.

One of these hormones is cortisol, which helps manage our stress. Understanding now that the third eye helps balance all the energy centers and their organs and senses, below it, we can understand how stress can be triggered and felt in a more powerful way when each of the energy centers, their senses, and connecting auric layers are not balanced. If imbalanced, we experience the world through our aura and senses in a less than healthy way. Once our third eye energy helps balance the chakras and the pituitary gland, thus balancing the organs, we establish peace, manage our stress, and experience peace and calm.

I have found an incredible pattern between those who are highly intuitive and those who are diagnosed with ADHD. I find those who come in for a session with a diagnosis are generally highly intuitive. The "attention deficit" is a result of the highly sensitive person following chaotic energy without regard to their physical senses. (More on this in the Counter Chakra—Third-Eye section of this chapter.) Their attention shifts because they are distracted by the next shifting energy experienced.

Color

The color that resonates at the frequency of the third eye is indigo, a blend of dark blue and purple, resonating at a frequency of approximately 670 hertz. This color supports deep concentration during meditation, which is why you will often see meditation pillows or blankets in this deep shade. You can use an eye pillow in this color to help bring balance into your third eye.

Emotions

Remember those moments where everything felt at peace and in order? It felt like you could finally exhale. It may have been because you completed your "to-do" list, perhaps on a physical level. With that list completed, what happens to your energy? You relax and let go. Your energy naturally flows, and you feel connected to a state of peace. The true clarity and inner connectedness obtained through the third eye brings about this feeling of true peace, knowingness, and contentment.

Lifetime Development

Ajna or third eye is the command center that balances the chakras below it. As such, there is no range of lifetime development for this energy center.

We are born with our third eye open, and often babies and toddlers seem able to see energies and spirits. Have you ever noticed babies appear to be smiling at someone when they are sitting in their bouncy seat? It is usually an ancestor who has crossed over and is helping the family out by entertaining the baby. The baby is able to see them because their third eye is wide open, while most parents cannot. Life hasn't closed the newborn's third eye yet.

Life causes us to close our third eye for a number of reasons. Were you ever told by a person of influence (parent, grandparent, friend, or teacher) that it is wrong to use your intuition or see spirits? Were you ever lectured on how your guidance is not real? Did you have an upsetting situation involving your intuitive guidance? Each of these experiences can close your third eye.

When this happens, you must then heal and strengthen your chakras to reopen this energy center. This is why there is such a varying degree of psychic ability in people. We all have equal access because the Divine is in all of us, but the openness to it is dependent upon how grounded we are, the strength of the chakra centers below *ajna*, and whether our third eye ever closed in the past. Children who are raised in encouraging environments will naturally be more psychic as adults because they've been strengthening this muscle for longer and have no fear attached to this process.

When my children were young, I would play the card game Go Fish with them. In the game, you create matches with the cards in your hand by asking another player for what you believe will be your card's match. Instead of asking arbitrarily, I taught my daughters to use their intuition first and *feel* where the card was located that they needed for their pair and then ask that person for it. They got so good at it, we stopped playing because the first player would just run the table every time. I was so proud!

When our third eye reopens (at any given time in our lifetime, if it needs to reopen), we begin to hear, see, and feel our Divine guidance. One noticeable trait of our third eye opening is seeing an open eye in meditation as a vision. We obtain this openness (without the use of mind-altering herbs or drugs) first by being grounded. Our body will not open up to this "seeing" without being grounded because it keeps us safe and balanced. Once we understand what our guidance looks and feels like, we must learn to trust it. Trust builds as we recognize our signs and witness our premonitions come to life. As this begins to happen more and more, we begin to trust our intuition more, too, and recognize our intuitive signals.

I once had a client who had attended many mediumship classes and desperately wanted to be able to "hear" messaging from the other side but couldn't tap into that communication. It was because her energy was completely ungrounded. I explained her energy system knew what was best for her, and it would not allow her to connect until she grounded herself and strengthened her root chakra.

Our third eye reopens naturally when it feels safe to do so. There are plant medicines that can expedite the opening of our third eye. However, if taken without being properly grounded and without the strength of the chakras below for support, one can experience hallucinations and negative, even dangerous mental side-effects.

The third eye shows us that everything is connected and sacred. When we can view the world through this spiritual "eye," life feels richer, more compassionate, and connected.

The Everyday Connection

- Has it been hard to concentrate lately?
- Have you been making up stories in your head about people that may not necessarily be true?
- Have you been struggling with hormone imbalances?
- Are you having trouble sleeping?

Once you have the awareness of these symptoms, you can begin to apply the teachings from this chapter and the techniques in the next to bring balance and a true sense of peace into your life.

An imbalanced third eye can cause each of these symptoms to show up in your everyday life. Our third eye helps regulate the body's internal cycles. Specifically, the pineal gland, which is connected to the third eye, is activated as it absorbs information through the light brought in through the eyes. This is how melatonin is produced in our bodies. If the third eye is not balanced, it will not produce the right amount of melatonin and will disrupt the sleep cycles. When my teenagers have a hard time waking up, I wake them up by doing Reiki on their third eye. They almost instantly wake up and are ready for their day upon getting up because their third eye is more balanced.

CHAPTER 30

The Counter Chakra to the Third Eye Chakra

AS YOU HAVE JUST LEARNED, the third eye balances the energy centers below it as all three energy lines integrate here, so the third eye chakra has no single pairing with one exclusive chakra. *Ajna* is the command center and balances each energy center underneath it. In return, this center draws wisdom from each of the five energy centers beneath it to obtain a sixth sense of knowing and understanding in this center. Our sixth sense is the integration of the five chakras, and their senses, below *ajna*. (We will expand on this more in the next chapter's Five Senses section.)

When this energy center is overenergized, it can sometimes lead to hallucinations. Hallucination is not always seeing crazy images or color designs. Hallucination can be false stories. We may tell ourselves stories, which we convince ourselves to be true, when in actuality, they are not. This type of storytelling causes worry based on assumptions, what-ifs, and made-up stories that create a powerful disturbance for someone believing them.

I once had a devoutly religious client who believed I had done something on purpose in class to make her feel upset. I explained I would not do that to a student and then realized it was a hallucination. She prayed all the time and had beautiful, amazing faith but was completely ungrounded. I explained this to her and put her on a root chakra regimen. It was illuminating for both of us.

Let me be clear. It is not a bad thing to be prayerful and faithful. I'd love everyone to be as prayerful and faithful as this client was, but the real strength for us is not just in having our Divine connection strong but to have all of our energy centers equally strong so that we achieve equilibrium. We can't have one singularly powerful chakra and find peace in our days.

The Antidote

Since the sixth chakra pairs with the five senses below it, when the sixth chakra is excessive, the missing piece is the connection with the five chakras below it, which connect the energy to the physical senses and the human experience. Without the equal pairing, the experience of the sixth chakra without its grounding physical world counterparts is one of illusion and detachment from reality because this energy is not attached to the senses that connects us to the physical world reality. When there is a reconnection made with the five chakras below, equilibrium is established and a more realistic view of the world is restored.

When the sixth chakra is stagnant, life feels tough and decisions are challenging. There is no intuitive guidance absorbed, only information from the physical senses. There is too much dependence on the five physical senses and no adherence to intuition. When there is a release of the physical chakras and a beginning of trust in the intuition's guidance, equilibrium is established.

CHAPTER 31

The Auric Effect:
The Third Eye Chakra

Deficient Third Eye Chakra

When the third eye is stagnant, decisions are difficult because one is not taking in insight offered by their intuition. They feel the pain of life more because the aura size is minimal, less than one foot. With minimal energy around them, they feel the drudgery of the physical world and only believe in the physical proof they are experiencing, negating intuitive guidance. This person is so pragmatic that life is more difficult than it needs to be. If they listened to their intuition, and followed its guidance, life could function more smoothly for them. This person may suffer from migraines, seizures, or vertigo and displays excessive behavior in the first five chakras: greedy, cheap, blaming, egocentric, critical, envious, jealous, and an overtalker. A balancing of the third eye and the welcoming in of Divine guidance will begin to assist this person and establish equilibrium. Remember the third eye balances the five centers below it. It is amazing how quickly this remedies once the proper attention and healing is given.

Excessive Third Eye Chakra

When the third eye is excessive, there is hallucination. This results in an excessive aura, as the individual sees the world only through their third eye. This person is challenged with discerning the difference between reality and nonreality. They depend on their sensing alone, leaving them with an excessive aura. There is a detachment from the deficient five chakras below, leaving this individual with no secure touch point within, or consideration of, reality because they are not tapping into their five physical senses. This person may seem lost or confused or live life according to their own rules and may struggle with a myriad of physical symptoms.

The Auric Effect ✧ *Third Eye*

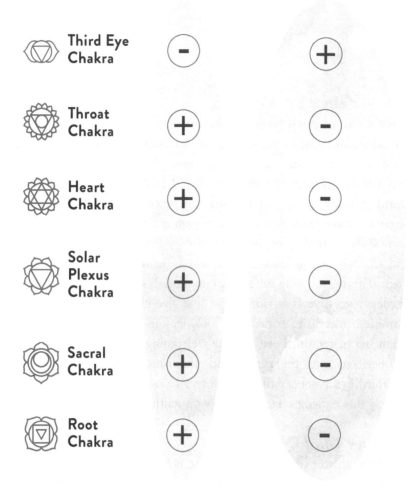

CHAPTER 32

Tools to Heal Your
Third Eye Chakra Marker

AS I SHARED EARLIER, when I asked my mom for help with the spirits in the hall as a young child, I didn't understand why she panicked. It felt as if she was afraid of me, rather than the situation, despite having done nothing but ask her for guidance on the reality I was experiencing. Mediumship and psychic ability are no different than being born with blue eyes and brown hair.

I think this is why I have worked with so many children in my practice. I have wanted to help teach them and their parents a better way to turn their gifts into their greatest superpower. When kids would arrive for their session, I open the door and say, "Welcome to Superpower School."

Because it is your superpower.

As you strengthen and balance your energy, you begin to foresee what is about to happen so you can be better prepared. Your reflexes improve. You think more clearly. Life becomes more effortless as you no longer waste time on things that will not matter in the long term.

There is a sense of peace and calm. Basking in a sense of peace and knowingness, comforted by the wisdom that everything is going to be okay, clear on what your next step is on your journey, no longer seeing a divide between all that is and yourself, witnessing the world as is, not as good or bad—these are all results of a balanced third eye. Your first step in working with your third eye, after balancing the chakras beneath it, is to empty it. Clear it from thought, perception, ideas, and opinion, and then *allow* Divine guidance to enter in to guide you.

When we create silence and stillness within us, it permits us to receive guidance toward our next step. In working with Divine guidance, however, we rarely receive the entire plan at once. It tends to be more step by step. Often, you are guided to "go buy a loaf of bread," for example. However, when you go to the store and buy the loaf of bread, you bump into an old friend who just "happens" to work in the same field as you, who, after reconnecting, wants to offer you your dream job.

Your guidance didn't say, "Go to the store for your dream job," because it may have caused too much confusion or worry about whether or not you were ready or worthy. Divine guidance shows up in simple steps. We just need to follow the one simple step that leads to the journey of a lifetime. When we begin to listen to and trust the guidance and the knowingness that exists with us, our path begins to unfold.

How do we begin to practice? Try experimenting first with small matters. Trust yourself to "see" into the truth of everyday matters around you, perhaps anticipating minor events. Guess who is calling on your phone before you look at the name. Anticipate when the traffic light will turn green. Predict who is at the door before checking or the precise time someone will arrive. If you are people watching at a park, see if you can figure out what the people at the park will do next. Experiment and have fun with this practice. It is thrilling when you've "guessed" right and it helps you to strengthen this muscle.

This chakra holds the guidance and the wisdom you've been seeking but is found only in the letting go of what you believe to be true. Trusting and knowing that as you let go of opinions and personal truths to journey to a state of neutrality within this chakra, it is possible you will be refilled with much of what you already believe. For many, this happens as they clear their energy and are renewed in spirit with the confirmation that they are "on their path."

However . . . we grow. We evolve. We change. There may come a day when you clear your third eye to receive your guidance and a new direction is introduced, leading you toward your life purpose one step at a time. The following tools and techniques will help you clear your third eye and strengthen it to reach a place of continual guidance.

Color and Clothes

We dress for what we need, and your soul knows which colors to wear. When you wear indigo, you will draw in the supportive energy to balance and strengthen your third eye. You can wear an indigo eye mask when lying down, sleep in indigo clothes, or lie on an indigo pillow, remembering your third eye releases from the front of your head as well as from the base of your head where your neck meets your skull near and below the occipital bone.

Element

Have you ever been out on a hike and turned toward the sun, while closing your eyes, to welcome in the sun's rays? Have you ever noticed your third eye tends to warm up first when you do this? Do you feel tingling between your eyes when you do this? The element of light balances your third eye. If you can't get outside, imagine the sun's warmth, light, and heat beaming down onto your third eye, inviting in balance, healing, clarity, and light. Intention is powerful. Lying out beneath the actual sun and welcoming in the sun's healing power and warmth helps balance this energy center.

On the *Huberman Lab* podcast, one of Dr. Andrew Huberman, PH.D.'s consistent messages is to absorb sunlight first thing in the morning to become more focused and regulate your circadian rhythm. He recommends five to ten minutes of sunlight every morning. Energetically, why do you think this is helpful? The sunlight begins to balance the third eye and the energy centers below it, awakening and balancing each of the chakras and their connected senses and ultimately the aura to awaken the senses and physical human experience. When all of your senses and their connections to the aura are balanced, you find focus, balance, and awareness throughout your day.

Our Five Senses

Have you ever guessed or knew who was calling, only to look at the caller ID and see you were correct? This energy center transcends our five most basic senses and uses them all together to create the sixth sense that sees beyond all senses. It is truly the integration of all of our senses that allows us to receive Divine guidance. *Ajna* draws wisdom from each of the five energy centers beneath it—thus each sense—to obtain a sixth sense of knowing and understanding in this center. It draws upon the energy, and sense, of each energy center. It also draws in the information from each layer of the aura that is connected to each chakra and sense. We sense and smell, taste, see, feel and hear the energy around us through our organs and our aura.

For every human sense we experience, there is a counterpart "clair" sense that contributes to a rich intuitive experience.

- **CLAIRAUDIENCE/CLEAR HEARING.** Hearing Divine guidance either through your psychic gate (located at the base of your skull) or as if someone is whispering to you. Sometimes, music or ringing in the ears is heard as messaging.
- **CLAIRVOYANCE/CLEAR SEEING.** Seeing images in your mind that can be pieced together to tell a story of either the past, present, or future; seeing energy and spirits.

Images can be symbolic or pictures from life. Many people experience this in the phenomenon of déjà vu.

- **CLAIRSENTIENCE/CLEAR FEELING.** Experiencing Universal confirmation (goose bumps) when you say something; feeling a nudge, hug, or subtle wind on your cheek. It is also being a true empath when you can feel the emotions of what another feels. This specific feeling is often referred to as clairempathy.

- **CLAIRCOGNIZANCE/CLEAR KNOWING.** Knowing in your gut or within your spirit the absolute truth of something. You don't know why, you just *know* it is true. The Divine blesses you with wisdom, knowledge, or a premonition.

- **CLAIRALIENCE/CLEAR SMELLING.** Smelling odors that do not exist in your environment. For instance, I will smell the aroma of the coffee my late mother used to brew when I know she is near.

- **CLAIRGUSTANCE/CLEAR TASTING.** Tasting metal is common as a Divine sign of awareness; tasting a favorite food from a loved one without consuming the food is another sign. Chefs and food critics tend to have a heightened sense of taste.

- **CLAIRETANGENCY/CLEAR TOUCHING.** Seeing images when you touch an object. When you hold an object, you see/hear/feel images that tell the story of the energy held by the object, which can then be read by sensitives. This art is also termed *psychometry* and is one of the ways in which the Dalai Lama is tested and chosen. Once a boy is found who is believed to be the reincarnated Dalai Lama, assorted objects are placed in front of him and he must select the ones that belonged to the Dalai Lama.

While I have taught several powerful courses on this topic, developing these senses and working through them would constitute a different book. But before you immerse yourself into that work, do complete your road map's work first. As I've already mentioned, your grounding process is your first and foremost most important tool to master in developing your intuition. As you strengthen your chakras, your third eye will naturally develop and then you can move onto specific mastery of your clairs through the clarity found within the chakra system.

Organh of Action

It is no coincidence that meditation calls for you to quiet and still your mind to reap the benefits of this practice. The mind is the organ of action for the third eye chakra. As you quiet and focus your mind and third eye chakra, you receive the guidance, direction, and peace you look to experience. Allowing Divine guidance and energy to be received by the third eye and the mind offers the meditator a path toward their Divine purpose.

Food

Modern science encourages the consumption of brain food and this same recommendation is echoed here as suggestions to strengthen the third eye. Eating foods rich in omega-3 fatty acids, such as fish and nuts, flaxseed and chia, and any whole purple foods including grapes, eggplant, purple cabbage and plums will strengthen and balance your third eye.

Essential Oils

The supportive essential oils for this center include the following:

- **ROSEMARY:** heals confusion; develops knowledge
- **FRANKINCENSE:** heals spiritual disconnection
- **SANDALWOOD:** heals disconnection from God
- **HELICHRYSUM:** helps intense pain, heals turmoil

Diffusing these oils can be helpful while meditating or sleeping to bring balance into your third eye. If you choose to rub them on your body, take care not to touch your third eye with your right middle finger. We hold our anger in our middle finger (again no coincidences), and if you were to touch your third eye with your middle finger, anger energy can be released there. It is a good practice not to allow anyone to touch your third eye due to its high sensitivity and perception. I am fiercely protective of this area. If you've been using your middle finger, utilizing the techniques within this chapter will assist you in raising your vibration to clear any lower energy of anger from this energy center.

Crystals

I've always liked crystals, but it was my experience with a moonstone many years ago that really made me appreciate the power of crystals and give them the respect they truly deserve.

One of my aunts had given me a beautiful moonstone pendant. A few months later, I was running out the door for a girls' weekend and tossed the necklace on. A few hours later, I started experiencing uncomfortably strong visions and messages, which I always had, but these felt more intense than normal. I didn't realize why this was happening. I assumed it was because I was more relaxed and was hanging out in the sun.

A little later, my girlfriend said, "Oh, I love your moonstone."

I looked it up online and found out what the moonstone does! It's known to stimulate intuition, visions, and psychic perception. Without even trying to make this process happen, I saw, firsthand, how powerful crystals can be and how the moonstone can ignite your psychic process. I gave total respect to my amazing moonstone and encourage you to do the same. For reference, this moonstone was probably smaller than a dime. It was tiny and powerful. From that moment on, I never wore the moonstone around crowds. I wore it only when I wanted my psychic abilities to be even more upleveled in meditation and when working with clients.

Crystals that balance this center include the following:

- **CLEAR QUARTZ:** master healer crystal and, like the third eye, can balance all chakras
- **LAPIS LAZULI:** protects *ajna* energy and shields against psychic attack
- **AMETHYST:** encourages serenity and peace
- **MOONSTONE:** increases intuitive ability and mental clarity

Mantra

The sound of OM is every note ever known. It is the sound of the Universe and unifies everything in it. It is the seed sound of all the chakra mantras below the third eye, making it holistically healing, as it heals each of the energy centers below it. Each mantra would sound like: L-AUM, V-AUM, R-AUM, Y-AUM, H-AUM. AUM is chanted in the keynote of A. The traditional "Happy Birthday Song" begins on the note of A and is a simple way for you to remember what note to begin your OM chant.

Environmental Shift

As light is the healing element for this energy center, we want to bring as much light as possible into our living spaces. Replace any broken light bulbs in your home. Is there a room that needs another lamp? Is your front door well-lit? Remember, if people have a hard time finding your front door, energy will have a hard time finding it, too.

Light candles during meditation. Clear out anything under your bed so energy can circulate while you dream. While we're talking about the bedroom, this is not a good place for electronics. Turn off routers at night and turn them on again in the morning. If you must sleep with your phone next to your bed, turn it on airplane mode. This helps alleviate the stress of electromagnetic frequencies, so your body can truly rest and receive the Divine guidance it's seeking.

Yoga

Positions that support this energy center include the child's pose . . . but not just any child's pose. When you're in child pose position, focus your third eye on the ground with the intention of clearing it and releasing your ego. Many religions use prostration as part of their ceremonies and prayers for this reason. It is powerful.

Sometimes if I feel my ego igniting, I will drop down and place my third eye on the ground in child's pose and stay there until I feel myself getting out of the way of myself. I also think it's really great to make this part of your total body workout and get double value—releasing the ego while releasing toxins from your body.

Archangels

Archangel Uriel is known as the Light of God and assists in developing your psychic and intuitive skills and heals any loss of self-respect. Archangel Uriel assists with intuition development, spiritual understanding, and taking back our power when necessary.

A good prayer is, "Archangel Uriel, thank you for helping me discern and understand the Divine guidance that I am already receiving." I recommend you say this every night, every time you meditate, and any time you are looking for Divine guidance.

Ten-Second Rescue

Ground your energy (go back to chapters 7, 10, and 12 on the root chakra if you need to refresh this) and look up at the sun with your eyelids closed or covered with a cloth. Do not stare into the sun and risk damaging your eyes. Just bask in the light with your eyes closed or at dawn or dusk. Allow the sun's energy to penetrate and balance your third eye. Receive that balancing, clearing energy and set the intention that light is clearing any debris away and recalibrating your energies appropriately. If looking up at the sun with eyelids closed is too intense for you, you can envision the sun beaming into your third eye and receive the energy of the sun through a visualized experience. It is all energy.

Homework

Trusting the guidance. It is important to use your intuition powerfully and elicit the proper guidance you seek. Here is what Divine guidance should and should not look like to you and what to do in each case.

- **DIVINE GUIDANCE.** Positive, service-oriented, helpful, and should fall within your interests or current life. Even if it is pushing you out of your comfort zone, there should be a logical next step. It should always be *loving,* even when warning you of danger. It should always be helpful information, and there should be a deep understanding, feeling, and *knowing* it is the truth and wisdom. Goose bumps or psychic chills are often associated with Divine messaging. Give gratitude for this guidance to continue to receive more of it.
- **NOT DIVINE GUIDANCE.** Harsh, negative, taunting, "get rich quick" schemes, or something that does not make sense within your current life. It will usually feel "icky." You'll know. If it happens that you get some guidance that doesn't feel right, call upon your own Divine bodyguard (Jesus, Buddha, or Archangel Michael) and ask for protection. Ask them to take away any cause of false guidance. Always protect your home or wherever you are while doing this work prior to tapping into this guidance. As you have learned, remain grounded and connected through your root chakra. Connection to Earth always keeps you safe. (See chapter 47 on how to protect your home.)

Archangel Michael is the angel of protection, who can instantly remedy the situation. He wields a sword and a shield and is here to protect you. Police and firefighters often wear his medallion for protection. Feel free to call upon another Divine bodyguard if you prefer—Jesus, Buddha, or someone that feels powerful and safe for you personally.

Testing your intuition. As you begin to open up to your intuition, you may find it difficult to discern between your Divine guidance and your thoughts. It is hard to move forward when you are unsure whether or not it is still just your thoughts suggesting you do something. This following chart is a fantastic way to track and learn what your intuitive language looks and feels like so you can begin to trust what you see, hear, feel, and know.

- **FIRST COLUMN.** What do I see/hear/feel? Was it in color? Was there a flash of light behind the picture? For example, my Divine guidance pictures tend to have a white flash behind them, while pictures I see with a gray background are typically someone else's real-life experiences. Begin to notice what your language is.
- **SECOND COLUMN.** What did it look like/feel like? Background? Sensations? Goose bumps? Again, by tracking your typical reactions—perhaps tingling or shivers as well as goose bumps—you can learn to spot when your intuition is speaking to you.
- **THIRD COLUMN.** Did it come true? Keep an account of any follow-up. You might be surprised. Even if things don't work out the way you saw them, you can begin to discriminate different types of feelings and warnings in your own personal "intuitive language."
- **FOURTH COLUMN.** When did it come true? How long did it take for it to come true? You might have to fill this out afterward because maybe you saw something in your mind's eye but didn't realize it was guidance until it happened. No worries. Do your best.

✦ *Daily Intuition Chart*

Date of Intuitive Experience	What do I see/hear/feel?

What did it look/feel like? Background? Sensations?	Did it come true?	When did it come true?

As you come to know your own personal psychic language, you will begin to trust yourself more and gain more confidence in moving forward with the direction you receive. You will start to recognize it as your own Divine guidance. Be gentle with yourself as you begin. There will continue to be times where you'll say, "Oh, I knew it! Why didn't I listen?" Trust that even ignoring the advice creates a stronger desire to follow it the next time. Everything happens in perfect Divine timing. It is possible the Divine needed you to follow the advice more strongly the next time and used the "missed opportunity" to teach you how to pay attention in subsequent messaging.

One incredible way the third eye chakra provides guidance is through visions and dreams. As we've addressed, you may often astral travel and collect a lot of important information at night. Keep a dream journal and write any dreams down when you wake so you can begin to see the patterns in the answers to the problems in your life. The answers are clear and there for you . . . if you are dreaming. Sometimes our dreams allow us to notice information our conscious mind has blocked out or not picked up. Some people also find they have telepathic or psychic dreams, accessing other levels of consciousness, particularly if they practice opening the third eye. Again, however, your spiritual disciplines need to be firmly in place to make the best use of this kind of dreaming.

What we do with our energy matters.

Third Eye Chakra Journaling

In addition to the dream journal mentioned above, we still need to keep up our wake-time journaling. Take some time to journal on these intuition-supporting questions. Where in my life do I need Divine guidance? Where am I most unclear? Where do I need focus for my life? What is my goal and what would my next step be? Are there any fears that I have keeping me from accessing my Divine guidance? Do these fears make sense anymore? How can my energy support my intuitive process?

Third Eye Chakra Mantra Review

Chakra	Mantra	How do I remember it?	Keynote
Sixth: THIRD EYE	OM	The seed sound of all the mantras.	KEYNOTE A: first note in the "Happy Birthday" song
Fifth: THROAT	HAM	This is the area where we hum.	KEYNOTE G: first note in "Itsy Bitsy Spider"
Fourth: HEART	YAM	Being in love is yummy!	KEYNOTE F: first note in "Come Together"
Third: SOLAR PLEXUS	RAM	I stand in my power like a strong ram.	KEYNOTE E: first note in "Mary Had a Little Lamb"
Second: SACRAL	VAM	V-V-Vagina—connected to sexual organs.	KEYNOTE D: first note in "Amazing Grace"
First: ROOT	LAM	L-L-Lowest energy center.	KEYNOTE C: first note in "Old MacDonald Had a Farm"

Third eye chakra meditation: "All you need to know is already contained within" (Proverbial saying). Let's delve into all the wisdom contained within you. This is a great meditation for opening up to even more Divine guidance. It is a little longer than some of the other meditations, so make yourself comfortable and meet me for meditation at www.LoveHealThrive.com.

CHAPTER 33

The Connection Between the Universe and Your Seventh Chakra Marker: The Crown Chakra

EVEN AS A CHILD, when something unwanted transpired, I dug deep and searched for the meaning, reason, and lesson the situation was attempting to teach me so I could learn from the experience and hopefully make it end sooner.

I had previously mentioned that my mom died when I was thirty-three. I did not mention we had just completed a two-year relocation plan to move near my mom so the grandchildren could grow up near their beloved Grandma. We had left our friends and first home to be close to her. Her passing sent me into the dark night of my soul. I didn't understand why we needed to move only to have her physical body taken away so shortly after moving. I read; I listened to speakers; I journaled; I questioned; I meditated; I healed; and I came to know all things happen for a reason.

We moved closer to family. My husband had been hand-selected by local companies to work for them and I have had the opportunity to learn from, work with, and know some of the best teachers in the area. While I, at first, believed I was moving to be closer to my mom, I realized I came here to build a life I never imagined would be so abundant. While living here, I became a Reiki master, hypnotherapist, ran a healing center, and met my illustrator for my first children's book, *Angel Birthdays*. All things truly happen for a reason.

The deepest Universal truth lies in knowing everything happens for a reason and for your good. A connection, a completeness, a coming home to, *and* a welcoming of the Divine—these all blossom as you willingly and lovingly offer yourself to the Divine—an integration of you into all that is.

The graduation to the crown chakra invites you to reap the benefits of the journey you have taken through the other six chakras. The seventh chakra, *sahasrara* in Sanskrit, connects you to the Divine and to a deep, transcendent understanding of why things must happen.

To recap, when we feel safe and secure, our emotions are balanced, we know who we are, *love* who we are, speak our truth, and feel heard. Because we are responding to the Divine guidance we are receiving, life unfolds in amazing ways we never imagined. As a result, we experience the truth of being connected to the Universe. By now, I hope for you, too, rather than just saying it, you feel it. I hope you begin to notice how your thoughts are affecting others, how your thoughts are impacting your own life and surroundings, and how much you contribute to the outcome of your life. *Sahasrara* is empowerment realized. With the crown energy center strong, you are able to process the themes of this high frequency energy as all the cells within your body begin to vibrate at this higher frequency now that you have made the journey from your root chakra up to the crown chakra.

When you've reached the crown chakra, the *kundalini shakti*, the energy that resides in your root chakra has ascended through the *sushumna nadi*, the central conduit of energy parallel to the spine, and has integrated with *Shiva*, the energy that resides in the crown chakra. When this happens, the *sushumna nadi* is awakened and there is a feeling of full integration, a balancing between the masculine and feminine energy in your body, and the loss of self-importance in exchange for the fullness experienced when you integrate with the Divine.

This entire process, from the feminine kundalini energy leaving the root chakra and rising up into the crown chakra, is called the awakening of the kundalini. The kundalini energy has traveled through the length of the *sushumna nadi*. It begins like the frog jumper carnival ride that moves up and comes down and then moves farther up and then comes down, until finally it makes its way all the way to the top.

Some people find this awakening to be overwhelming and should be sure to take care. If you have strengthened your chakras along the way, you should feel well supported and strengthened and be able to enjoy this experience and bask in its wonderment.

Sometimes, there may be an achy feeling in your back that is undiagnosable by Western medical doctors. I've seen a few clients who have come in this way, and their energy was blocked within the *sushumna nadi* and needed to be released. After one energy healing session, they felt better and were able to walk away pain-free with their energy flowing. If you experience an achy back, seek out assistance if you feel called or return to tools and techniques you have already learned along your journey. In passing through these healing markers, you should be well prepared for this stage, but if you have any issues, an energy practitioner should be able to assist you in unlocking the stagnant energy. Always consult your doctor if you are concerned with any pain that may be more than stagnant energy.

When the crown chakra is balanced, you will find yourself in a place of quiet self-confidence and faith-filled trust. You know that all things really do happen for a reason and in perfect Divine timing. There is no hurry; you are accepting of the Divine pace. All of life is blessing you, including the blessings disguised as challenges. When you begin to realize everything is connected, you live from a place filled with gratitude, faith, and trust, rather than from fear and anxiety.

We experience *gratitude, not attitude* for everything that happens. However, when anxiety strikes, we can experience irrational thoughts that cause us to be fear-filled. These irrational thoughts spiral us downward to believe that the worst-case scenario has occurred or will occur. We often reach this state when our thoughts script a generalized negative outcome for all such as, "Everyone must be talking about me." Or our fears are heightened by the catastrophic thinking of believing only the worst can be true. "If something hurts, I must have cancer."

These irrational thoughts and false logic can trigger even greater anxiety and cause you to live a life full of fear and worry. But it doesn't have to be this way. Once you read through this chapter and the next, you can shift your perspective and begin to soothe away such thoughts. Having reached this depth within *Establishing Equilibrium* itself, you may already be finding that you experience fewer fearful thoughts with the strengthening of the first six chakras and the perceptual shift and healing from your journey up to this point.

When your seventh chakra is balanced and strong, in addition to experiencing a life that feels blessed and connected, some people experience a brightening of energy manifested as white light surrounding the body. Those who have strengthened their third eye and are beginning to become more clairvoyant can see this white energy emanating around you. Perhaps now you do, too. With this brighter energy surrounding you, it seems that you stand out in your surroundings.

Have you ever noticed people looking at you for no apparent reason? Or have you ever been drawn to someone who just seems to have "something about them"? When your seventh chakra is balanced and strong, the divinity within you attracts people. You attract their attention along with their desire to be closer to you because they are drawn to the higher vibration you are now offering. They feel good around you because of this vibrational frequency and want it for themselves. If you find this overwhelming, you can share some of these teachings with them and help them begin their own journey toward their higher frequency and their own personal connection with the Divine.

This surrounding energy can be found in religious paintings, too. Saints are often painted with halos around their head, representing an activated crown chakra. But maybe you've also noticed halos painted over people who are not angels in certain paintings?

I imagine some painters were so attuned to their subjects they probably saw the white light energy radiating from the top of their heads and painted precisely what they saw.

True opening of your seventh energy center means you have a profound understanding that you are pure consciousness and a part of everything. There is no division. You are in union with all that is and connected to your higher self at the exact same time.

This is where enlightenment lives. I have found the word *enlightenment* can often trigger apathy in one's spiritual practice. Not that you wouldn't desire enlightenment, but it can feel so far-reaching that you may wonder why you should even try.

How would you ever get there with your crazy, busy schedule? Well, I've got great news for you. Enlightenment doesn't have to be that far off. Enlightenment can be found in moments of pure connection and pure awareness.

- Have you ever felt unconditional love for someone?
- Have you ever experienced a miracle?
- Have you ever held a newborn baby or a puppy?
- Have you ever experienced kairos time?
  Or experienced "flow"?

These are all moments of enlightenment. So instead of feeling it's unobtainable, hold on to that one moment of enlightenment and let it grow within you. You may find that each of those moments will connect, and you begin to experience a state of continual contentment and bliss.

Kairos time, from the ancient Greek word meaning a proper or appropriate time, is a powerful way to experience the Divine. Have you ever spent all afternoon with a friend and felt as if only an hour had passed? Or you do something your soul is calling you to do—painting, playing music, or writing—and all of sudden, three hours have passed? Author Mihaly Csikszentmihalyi PhD calls this a state of flow. This flow is experienced in kairos time, which means you are working from your crown chakra, feeling connected to all things, and pulling down inspiration and wisdom from the Divine. It's a wonderful experience.

In contrast, chronos time is the clock ticking—*tick-tock-tick-tock*—the minute-by-minute, stress-inducing gauge of time experience. As it sounds, chronological time is measured by sequence, not flow.

As with all things, balance is key. To rock it as a human on Earth, we must be aware of both versions of time and use both to live a balanced life—feet on the Earth, head in the Divine. You can be grounded, present, and Divinely guided simultaneously.

The Divine showers this chakra with Divine energy, and often in meditation and sleep, we connect to the Divine with this energy center by sending our energy up to the Divine and the collective consciousness. When all of our energy centers are balanced, we find a knowingness and peace that we are held and blessed by the Divine. The Divine nourishes this space within us as we offer our energy back up to it. A beautiful energy exchange takes place, and presence, contentment, peace, and spiritual bliss are experienced.

Everything Happens for a Reason

I'm sure you've heard this saying before, but this is probably the hardest attribute of the crown chakra for people to process and really accept. "Everything happens for a reason" is the real work of the seventh chakra. This energy center calls us to find a way to put into practice that all things happen for a reason. We may be called on to answer questions such as the following:

- What's the teaching of this experience?
  What's the learning?
- How can I strengthen or grow from this happening?
- How can I find more compassion for others as
  a result of this?
- Where is the blessing in this?

Since I was a little child, when presented with a challenging situation, I would think to myself, *What is God trying to teach me here?* Even then, I realized if I could just figure it out and learn it, then that particular situation could be over faster.

This is truly the question of the crown chakra: "What do I need to learn here to graduate to the next level of awareness in my life?" As we ask, we find our way and our path into the most intimate parts of ourselves—the place where the Divinity within us exists. The crown chakra is about shifting perspective.

In an interview on *Super Soul Sunday*, Deepak Chopra talked about his time as a monk. He had to walk for miles and miles and his feet would hurt and his skin would become torn. His teacher told him to focus on the foot that was up, instead of focusing on the foot holding the weight.

How many struggles can we think of in our life that might shift if we just focused on the other foot?

Another way to look at this is to ask, "What blessings might be coming from tragedies?" What new organizations, groups, products, or inventions were created as a result? Meetup is a great example of this. Meetup was started in New York right after 9/11. The founders realized there were groups of people with many different hobbies and interests in common but who had no idea of this because they never knew their neighbors. Life paused after 9/11. Work halted and brought people out into the streets as they looked to see what had happened and to nurture each other. Many people found that by being out in the streets together, they met each other and found much commonality. They appreciated the sense of community born from this disaster. At that time, there was not a platform to bring neighbors together. Thus, Meetup was born, an online platform used everywhere to bring like-minded people together for countless subject matters offline and to build meaningful communities. This format was an incredible blessing brought about by this terrible tragedy.

This is role of the crown chakra. How can I put my fears and myself aside and help? How can I serve? How can a blessing be born from tragedy?

Seventh Chakra Description

How do we know if the energy in our crown chakra is excessive, deficient, or balanced?

Excessive Crown Chakra Energy

Have you ever walked outside and squinted because the sun was too bright? Have you ever felt like music or the television seemed to be fine for everyone else but felt it was too loud for you? If your crown chakra is excessive, you may find yourself sensitive to light and sound, with endocrine or neurological disorders including hormone imbalance, ADHD, and dyslexia. You may also experience boredom, frustration, migraines, or vertigo. These are the results of the excessive Divine energy being received and seeking to find balance with its physical form.

Deficient Crown Chakra Energy

Have you ever felt like you just didn't have enough energy to move forward and think straight? Have you ever felt so depressed that you just couldn't get out of bed? If your crown chakra is deficient, you may experience depression, mental fog, chronic fatigue, and apathy.

Balanced Crown Chakra Energy

Have you ever had a moment where life just felt fully complete? Everything felt right and orderly in your world? This experience is called syzygy. You feel you can exhale and let go because all is well and in order. This is also how it feels when your crown chakra is balanced. You feel grounded, prosperous, energized, and full of Divine guidance. This is the result of the kundalini energy (known as kundalini Shakti: Divine feminine energy, flowing with endless, powerful flexibility and possibility) rising up from the root chakra through the *sushumna nadi* and meeting Shiva (Divine masculine energy, sheer presence and unwavering source of all) in the crown chakra where these two energies merge. Shiva is formless and Shakti is all that is manifested. Shakti holds the space for the Shiva energy

ERIN GARAY • 257

to flow, and it is believed these two sources of energy are always intertwined. This meeting is the integration of the individual person and Universal energy resulting in this powerful Divine alignment.

Location

The *sahasrara* chakra is located just above the top of the head above the *Brahmarandhra*—the cave of Brahma—also called the door to pure consciousness or the door of liberation, a space on the crown of the head where the soul departs upon death and connects during meditation.

I had the honor of being at my father's deathbed more than twenty years ago. When he passed, I was able to bear witness to his personal *Kapala Moksa*, the moment when the life force leaves the body. This process felt so sacred, honoring, and humbling. I believe it is an equal honor to be with someone at the beginning of their life as it is at the end of their life. I did not know then all that I know now about energy.

At the time, it appeared to me like a distinct light bulb turned off in his root chakra, then in his sacral chakra, and then continued, ascending upward with each center's light bulb extinguishing until I saw his spirit leave through the crown of his head and all was "dark" in his human body. I didn't entirely understand what I had seen. Back then, I didn't even know I was seeing chakras— I saw only energetic light bulbs, but I saw very accurately this ascension of light bulbs "turning off." Or so I thought. However, I *did* know this was something very sacred.

I remember looking around the room afterward at everyone, moved by this profound experience, seeking others' reactions and thinking, *Did you just see that?* But I quickly realized the visual energetic experience was my personal treasured moment with my father to know he, indeed, had connected his soul with the Divine.

In addition to *sahasrara* (the seventh chakra), *Bindu visarga* is a higher-consciousness chakra center located at the top back of the head. It is believed this is the source of creation and all the karmas of the embodied soul from previous lives exist here in this space. This center feeds the optic system within the body and holds the energy to immortality.

The door to pure consciousness is not only used for us to connect upward during meditation and death but also allows the nectar of the one-thousand-petal lotus, located approximately four fingers above the head, to drip down into the space between the two brain hemispheres, the *Shunya Mandala*, where a pure void resides—no activity, no desire, no knowledge, no individual. This is where samadhi is experienced, the pure bliss of meditation and stillness. The spiritual nectar, *amrita*, can be experienced and even tasted during meditation when the *sushumna nadi* is connected and awakened to the Divine.

When you are looking to calm your thoughts and irrational fears, bring your attention to your root chakra first (always) but next bring your attention to this space between the hemispheres, the *Shunya Mandala*, and be still and welcome this healing power of the Universe in to still and calm your mind and thoughts.

Physical Correlations in Body

The correlations within the body connected to the crown chakra include the brain, pineal gland, central nervous system, and cerebral cortex. The pineal gland is responsible for the production of melatonin. Just as light balanced the third eye and the pituitary gland, drawing in homeostasis within the body, the *absence* of light balances the pineal gland in order to release melatonin for sleep. Light ignites and balances the third eye, and the absence of light allows for the crown chakra to prepare the physical body to restore while the soul connects to the Divine. Melatonin allows for the physical body to rest so the energetic body can repair by connecting to the Divine.

As you learned in chapter 29, the three energy lines of the body, the *sushumna*, *pingala*, and *ida* integrate within the third eye. Together, they move to the crown chakra to connect with the Divine while we sleep and meditate. While our soul is connected to the Divine, it processes past life memories and organizes the day's events for filing within the subconscious mind and Akashic records. At the same time, our physical body is restoring with its sleep as a result of its melatonin production ushered in by the darkness.

This subconscious process of healing the soul concludes with the drawing in of the morning sunlight. The early morning sunlight draws the soul and its energy back into the body, and into its third eye, to begin its day, awaking and balancing the chakras and senses. When we are startled awake and feel groggy for the day, it is because we have not fully completed this Divine process. If you are finding yourself groggy, allow the sunlight to warm your third eye and see how this may help you feel focused and balanced as you draw your energy back in.

Imbalanced crown chakra energy can also play a role in learning disabilities, comas, mental illness, Parkinson's disease, vertigo, and migraines. We will examine the root cause of these ailments in the counter chakra chapter that follows.

Our thoughts trigger emotions, emotions move energy,
and energy manifests physically.
What we do with our energy matters.
If our energy isn't weak, our body doesn't weaken.

Color

The frequency of the energy in this chakra can be seen on the color spectrum of light as violet and white, with violet resonating at a frequency of approximately 750 hertz. This is the shortest wavelength and highest vibration of the colors visible on the spectrum of light. Violet is the color for transformation and transmutation. How can we transmute the pain? Turn fear into faith? Violet also represents grief and helps us in transforming the grief we feel into preparation, strength, and wisdom for what is to come in our lives.

Emotions

There is much grief in transformation as we close the chapter of our prior awareness and open up to new understanding. Recognizing it is a process of grief that we are experiencing opens us to be more compassionate with ourselves, more loving, and more accepting of our shift, change, and circumstance. We do not just grieve when people pass away. We grieve every life change and chapter. We grieve the life we had before we were aware our emotions were making us sick and now have to process and heal them to make ourselves better. We grieve the stories that have come up throughout these chapters.

As we allow ourselves to grieve, we strengthen, we ready, and we prepare ourselves for the next chapter in our life. Sometimes, we shift so much that the friendships that once enlivened us no longer feel satisfying. We grieve the state of that friendship but recognize we are vibrating at a different level and will attract new friendships that match our new outlook on life. Other times, friendships do not fall away but the unhealthy interaction of the friendship falls away, leaving both of you with a healthier and happier relationship. Honoring and showing compassion for yourself and your emotions is a meaningful step in your self-development.

There is balance felt here. There is peace felt here. There is transformation that changes us here. This is where we resolve to let go of ourselves for something greater than ourselves, not just with the guiding purpose of our life but with the simple gift of our pure self. An offering of ourselves to the Divine that we might sit in the Divine's presence as we anticipate the fullness and the bliss we know is available to us when we pause, honor, and welcome the Divine into our humbled mind.

Lifetime Development

Unlike the previous chakras, age range does not apply here. This energy center is beyond our bodies and our age. It is about being connected to the collective consciousness and to the Divine, which is significant throughout our entire life.

The Everyday Connection

- Have you been struggling with migraines?
- Have you felt depressed?
- Are you struggling with trusting that all things happen for a reason?
- Do you have Parkinson's disease, ADHD, or dyslexia?

Each of these challenges is the result of an imbalanced crown chakra. As we strengthen the crown chakra and its counter chakra, we begin to live a life free of these challenges. If you are experiencing any of the previous frustrations, take a moment and choose one technique from the next chapter to add to your week and see how that begins to alleviate your symptoms.

CHAPTER 34

The Counter Chakra: The Crown Chakra

THIS SEVENTH ENERGY CENTER, crown chakra, is paired with the third energy center, the solar plexus chakra, which is where our fear and faith exist. As you learned in the solar plexus chapter (chapter 17), the sense fed by and connected to the solar plexus is the sense of sight. The *Bindu visarga* within *sahasrara* feeds the optic system and nourishes the eyes. However, it is not just our eyes that are fed.

Are you a worrier? Are you an overthinker? Do you also struggle with stomach issues?

There is great research that confirms the connection between the gut and the brain. Many call the gut the second brain because it is the home to our enteric nervous system, with more than 100 million nerve cells activated within the intestines. While these nerves focus on the digestion process, they are disrupted by the thoughts released from our brain. Gastroenterologists have been known to prescribe certain antidepressants for IBS because these medications have remedied the symptoms by calming cells in the gut.

We feel nervous before an important conversation. We feel nauseous when we have vertigo. We often don't feel hungry when we are overthinking or are overworked. It is the connectivity experienced through the chakra system that has always connected these two areas. As we welcome this partnership and the entire system itself into our breadth of healing, we will heal our mind, body, and soul in a collective holistic process. The crown chakra strengthens the solar plexus, and the solar plexus strengthens the crown chakra. These energy centers work in partnership to bring balance and peace to our energetic, physical, and emotional bodies.

Together, this partnership creates faith that is unbreakable. The physical energy and "self-worth in gold" derived from a healthy solar plexus combines with the spiritual energy of trust, faith, and understanding of the crown chakra. Together these two energy centers establish an equilibrium of faith and a trust in the Universe that cannot be broken.

Our crown chakra can become excessive and result in migraines when the third chakra is more deficient (triggered by fear or lack of self-worth) because the crown chakra is in excess as it overworks to balance the solar plexus. For example, I had an adult client who had been working to heal her childhood experience of an abusive mother. Her mother inflicted the greatest pain on her between the ages of fourteen to twenty-one. This time period and experience caused great fear and left my client feeling powerless, afraid, and with little self-worth during those formative years—all symptoms of a deficient solar plexus. My client continued to struggle with migraines and sleep apnea because the seventh chakra was working overtime to bring strength back to the third chakra and reach shared harmony within this pairing.

The emotional source of migraines and sleep apnea is very similar and is found to be the longing for mother's love—"love-starvation," according to *Illnesses and Ailments—Their Psychological Meaning* by Narayan Singh Khalsa, PhD (February 1991).

We can assess this client's symptoms from two directions. It is the lack of mother nourishment and an imbalance between these two pairing chakras. Through energy balancing and hypnotherapy on her relationship with her mom, she was able to relieve her migraines and sleep apnea.

Our thoughts trigger emotions, emotions move energy,
and energy manifests physically.
What we do with our energy matters.
If our energy isn't weak, our body doesn't weaken.

Many of us experience exhaustive focus throughout our day when we have focused so hard that we have nothing left at the end of our day. This is a presenting symptom of a deficient crown chakra. When you are experiencing exhaustive focus, the crown chakra energy is being driven by the fear and need for control; this fear is sourcing from the excessive solar plexus. The traumatic event that occurred between the ages of fourteen to twenty-one years old established a false imprint of the need for fear and control that is continuing to influence this partnership. As a result, the crown chakra, the solar plexus chakra's partner, is feeding the solar plexus energy to its exhaustion in an attempt to soothe the solar plexus's fear.

Your brain is exhausted from focus because it is being fueled by the story of fear and need for control, originating from the fear of the solar plexus. This looks like the person who needs to control and who can never relax because they need to think through more outcomes or solutions. This process leaves you feeling exhausted and yet oddly still afraid. While the presenting symptom is exhaustive focus, the true healing is found in the counter chakra, the solar plexus. When Divine faith and trust is added to the fearful solar plexus, equilibrium is established. Once the driving fear and control is balanced by faith in a Divine plan, there will be less demand for the crown chakra to exert its energy.

Alternatively, another client who was diagnosed with dyslexia had grown up in a large critical home. She experienced so much fear about being perfect for her family that it left her solar plexus weak and her seventh chakra excessive. She was unable to process letters and words properly. The crown chakra worked so hard to produce energy to strengthen the solar plexus (to help her feel good enough about herself) that it left the crown chakra excessive.

In strengthening her solar plexus, she was able to balance her body, mind, and energy.

The Antidote

The solar plexus energy is the antidote to the imbalanced crown chakra energy. When the seventh chakra becomes excessive because it is lacking the control and drive of the third chakra, the excessive seventh chakra floats about without the regimen of the third chakra and struggles to accomplish tasks and being responsible within the material world. Adding the antidote of the solar plexus energy of control and structure allows the seventh chakra to thrive within this construct, establishing equilibrium between both Divine guidance and material pragmatism, regaining balance.

When the seventh chakra energy is stagnant, there are control issues and a struggle with fear. When the seventh chakra antidote of trusting the Divine plan and the belief that we are always being blessed is applied, fear subsides, control issues dissipate, and equilibrium is established as we come to know our material-based choices are always being guided.

Counter Chakra Seed Planting

We can now allow the people, situations, and circumstances we once wanted to control to be who and what they are meant to be for us. What is meant to be will be; what is meant to fall away will fall away. What were you afraid of from fourteen to twenty-one years old or felt the need to control? Can you allow it to be now? Through my energy-healing process, I no longer feel compelled to be the president of everything. I am the president of my peace. I lead groups when I feel inspired and am equally content being the helper as needed. The balance I have struck here is one of the most powerful spiritual gifts I have received through my decades of inner work and healing. My hope is this road map brings you to this powerful place as well.

CHAPTER 35

The Auric Effect:
The Crown Chakra

Deficient Crown Chakra

When the crown chakra is stagnant, the solar plexus chakra is excessive. This leads to a state of desired fierce control. As such, the aura remains minimal and tight to the body as to not allow anything in. This aura would be within a foot to ensure minimal energy is gained admittance. This person often struggles with control issues, exhaustive focus, migraines, dizziness, and eye issues.

When the crown chakra is excessive, the solar plexus is stagnant and feels unsafe in its surroundings, resulting in a larger aura to gather data about what dangers need to be averted. This person struggles with overthinking, analysis paralysis, digestive, eye and feet issues.

The Auric Effect ✧ Crown Chakra

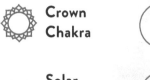 Crown Chakra

 Solar Plexus Chakra

CHAPTER 36

Tools to Heal
Your Crown Chakra Marker

I VOLUNTEER FOR AN ORGANIZATION as a tutor to help bridge the gap created by the pandemic for students who did not have internet access during that time and essentially missed two years of school. I helped one student for several months who was learning English. While we were bonded in heart and soul, our language difference created some challenges, and she agreed a tutor who spoke Spanish would be a better fit. The following tutoring day arrived and a stranger walked in, a friend of a friend who had heard about our program and came to help out. This amazing tutor not only spoke Spanish but was an ESL (English as a second language) teacher by profession. I was in awe of this manifestation as she would be able to support this student exponentially better than me.

I have come to know this is how the world works. When we live from a place of trust and expectation of blessing, miracles arrive daily. Experiencing repeated awe-inspiring events such as this cause us to elevate our beliefs and ultimately our energy frequency, leading us to the state of enlightenment and abundant manifestation.

Enlightenment is a state, an understanding, a way to interact with and experience the world . . . and only has to feel as unobtainable as you make it. Don't be intimidated by the word *enlightenment*. Remember that a sense of oneness can come from inconsequential events, such as holding a baby, as described in the last chapter. Exchanging a connected smile with a stranger in the supermarket, even standing at the top of a hill in the wind, these are subtle blessings easily missed if we are straining for great effects. Some people do see angels and experience visions of light, of course. But, in my experience, it's always best to start small and appreciate each experience as it appears. Remember to work your way up from your lower chakras, grounded in Earth but soaring upward as you integrate Divine energy into your mind, body, and spirit.

Strength and balance are obtained through the stillness and quiet established in this center. This strength and balance will bless you with a life that allows you to socialize with your friends without worrying how you're accepted and to live without your compulsions. You no longer have cause to fear the worst. You have come to know and understand how your anxiety may have crippled you in the past. Now that you have strengthened yourself, you know you no longer need to be a victim to your anxiety.

It begins with stillness and the powerful welcoming of the Divine. There are fewer tools in this chapter because the most powerful tool you can implement here is the tool of *being*. As you quiet your mind, invite in a knowing anticipation that the Divine will whisper its guidance and calm you with its peace when you're still and quiet. The blessing of the Divine will be a knowingness, a clarity, and a message that will guide you and direct you to a life full of presence, calm, and balance.

Silence is the great activator of the crown chakra. Sit in silent meditation as you maintain your focus on the *Shunya Mandala*, the place of void that resides between the two hemispheres of the brain. Feel this space being nourished by the one-thousand-petal lotus, located four fingers' breadth above the crown, that drips sweet nectar of immortality—*amrita*—to nourish and heal you. If you find yourself anxious, afraid, worried, or frustrated, remain in silence with a steadfast focus on this point within your mind. We bring in more of what we focus on and talk about, so if you are experiencing irrational thoughts, find your Divine silence and connect to the power of stillness and peace found in this nourished chakra to experience peace and Divine connectedness.

Color and Clothes

Violet represents spiritual wisdom and humility. Wearing violet scarves and accessories can transform a white outfit, accessorized with amethyst earrings and jewelry. Sleeping on a violet pillow or putting a violet scarf down on your pillow while you rest on it can assist in the rejuvenation and balancing of your crown chakra.

Element

In the same way the third eye is balanced by the element of light, the crown chakra is balanced by the absence of light. It is darkness and stillness that prepares this space to receive energy from the Divine to establish its own balance.

Our Five Senses

The third eye's sixth sense is made up of the integration of all the senses here within this energy center. Conversely, the withdrawal of the senses from the outside world invites the crown chakra to balance and find your inner sacred center. This withdrawal of senses from the outside world creates stillness within the mind, body, and senses to create a safe place for the Divine energy to flow into the *Shunya Mandala*, the space between the two hemispheres of your brain.

Organ of Action

There is no organ of action associated with this chakra because this chakra is beyond the body. This chakra has been described as a gateway to the Divine and looks to connect you with this Universal truth, rather than being confined by the body. There is no connected organ, and to receive optimal results from this chakra, there should be no action. It is stillness, in body and mind, that strengthens the crown chakra.

Food

There is no specific healing food associated with this chakra because this energy center is fed by spiritual nourishment, the nourishment beyond our physical needs. You may fast with the intention of becoming closer to God to strengthen this center.

I once attended a class hosted by a teacher from India. He told a story about how he and his students had traveled all day via planes and buses, finally to arrive at the ashram only to find the kitchen closed.

The students were complaining and hungry, and the teacher said, "Instead of being hungry, we will fast."

By shifting their intention to a fast and dedicating their thoughts to something outside of themselves, they were able to shift the whole experience and their perspective, which is the key to this energy center. This perspective is similar to the foot focus shift and to the principle of polarity in general. As we shift our perspective from the theme of one chakra to its partner, equilibrium and healing is established.

Essential Oils

The supportive essential oils for this center include the following:

- **SANDALWOOD:** reconnects you with the Divine
- **ROSE:** aids in helping you feel the love of the Divine
- **JASMINE:** supports the healing of anxiety by connecting you with the Divine

You may apply this oil to a tissue and place it near your pillow or inside your pillowcase, ensuring the oil doesn't touch the fabric and make it oily. Diffuse these oils during meditation or while you sleep. Rub the oils on the crown of your head with your right index finger, either clockwise to energize this chakra or counter-clockwise to clear it.

Crystals

The crystals that bring great balance and healing to this center include the following:

- **CLEAR QUARTZ.** The Universal healer that connects to all the chakras and brings clarity to this center. This crystal also accentuates and magnifies the power of any other crystal coupled with it.
- **AMETHYST.** Calms the mind, assists with sleep, and brings in peace and harmony while balancing your crown chakra.
- **SELENITE.** Clears our energy and brings in mental clarity and deep peace. It is used to clear energy from the body as well as to clear other crystals. Selenite wands are helpful in clearing your entire body's aura and energy. Just wave the selenite before you and behind you, to the right and left, and above and below you. You can also place your crystals directly on the selenite to clear them. Clearing your crystals will ensure you are clearing your energy with the highest vibrational crystal possible.

You can place these crystals next to your bedside table or under your pillow or mattress as you sleep or hold them in your hands while you meditate. If you are unable to sleep with them next to your bed, be sure to remove them from your bedroom. Some-times crystals can have such a radical effect on our system that we are too stimulated to sleep with them nearby. Remain attuned to your body and sleep schedule and be aware of this and make changes accordingly.

Mantra

The *sound* that heals this center is silence. A mantra for this energy center is a silent OM. This can be achieved by focusing on the OM symbol itself, a combination of curves, a crescent, and a dot, as a focal point while remaining silent. This focus assists in calming the irrational thoughts and fears. AUM, the Universal sound for clearing, makes one whole again. Often singing bowls are used to balance our chakras. In this case, the keynote of B would balance the crown chakra.

Environmental Shift

Just as your goal for this chakra is to clear your mind and settle into the void of the *Shunya Mandala*, the space between the hemispheres of your brain, the goal for your home is to clear the clutter so there can be room for the Divine to be welcomed into your home. Clear your counters and desk to achieve a peaceful mind. As you begin to surround yourself with only items you love, your entire home will resonate at a higher vibration. As you declutter your space, you declutter your mind. If you feel called to set up an altar, create one that feels good to you and add the spiritual guides you feel drawn to, along with crystals, candles, incense, and so on. Create a space that has meaning and resonance for you.

Yoga

Downward dog (*adho mukha svanasana*) is a good pose to calm the brain and rejuvenate the body. Think in terms of a mental shift.

Do not push boundaries and strive for difficult poses, but rather work on mindfulness, meditation, and accepting yourself. You are exactly where you're supposed to be. If downward dog is unavailable to you, proceed to the meditation section and complete a few rounds of *nadi shodhana*—alternate nostril breathing—to bring calm and focus to this center.

Archangels

Archangel Metatron is the archangel who can extend from Earth to heaven and deliver prayers instantaneously. Simple gratitude forms a lovely prayer to be delivered because it is a high-vibrational message.

"Thank you, Archangel Metatron, for connecting me to all that is. *So* grateful." Offer this prayer, or one that speaks to your desire to be fully connected to the Divine, in the morning upon awakening and before you go to sleep. As you create this bookend experience of connecting to the Divine, your days will flow more easily and you reach a place of effortless joy.

Ten-Second Rescue

Ground your energy through your pelvic floor, the base of your spine, and your perineum, and then connect through the top of your head into your Divine source. Once connected, invite the golden white light of Divine love to pour down through the top of your head, filling in the *Shunya Manadala* first. Once it is filled and overflowing with this beautiful golden light, invite this same energy into every cell in your body until every cell is overflowing with this golden white light. You will experience waves of golden light filling you up. Being flooded by this golden light helps you clear fear and irrational thoughts.

Homework

Meditate for at least one minute before putting your head down on your pillow when going to sleep. Make the commitment that you are not going to put your head down until you meditate. It can even be a ten-second pause. Breathe calmly and count ten breaths with your focus on your root chakra to begin this practice. One minute leads to five to ten to twenty, but you will sleep better because you meditated and surrendered to your day. An incredible thing will begin to happen. Your body will wake up earlier than you need in order to meditate again before you start your day. This is the easiest way to begin your meditation "bookend" practice, meditating in the morning and night. By committing to your nighttime meditation, your body will crave meditation in the morning as well. It will not feel forced or like one more thing to do.

Daily meditation, prayer, and silence are practices that lead to increased moments of spiritual connection, which will heal your illness. The more time spent in prayer and meditation, the greater your connection to the Divine and the greater increase in grounded, connected energy. Like all relationships, you get out of it what you put in. As you commit yourself to an intimate relationship with the Divine, you will experience that intimacy in return. It will show up in your everyday life. People will notice there is a peace and calm about you, and you will find life feels more calm and peaceful. As a result of this continued renewal with the Divine, your stress, worry, and illness will lessen, and you will experience fewer and fewer symptoms because your energy system has been strengthened and balanced.

Once you establish this practice, you will begin to experience unconditional love on a consistent basis because you really do recognize how much you are connected to everyone and everything. It's an awe-inspiring and very responsible state as you realize how much your thoughts dictate your life.

Crown Chakra Mantra Review

Chakra	Mantra	How do I remember it?	Keynote
Seventh: **CROWN**	Silent OM	A connection to all that is—a symbol for the infinite.	Silence. KEYNOTE B
Sixth: **THIRD EYE**	OM	The seed sound of all the mantras.	KEYNOTE A: first note in the "Happy Birthday" song
Fifth: **THROAT**	HAM	This is the area where we hum.	KEYNOTE G: first note in "Itsy Bitsy Spider"
Fourth: **HEART**	YAM	Being in love is yummy!	KEYNOTE F: first note in "Come Together"
Third: **SOLAR PLEXUS**	RAM	I stand in my power like a strong ram.	KEYNOTE E: first note in "Mary Had a Little Lamb"
Second: **SACRAL**	VAM	V-V-Vagina— connected to sexual organs.	KEYNOTE D: first note in "Amazing Grace"
First: **ROOT**	LAM	L-L-Lowest energy center.	KEYNOTE C: first note in "Old MacDonald Had a Farm"

Crown chakra meditation: Join me as we bask in this place of knowing all things happen for a reason. Join me for the crown chakra meditation at www.LoveHealThrive.com.

Crown Chakra Journaling

How could one of the biggest struggles in your life have been a blessing to your life? What is the lesson? How did you get stronger? How are you serving now as a result of this event? How can you serve because of it? What do you feel gets in your way to connecting to the Divine? What can you offer up today that can be cleared so you can be more connected?

CHAPTER 37

Cultivate Your Witness

AS THE LATE Ram Dass would teach, begin by "cultivating your witness." This means creating a separate consciousness so you can begin to witness the events in your life without attachment or judgment. You can see them or witness them happening instead of living them.

Imagine yourself in your own private, pristine movie theater settled into your favorite seat. See the movie screen in front and above you and begin to place all of your thoughts up on the screen. Any thoughts that come up, place them on the screen.

Notice how you watch those thoughts. Then notice the viewer.

The viewer is you. Capital *Y-O-U*. This connection to the Divine.

Continue to watch your thoughts on the screen separated from you.

You are not the stories you tell yourself.

You are not the experiences that happen in your life.

You are not those emotions.

You are the *Y-O-U* watching the movie.

The *Y-O-U* is not triggered by your emotions, by your stories, or by your experiences.

Sit in that separation for a moment.

You can begin this practice in meditation, but as you practice more and more, you will find you are able to witness the events in your life consciously in your everyday life and can respond from a place more healed and centered, rather than triggered and impulsive.

When you are witnessing the movement of your energy and your life (also known as Shakti), it is in this place that you are resting that is considered your Shiva nature. Shiva is the experience of holding space for the movement of this feminine energy to flow, the witness. We experience this profoundly here when we cultivate our witness.

CHAPTER 38

Time to Review

IT IS IMPORTANT to have your foundation in place. Each chakra is a building block of prevention toward illness, and once your system is fully integrated and strengthened, you may find even your chronic illness dissipates. Each energy center builds upon the next, supporting the development and strength of the next one. Rushing spiritual development and healing can result in frustration from not achieving the outcome you desire, finding yourself stuck in a pattern, or reaching uncomfortable stages because you are not grounded enough. All these can lead to a lower frequency, which, as you have learned, can result in a number of manifestations within your body, mind, and soul.

Take the time to build your foundation. The way to your true self freed from your illness is best journeyed one careful step at a time. There will be moments of increased spiritual expansion and then a time of plateau, where you will find yourself getting acclimated to a new way of viewing life where you adjust and ground. Then you begin to climb up another mountain. Expansion, plateau, expansion, plateau. It is how you will reach great spiritual connection, heal your illness, and remain steady on Earth.

Take a moment and reflect on what you've learned so far. Where was your biggest struggle? Where have you seen yourself grow the most? Go back to individual chapters and absorb them again slowly if needed. I want your neuropathways to be strengthened before you meditate on your own.

Here is a final comprehensive road map of what has been covered so far. Each chakra includes a quick meditation to help you remember its essential characteristics. I suggest one minute to make this something you can complete anywhere, anytime, but of course, as I said earlier, feel free to let one minute expand to two, five, and further . . .

First Chakra: Root Chakra

- Location: Perineum, base of spine, and pelvic floor.
- Emotions/themes: Feelings of safety, security, and protection; feeling safe and provided for by the Divine. This chakra holds responsibility for what is physical—in our body and our life.
- Symptoms: Losing your keys, forgetting what you are saying, or double-booking your schedule.
- Development: Zero to seven years old, when we come to learn what tribal acceptance will mean to us and what safety and security look like in our life.
- Mantra: LAM—lowest and slowest sound.
- Element: Earth.
- Organ of action: Anus.
- Sense: Smell.
- Sense organ: Nose.
- One-minute meditation: Use grounding to settle and calm you and bring you into the present moment. This can be done in a second. Grow a quick tree root from your pelvic floor and click your root in like a seat belt would click in and pull taut. Draw up Earth's energy, filling up this space until you feel this energy center is weighted—not too heavy, not too light. Allow this nutrient-dense Earth to nourish your pelvic floor. This can be super quick and super powerful. If you could take just one thing from this entire book, it would be this.

Second Chakra: Sacral Chakra

- Location: Two or three inches below the belly button.
- Emotions/themes: This is the warehouse of all of our emotions, where creativity, passion, and desire live.
- Symptoms: Indulging in the blame game, feeling overemotional, constantly getting sick, struggling with drug or alcohol addiction, hoarding, OCD, depression, or social anxiety.
- Development: Seven to fourteen years old, when we create emotional connections and ignite our desires.
- Mantra: VAM—connected to sexual organs, like V for *vagina.*
- Element: Water.
- Organ of action: Genitals.
- Sense: Taste.
- Sense organ: Tongue.
- One-minute meditation: Our emotions flow like water. Sometimes they can trickle or drip, sometimes they rush like a waterfall. Visualize the faster-moving emotions speeding up the slower emotions, and the faster emotions being slowed by the slower emotions to reach a place of emotional and energetic balance and equilibrium in this center.

Third Chakra: Solar Plexus Chakra

- Location: Between navel and breastbone.
- Emotions/themes: This is where we turn fears into faith. The home of our personal power, here is where we can surrender our ego to open up to Divine power, purpose, and guidance. This is where we know our worth in gold.
- Symptoms: Being overreactive, stressed, angry, or struggling with perfectionism or control issues.

- Development: Fourteen to twenty-one years old, when we begin to figure out how the world works through our own eyes and experience personal power and strength.
- Mantra: RAM—like a powerful ram.
- Element: Fire.
- Organ of action: Feet and legs.
- Sense: Sight.
- Sense organ: Eyes.
- One-minute meditation: We build an inner fire and use it to burn up anything that does not serve us or holds us back from the life of our dreams. Then we allow Divine light to come through and fill in the area previously occupied by the stagnant energy, beliefs, and illusions we have just destroyed and allow that golden light to grow bigger than any fear, worry, or obstacle.

Fourth Chakra: Heart Chakra

- Location: Heart and chest area; the astral bridge that takes us from the physical chakras into the spiritual chakras.
- Emotions/themes: Love, self-love, love for others, connected love, pure healing. Here we release our attachments to people, places, things, and outcomes. We let go of the *should've beens*, *would've beens*, and *could've beens* so we can receive even more blessings.
- Symptoms: Feeling closed off or aloof, overgiving, or having a lack of boundaries. We experience PTSD and depression.
- Development: Twenty-one to twenty-eight years old, when we learn to love ourselves first and then begin to love others.
- Mantra: YAM—being in love is yummy.
- Element: Air.

- Organ of action: Hands.
- Sense: Touch.
- Sense organ: Skin.
- One-minute meditation: Grief and sadness play an important role in our lives. They help us have a greater appreciation for our blessings and our lives and create greater compassion for others and ourselves. But grief won't leave until it has done its work. Think about when you're sad. You feel you have a weight on your chest. It's stagnant energy. It needs your permission to leave, so now, give it that permission. Breathe in and let the air fill your lungs and heart. Fill sadness with air and release what is ready to be released as you breathe out. Set an intention for any other grief and sadness to leave once it has completed its purpose. Allow a beautiful emerald-green energy to come in and fill in the space that needs healing. Allow this green energy and love to emanate through this energy center and out to you and to all of your loved ones.

Fifth Chakra: Throat Chakra

- Location: Throat, in the V of your collarbones.
- Emotions/themes: Conveying our truth and feeling truly heard.
- Symptoms: Unable to speak up for ourselves or we keep talking without conveying much because we are unclear about our truth. We won't let anyone else talk. We experience social anxiety.
- Development: Twenty-eight to thirty-five years old, when we learn to speak our truth.
- Mantra: HAM—we hum in our throat and mouth.
- Element: Ether.
- Organ of action: Mouth.
- Sense: Hearing.

- Sense organ: Ears.
- One-minute meditation. This is where we release lots of hot air! Use this chakra to release stagnant energy from the chakras below stuck in your system. Visualize a tube connected to the outside of the V of your collarbones. See ether flowing through this tube into your fifth chakra, open your mouth in lion's breath (see chapter 28 for how to do lion's breath), and release what is stagnant in this center, feeling the ether cleanse and balance this energy center.

Sixth Chakra: Third Eye Chakra

- Location: Just above and between the eyebrows.
- Emotions/themes: Clear intuition and Divine guidance. It is our true source of guidance.
- Symptoms: Have a hard time concentrating, or experiencing hallucinations or depersonalization.
- Development: Thirty-six to forty-two years old. We are born with our third eye open, but it tends to close as we grow older and we learn to listen to others rather than to our own inner and Divine guidance. We need to reopen it as we go through our spiritual reawakening.
- Mantra: OM—the vibration of the Divine. The primal sound of the Universe.
- Element: Light. It is the element that illuminates our minds so we can receive Divine guidance.
- Organ of action: Mind.
- Sense: Sixth sense.
- Sense organ: Mind.
- One-minute meditation. When you feel you might be experiencing hallucinations or are having difficulty concentrating, envision the sun's healing warm light shining into your third eye, bringing warmth and balance.

Seventh Chakra: Crown Chakra

- Location: Top of head.
- Emotions/themes: Connection to all. Connection to the Divine. Everything happens for a reason.
- Symptoms: We have migraines, feel disconnected from others, and have depression.
- Development: This is the culmination of our spiritual development, so specific ages do not apply here.
- Mantra: Silence or focusing on the silent OM.
- Element: This is the chakra beyond elements, where we connect to and are the Divine.
- One-minute meditation: Ground. Then visualize gold cleansing energy rising from the center of the Earth through your spine and your chakras from root to crown and up through a tube that connects from your crown to the Divine. Cultivate your witness and see your life as a witness, with compassion and without judgment. See this beautiful golden energy flow down from the Divine and fill in the void between the left and right hemispheres in your brain.

When you have balanced your chakras from the root chakra up through to the crown chakra, you

1. Feel safe and secure
2. Have your emotions balanced
3. Know who you are
4. *Love* who you are
5. Speak your truth and feel truly heard
6. Receive/respond to Divine guidance and trust everything happens as it should
7. And *then* you feel connected to the Divine and to everyone, and you trust everything is happening as it should.

That we are all connected has been a continued theme throughout this journey. But instead of just saying it, I hope you really do feel it. I hope you are beginning to notice how your thoughts affect others, how your thoughts affect your life and your surroundings, and how much you contribute to the outcome of your own life. When all these chakras are vibrant and working together, it is an empowered place to be. You are the master of your life, and you feel it!

The chakra system will become an integral part of your physical, emotional, spiritual, and energetic health. Review this chapter as part of your daily practice until it becomes second nature. You can naturally pull up these images and themes in your thought process, during conversations, and as you are clearing your own energy centers before meditation. By reading through them regularly, you will have them memorized. This constant review will make such a difference to your daily practice.

CHAPTER 39

Establishing Equilibrium: How the Energetic Pairings Lead You to the Source of Your Healing

"The whole is greater than the sum of the parts."
—*Aristotle*

THE SAME IS TRUE of our energy system. The chakras work best in combination rather than in isolation, and it is the symphony of these energy centers performing together that is going to heal your illness and help you live an empowered life. Each of the chakras pairs with another chakra within the system, one physical chakra with one spiritual chakra, with *ajna* as the exception. Typically, when one is out of balance, its partner is out of balance as well. The reverse is true, too. When one chakra is powerful and strong, it will help its pair to be stronger, too. If one is weak, you may feel it, as the other may become excessive because it is working to strengthen its partner. When both fail, illness quickly follows.

You can imagine this partnership like a seesaw in a playground. One child must push themselves to lift the other up as the other descends, and then the other child takes their turn pushing the other one up. If one child is larger than the other, it takes more effort for the smaller child to raise the larger child. The smaller child becomes more exhausted more quickly because they are working so hard. This leaves one child with excessive energy and the other child with deficient energy from attempting to support the other child. For a fleeting moment, both children reach a moment of mutual energetic consumption and equilibrium is established as the seesaw passes through equipoise when both are at an equal state. The perfect energetic partnership can continue to flow when both sides of the seesaw are balanced, rising and falling, flowing back and forth with no constricted energy.

I often find the deeper answer to a client's symptom in the relationship between two chakras. This partnership tells the whole story, with all the hidden details. Often, the answer or root cause of an emotional or physical ailment lies in the "quieter" or asymptomatic energy center of the pairing.

How the partner chakra is the antidote to the disruption of the symptomatic chakra

I have helped countless clients heal by discerning the antidote to their presenting symptoms and addressing the partner chakra to create balance within the partnership.

Here are the chakra pairings:

- Solar plexus–crown
- Sacral–throat
- Root–heart
- Third Eye–root, sacral, solar plexus, heart, throat

The third eye chakra uniquely pairs with the chakras below because, as you've learned, it is the role of the third eye to balance these five chakras and draw upon the five senses to establish its sixth sense.

The colors of each chakra pair are color complements, too.

- Solar plexus (yellow) complements crown (purple)
- Sacral (orange) complements throat (blue)
- Root (red) complements heart (green)

As we've discussed, each chakra has a frequency and a keynote. So the notes of each of these pairings strike a harmony chord:

- Solar plexus (E) and crown (B)
- Sacral (D) and throat (G)
- Root (C) and heart (F)

When our colors and sounds are complementary and in harmony, we are balanced. In meditation, you can almost feel and hear the harmony between your organs. It is when these centers are all balanced and your root chakra is grounded that you will find your parasympathetic nervous system to be activated. The result will be a calm and peaceful state of being. Let's investigate the counter chakras a little deeper.

CHAPTER 40

Establishing Equilibrium Between the Root Chakra and Heart Chakra

THE FIRST CHAKRA, the root chakra, is paired with the fourth chakra, the heart chakra. The color complements are red and green, and the keynote harmony is C and F.

The first chakra is about safety, security, and acceptance. Our heart, the fourth chakra, tends to open only to another person when it feels it is safe to do so. Think about a past relationship or friendship. It is likely you did not really open up to this person until you felt safe and you quickly shut down once you no longer felt safe.

The heart chakra will feed the root chakra when it does not feel safe and secure, and the root chakra will feed the heart chakra when it does not feel safe and secure. Here's how that looks.

What happens when someone is in a life-threatening situation? They no longer feel safe (deficient first chakra energy). Their heart begins to race, and they find themselves out of breath (excessive fourth chakra energy attempting to strengthen the weakened first chakra and expanding its aura to search for danger). This is a perfect example of how these two energy centers work synergistically together, particularly under stress. This is a natural and important response to a threat. But, allowing the body to remain in this state can cause long-term problems. Learning how to rebalance these energy centers is the key to long-term emotional, energetic, spiritual, and physical health.

My clients who have heart problems often have a root chakra issue first. They don't feel safe, secure, or accepted. Perhaps they had a traumatic childhood and never felt included, wanted, or safe or that they could trust anyone. Again, the health of the root chakra is ultimately determined by feeling Divinely safe, secure, and accepted. So when our childhood did not feel safe or accepting, we can look to the Divine to heal this space and provide this safety and security. When we can feel safe, secure, and accepted in our first chakra, we are able to just *be* there feeling Divinely safe and secure. We can exhale, let go, and relax. When we feel *that* safe, we are able to open our heart and be in communion with others. We know we won't be so sensitive because we are loving from a more secure place. We have built energetic resilience.

These two centers also support each other through the balance of attachments. Our root chakra is about our physical world, and we tend to create physical attachments in order to feel secure. We hold certain expectations about these physical attachments/experiences. When we own a home, we expect to feel safe inside it. When establishing community, we expect people to be considerate of us. When we have a job, we expect it will continue. Our ultimate goal is to feel secure *without* attachments to things outside of us, knowing we are always provided for in every moment. We can enjoy our home, community, and job but without the expectation it is going to fill us and offer us happiness. Lasting happiness comes from within. When our energy here is vibrant, we know we are being blessed and provided for by the Universe and maintain a healthy balance between material demand and human relationship.

While the root chakra leans toward physical attachments, often recognized as expectations, the heart chakra struggles with emotional attachments, more commonly resembling resentments. Often, the resentments we build up in our life are a result of our own physical attachments because we believed something *should* be a certain way in our physical life and it proved otherwise.

- My house wasn't supposed to [catch on fire/have rats/be moldy].
- He/She/They/My community *should* have done this for me/been there for me.
- This wasn't *supposed* to happen at my job.

When we believe our life does not mirror our root chakra's expectations of life being a certain way (deficient first chakra), the result is often deep hurt and resentment (excessive heart chakra). It is tempting to blame other people and circumstances for our feelings of discontent and injury. However, healing lies within. When we can recognize the origin of the hurt as being our physical attachments and expectations, then we can allow our root chakra to strengthen, our hearts to soften, and our attachments to release. Equilibrium is established and a beautiful harmony develops between these two energy centers, leaving you grounded, strong, and emotionally and energetically connected.

As we strengthen our own internal security, safety, provision, and acceptance and look outward less, we strengthen this first chakra. With a strengthened first chakra, we recognize the internal source of our attachment and resentment (rather than projecting it outward onto other people and events). We are able to heal this partnership by finding a secure, safe, accepting, and openhearted way of looking at life.

The next time you begin to feel anxious or resentful, bring your attention down to your pelvic floor, repeat the mantra LAM, and imagine the Earth filling in and creating this nourishing garden within your pelvic floor. As your first chakra reinvigorates, you will feel your chest (heart chakra) relax. Your body will naturally take in a big inhale because it has balanced enough to do so. Take a moment to witness this within your own body. Continuing to take in deep breaths is extremely helpful. But do not force it. Your lungs will take that first deep breath when the energy releases on its own. (Note: This is not about holding your breath. This exercise refers to the natural energetic release your heart chakra will experience once the root chakra is strengthened and balanced and releases the tension in your heart chakra to achieve a full-bodied breath.)

The same application of this system also applies to heart, lung, and adrenal issues.

Here is a direct navigation for your road map toward establishing equilibrium for this root/heart chakra partnership.

- **REREAD:** Chapters 7 and 12 on the root chakra and chapters 21 and 24 on the heart chakra to review the many ailments associated with these road map markers.
- **EXPLORE:** Root issues such as childhood trauma, with a trained counselor, if necessary. If you find yourself getting overwhelmed, stop, ground, and seek professional advice.
- **ROOT CHAKRA PICK-ME-UP:** Sweet potato, red onions, strawberries, and red peppers
- **HEART CHAKRA PICK-ME-UP:** Green vegetable soup including kale, broccoli, and spinach. Add parsley or basil to taste. Log onto www.LoveHealThrive.com for some great chakra recipes.

CHAPTER 41

Establishing Equilibrium between Sacral Chakra and Throat Chakra

THE SECOND CHAKRA, the sacral chakra, is paired with the fifth chakra, the throat chakra. The color complements are orange and blue, and the harmony pairing is keynote D and G.

The second chakra is about emotions, desire, and creativity, and the fifth chakra is allowing that emotion, desire, and creativity to be expressed, individually and collectively. When these two chakras are balanced and working together, you don't just have the ideas—you will be able to act on them and speak them into existence. You will feel vitalized by speaking your truth and by bringing your ideas to fruition, thereby speaking your life, creativity, and purpose into existence. You will feel desire flow through you. Your second chakra will rev up when your fifth chakra is releasing what it is creating, and together these two energy centers will create a powerhouse of creativity and expression. I find this very inspiring.

A great physical example of this relates to when someone is freshly falling in love and *wants* to experience all those emotions, pleasure, and desire in the second chakra. They enjoy the feeling, so the energy is balanced, and as a result, the fifth chakra balances. In the beginning of a relationship, there are no emotional blocks, so both partners talk and share. There is no holding back of thought, expression, emotion, or energy in the throat chakra. This openness in the throat chakra maintains the balanced and vibrant energy in the second chakra. This is why many people find they lose weight when they first fall in love. Both energy centers are vibrant, balanced, and healthy.

The opposite is true too. Often, when I see thyroid conditions, the client has been trying to keep their true desires from being expressed. In forcing the sacral chakra energy (home of our desires and emotions) to be stagnant, its partner, the fifth chakra, becomes stagnant, too, or sometimes it can become overactive, trying to strengthen and balance the stagnant energy of the second chakra. The result is often weight gain and a thyroid condition. When people are healing their grief, they often gain weight, even if they have not been overeating. In trying to process the over-abundance of emotion they are experiencing in the second chakra, the fifth chakra attempts to balance and assist the second chakra. This attempt leads to depleting the energy in the fifth chakra, thus leading to thyroid symptoms including weight gain. This is often why journaling is a helpful grief-healing suggestion. The sharing of one's truth through journaling helps move this stagnant energy.

With social anxiety, our second chakra emotions, such as insecurity or lack of desire for connection, can show up as fear of public speaking or of being unable to convey our truth. If you are struggling with social anxiety, look back to your life at age seven to fourteen and see if you can correlate the events of that time to any anxiety you feel in social situations now. Did something happen then when you were embarrassed in a group setting or shamed for expressing your creativity? How can you work through this childhood experience to help bring peace to your social anxiety now? You no longer need to fall victim to this struggle. When we hold on to our guilt, it stagnates the throat chakra (chapter 25). Blame is the unspoken guilt energy we project as a result of us feeling guilty that we didn't act, speak, or connect in a certain way.

This stagnation is the recipe to turn this guilt into blame (chapter 13). As both energy centers balance, guilt and blame subside.

Here is your direct navigation to establish equilibrium within the sacral/throat chakra partnership:

- **REREAD:** Chapters 13 and 16 on the sacral chakra and chapters 25 and 28 on the throat chakra.
- **EXPLORE:** Blocked creativity. What have you always wanted to do and told yourself you never could? Start cooking, planting, writing, or painting, even if it's just for your eyes.
- **SACRAL CHAKRA PICK-ME-UP:** Mango, orange, and melon salad, or blend with coconut water for a delicious smoothie.
- **THROAT CHAKRA PICK-ME-UP:** Blueberry, blackberry, and plum salad; again, blend with coconut water for a smoothie.

CHAPTER 42

Establishing Equilibrium Between the Solar Plexus Chakra and the Crown Chakra

THE THIRD CHAKRA, the solar plexus chakra, is paired with the crown chakra. The color complements are yellow and purple and the harmony pairing is keynote E and B. The crown chakra also nourishes the optic nerve, which is the organ of sense in the solar plexus.

Remember the third chakra is about surrendering the ego and personal power to allow Divine power to come through you to create the life meant for you. It does not mean you are powerless. You are Divinely powered, and you no longer have to "effort" so hard to complete your task at hand. Divinity flows through you to provide the strength necessary to temper your fear and your ego, found in the solar plexus.

When these two chakras are balanced and working together, you are fearless. From a sense of total connection to God, you can work by surrendering your plan, or ego, and allowing direction to flow through you with step-by-step guidance and strength. The Divine plan gives you the presence and peace to turn fear into faith and move forward, executing the life that is Divinely planned for you. You live life from a state of feeling power-*full* instead of over-extending your efforts, exhausting your personal resources and living like a power-*fool*.

I have helped many clients with vertigo, and its root cause has almost always been found in the third chakra. It tends to come at a moment when the person has forgotten their self-worth in gold and that they are Divinely special and unique. This can show up when a client is working toward a goal where they are over-thinking their process or questioning whether or not they deserve to reach their goal. It can also show up when there is a need for decision-making or control over many different details because the solar plexus becomes excessive in attempting to manage and control their thoughts, foregoing the faith that the Divine has a perfect plan for you.

Vertigo may occur, but is not limited to, when someone is in the midst of a physical or emotional affair or when they forget their worth. The ego is using the affair to find importance, uniqueness, and a way to feel special because the person believes they are no longer receiving it from their partner and have forgotten it for themselves. However, the true lesson is an affair of any type is just a longing of the innermost self, which is wanting to embody the most desirable traits of the other person. When my client has found their *own* true worth in gold, knowing it is their own Divine uniqueness that is going to bring them their greatest amount of happiness, their vertigo (and often the affair) dissipates.

This imbalance is a result of the third chakra being in excess as it is working from ego, rather than Divine self-worth, and the seventh chakra is exhausted from trying to bring balance to the third chakra. Stagnation and deficiency of energy in the seventh chakra results in vertigo. According to the *Heal Your Body A-Z* app based on Louise Hay's book, *You Can Heal Your Life*, the emotional correlation of vertigo is scattered thinking, which is quite true when one is offering attention and energy to multiple relationships. (Having said this, do also check with your doctor in the case of persistent vertigo.) This same energetic pattern holds true for being obsessed with social media and the scattered content to manage.

This external focus is seeking to find self-validation, importance, or control, and often results in lack of self-respect, leading to a greater energetic dissonance in this partnership.

Could you recognize this energetic state in your life? Have you ever worked with, or been, a micromanager? Controlling people who are micromanagers lack faith in people and the Divine (deficient crown chakra) to take care of things and believe only they know best (excessive solar plexus).

Many of us experience exhaustive focus throughout our day when we have focused so hard that we have nothing left at the end of our day. This is a presenting symptom of a depleted crown chakra. When you are experiencing exhaustive focus, the solar plexus has a greater draw of energy because of everything that happened to you during this window of time because the body is trying to heal those energetic imprints of fear and need for control. The crown chakra, the solar plexus chakra's partner, is feeding the solar plexus energy to its own exhaustion in an attempt to bring the collective partnership into balance and faith-filled peace.

Your brain is exhausted from focus because it is being fueled by the story of fear and need for control from the solar plexus as a result of the imprinting experienced between the ages of seven to fourteen. There is a need for extreme control, leaving this person exhausted with headaches and dizziness.

While the crown is the presenting symptom (exhaustive focus) the healing is found in the counter chakra, the solar plexus. Offering faith and trust that all will work out here will draw in balance and healing.

When the opposite condition exists and the crown chakra is excessive and the solar plexus is deficient, there is extreme over-thinking with more passive control. Analysis paralysis and lack of courage often exist during this energetic state along with digestive, eye, and foot conditions. When healing is offered to the crown chakra, equilibrium is established. While the solar plexus is the presenting symptom (digestive, eye, and foot issues), the healing is found in the counter chakra, the crown chakra. Meditation and the healing of the *Shunya Mandala* would be very beneficial here.

Here is your direct navigation to establish equilibrium within the solar plexus/crown chakra partnership:

- **REREAD:** Chapters 7 and 12 on the root chakra; chapters 17 and 20 on the solar plexus chakra; and chapters 33 and 36 on the crown chakra.
- **EXPLORE:** The concept of surrender. Practice handing one fear at a time over to something greater than yourself. Listen out for the "little voice" guidance that nudges you to small, everyday choices, such as when to eat and when you need rest.
- **THIRD CHAKRA PICK-ME-UP:** Chamomile tea, lemons, and yellow peppers.
- **SEVENTH CHAKRA PICK-ME-UP:** Fasting and refraining from food. Take in spiritual nourishment.

CHAPTER 43

Establishing Equilibrium Between the Third Eye and Counter Chakras

THE PURPOSE OF THE THIRD EYE is to balance the chakras below it. This energy center is paired with the chakras below the third eye. When we quiet our mind and detach from our physical senses as we do in meditation, we receive our Divine guidance directly into the third eye and welcome in this Divine healing knowledge to know what each chakra needs. When we initiate our chakra-balancing session with our third eye, we can view it as the Divine delivery of the healing blueprint we need, to be distributed, in turn, to each chakra. The plan is placed in the third eye and then disseminated to each individual chakra. As you follow up with an individual healing and intention for each specific chakra, the blueprint plan, delivered by the third eye, is executed locally in that energy center.

Here is the direct navigation for you to establish equilibrium to your third eye chakra center.

- **REREAD:** Chapters 29 and 32 on the third eye chakra.
- **EXPLORE:** Inner seeing. Sit back and visualize your entire energy system in balance with the third eye. Practice trusting the flashes of insight and intuition that come to you at such times.

CHAPTER 44

Establishing Equilibrium: Using the System

NOW THAT YOU KNOW THE PAIRINGS, it's time to use the system and begin diagnosing your own energy patterns so you can begin to heal your body and energy system.

What I love about this intricate system is the empowerment it brings. I feel empowered and strong knowing I am not helpless when something presents itself in my life. I can locate it, diagnose it, and heal it. I want that for you, too. I encourage you to use the system. Use the information and signs your body is offering to you! Use the tools and watch what happens to your health and your life.

I find it interesting to listen to each client's ailments and symptoms, delve into their history, and then work out what experience needs to be cleared from the chakra, creating their energy stagnation and physical and emotional symptoms.

Now it's your turn to do some detective work! You are now set to heal your own body, mind, and spirit. Let's make SENSE of your healing and establish your equilibrium.

SENSE Your Chakra System

S: Sense
E: Evaluate
N: Nurture
S: Select
E: Establish Equilibrium

S: Sense your symptoms—Figure out which symptoms are presenting within your body. Use the summary chart found in chapter 38. If you have a physical ailment, match the physical ailment to the chakra and determine where this theme presents in your life. See if you can source the life experience that might be its root cause. Is it stuck in the original chakra, creating the energy stagnation, or is it in its counter chakra? Is the ailment found on the left side or the right side of your body? Left side of the body = feminine energy and the right side of the body = masculine energy. Go back to the relevant chapter and use the available tools to clear and balance the energy.

E: Evaluate Emotions—Match the emotion to the chakra. Are you going through an emotional struggle? Do these emotions align with the same chakra in step 1 or do those emotions match with its counter chakra? Go back to the emotions section in each chapter and see which chakra refers most closely to you. Then use the tips in the tools chapter to work on that particular chakra.

N: Nurture the Counter Chakra—Use the principle of polarity to draw healing in by drawing the strength of the counter chakra into the chakra that needs healing and balancing. What aspects of the counter chakra need to be infused into the asymptomatic chakra to establish equilibrium?

S: Select Technique—Select the techniques and tools that feel right to you that match the chakra you self-diagnosed and begin to integrate them into your life. Pair each new technique with an existing habit such as grounding when you put on your seat belt or right after brushing your teeth. Complete the journaling and utilize the meditation to bring more healing into this energy center.

E: Establish Equilibrium—Beginning to understand the core issue and where its root cause was initiated within your timeline, emotions, and energy will establish equilibrium. As you heal, you will find yourself less triggered when it pops up again. This will create healing momentum as you begin to notice your lack of reaction to the original trigger. Once it is truly healed, the pattern and ailment should no longer continue to present itself, maintaining your energetic equilibrium. This net result will help you find yourself living in a higher energetic vibration, healthier state, physically, mentally, emotionally, and spiritually.

As discussed earlier, often when one of these chakras is imbalanced, its partner is imbalanced, too, or it works to keep the other balanced on their energetic seesaw. What life experience might be affecting the chakra partnership? Here are a few effective and efficient ways to establish equilibrium to all your chakras all at once:

- **USE THE CHAKRA SHOWER.** Here's an efficient way to clear all of your chakras if you don't have time to meditate in the morning. While in the shower, let the water run down the front of your pelvis/root chakra (facing the shower head) and move your body left to right, allowing the water to run back and forth across the front of your root chakra, visualizing blockages and negative energy draining away. See the energy flow up all the chakras, moving from left to right, and over your head. Then turn around and clear the front side of your body, allowing your body to move in sync with the energy flow and water from right to left through each chakra, releasing anything that does not serve you and allowing it to release down the drain as you move through the chakras.

- **BREATHE.** Take a moment and breathe in all that we just covered. A profound, fully integrative system of healing like this takes some time to absorb and process.
- **INFORMATION OVERLOAD?** We have covered so much information so far! If you are ever struggling and don't know what to do, just ground. By grounding, you set the basis for your entire energy body to rest on a strong and powerful foundation.

Mantra Sharing

One powerful way to help balance the seesaw of the chakras is to share the counter chakra mantra. When you are feeling upset and your heart aches and pounds, try focusing on your heart chakra and chant the mantra LAM. Also bring in the safe, secure, and accepted energy of the root chakra into the heart. When you feel excluded, chant YAM with your focus on your root chakra and watch yourself naturally inhale as you begin to experience loving inclusion energy here in this center. When you are having a hard time expressing your emotions or before you have an intimate talk with someone, chant the mantra VAM while focusing on your throat chakra to assist in expressing those feelings, and the mantra HAM while focusing on your sacral chakra. Are you feeling overly controlling or nervous? Apply the OM symbol on your solar plexus and remember everything happens in the perfect Divine way at the perfect Divine time.

As a quick review, you can apply these mantras interchangeably as you feel necessary and in a way that helps you feel balanced.

LAM + YAM

LAM—Root chakra: offers safety and security
YAM—Heart chakra: offers self-love, compassion and nonattachment

VAM + HAM

VAM—Sacral chakra: offers balanced emotion
and creativity and releases blame
HAM—Throat chakra: offers a feeling of speaking
your truth, feeling heard, and releasing guilt

RAM + OM

RAM—Solar plexus chakra: offers a knowing of
your self-worth in gold, letting go of control

OM SYMBOL—Crown chakra: offers faith in the
Divine plan

It is in the sharing the aspects of each of the chakras with its counter chakra that creates less energetic polarity and establishes equilibrium. What is one lacking that the other needs? Together they find balance and equilibrium. Together they find wholeness, and so can you.

CHAPTER 45

Final Meditation

OUR BALANCED CHAKRAS ATTRACT a life that exudes
harmony and balance. This final meditation offers you an opportunity to bring together all you have learned to create a symphony
of healing for your body and your life.

This process will utilize our complete set of mantras to bring
full harmony to your body. I have been reviewing your mantras in
previous chapters (see especially chapter 38) so you are prepared
for this healing. This process will shift your life so much. It has
mine. I use this every single day, even twice a day, to keep my
energy vital, strong, and flowing.

Here's how it works.

We are going to begin with the third eye. Why? By inviting
the Divine in first, we are able to balance the chakras below it
more easily because we receive the healing blueprint here from the
Divine for what is currently needed. Bear in mind the third eye's
role is to balance all the chakras below it and will use this Divine
blueprint to complete the balancing.

In the crown chakra meditation, we completed this very
active meditation in which we regenerate each chakra by clearing
each one individually and collectively. This time, we are going to
work with the same general concept but will take a more passive

approach. Instead of vacuuming and working so hard, I invite you to surrender to the Divine energy of each energy center, and each counter chakra. Be still and allow the Divine to do the cleaning and rejuvenating for you. With each chakra, surrender to the energy that is there and allow the shift and change to happen, while feeling and visualizing the element of that chakra.

You may also invite the Divine to transform your illness with the repetition of every mantra or to focus on the specific chakra that correlates to your specific symptoms as you have learned throughout this process while you see your energy and body whole and complete. Either way, welcome in this energy shift to create a change in your state of illness and in your everyday life.

Final Chakra Meditation

Join me for this powerful receiving meditation as you clear and balance every single one of your energy centers. Join me at www. LoveHealThrive.com.

CHAPTER 46

The Connection to Others

OUR CONNECTION TO OTHERS is significant. Without human connection, we perish. But with a faulty connection to others, we can find ourselves exhausted, tired, depleted, anxious, angry, apathetic, depressed, and unmotivated. Sound familiar?

Why does this happen? We are all empathetic. We may have varying degrees of empathy, but we are ultimately all empaths. Empaths are sensitive people who have the gift of experiencing and feeling the present, past, or future states of others. Empaths often absorb the emotional energy and physical pain from the people or situations around them and take it on as their own, until they learn how to empower themselves with Divine energy.

This doesn't have to be a passive experience. In this chapter, you will learn how to use your God-given gift of empathy and turn it into one of your very best assets.

The empath is empowered by remembering what a powerful role the aura plays in sensing others, and by learning how to manage it effectively. To recap what we learned in chapter 4, your aura is an electromagnetic field surrounding your body, formed by the layers of energy flowing from each of your individual chakras to create a seven-layer energy field around the body. Beginning with the root chakra, each chakra clears and releases energy in a clockwise direction (when healthy), absorbs energy from its surroundings in a counterclockwise direction (when unhealthy), or is stagnant (also unhealthy). Each chakra creates one layer of this seven-layer aura. Now that you have cleared and balanced your chakras, the energy within your aura is purified and heightened too.

Your aura can be your greatest tool in navigating life, people, and situations. This amazing aura of ours gathers and collects information, and then transmits it into our system for our use. Like all things, when our chakras and aura are healthy, they form the ultimate fact-gathering detective system, where we receive intuitive guidance, a sense of knowingness, and an innate understanding of the world around us.

Have you ever had someone walk into the room and you knew they were sad or upset? Have you ever met up with a close friend while trying to pretend all is well only to have them ask, "What's the matter?" because they "could tell" something wasn't right? In both of these instances, it is the aura being read and felt by the other. This system is twofold. Just as you can take in information through your aura, people can feel your energy through your aura, too. What message are you sending out? Our vibe speaks louder than our words. I have built entire workshops on teaching people how powerful their energetic expression can be.

While the aura gives us a great deal of information, it can also create life struggles when imbalanced, much like our physical and energetic bodies. Have you ever had a conversation with a friend and then an hour later found yourself feeling the same way as they did? This is the result of absorbing someone's energy through your aura. If your aura is extending, you begin to absorb energy from many different sources.

As you have learned, when your aura extends too far out, your energy is dispersed too widely, so you feel scattered and spread too thin. You end up feeling the emotions and taking on the energy of anyone who walks through your auric field. A person struggling

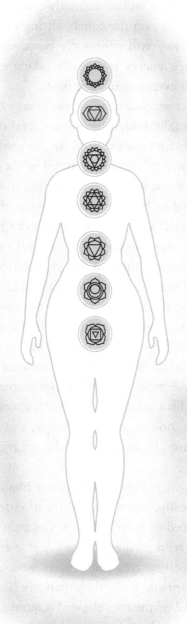

Chakra Aura Image, Erin Garay, 2022, www.LoveHealThrive.com

with an extended aura may feel they never have enough space to live and enjoy life. They will consistently complain that they don't have enough room . . . on the couch, sitting next to someone, or sharing a room. They will constantly be needing more "space." This is because their energy is actually taking up a great deal of space and they feel everyone in their field.

Although unseen without training, the energy of an empath with a large aura *is* actually taking up a great deal of energetic space. As a result, the empath feels the need for the physical accommodation of this space as well. As you learned in the aura chapter, the larger aura can be a result of an abusive childhood where the child always felt the need to be on high alert about their surroundings and be aware of what was happening in order to stay safe. Does this sound like anyone you know? Or maybe it's you? Teach others about their aura and the tools in this chapter to help you all feel more peaceful and that you have enough space.

In the chapter on the aura, we covered the story of the little boy who had an aura six feet wide and who had continued tantrums. He felt overwhelmed because he was taking in everyone's energy and emotion. He did not have the tools to release the excess energy other than via these meltdowns. Once he learned tools and techniques to draw in his energy and release its excess, he felt more in control, no longer took in so much energy, and ultimately experienced fewer tantrums. In his case, he did not have an abusive home, but he was adopted.

Adoption is an incredible and amazing blessing to our world. However, energetically, it can cause disruption for the baby's root chakra that will need to be rebalanced. Once the sense of the new home is physically reestablished for the adopted child, home in their root chakra needs to be reestablished, as well. Assisting them in learning how to plant and water their own tree (see our tree imagery in chapters 7 and 12 on the root chakra) is monumentally helpful in teaching them to draw their aura in and to feel more grounded, safe, and secure in the new roots of their new home. I have seen this larger aura energetic experience in 100 percent of the adopted clients I have worked with in my practice. With a little bit of awareness and root chakra healing, the adopted child, or adult, will feel safe, secure, and unshaken by the environment around them.

I have had many clients report severe ADD/ADHD and distraction, and when we measured their aura, it invariably tended to be notably wide. When I explained to them this energy state absorbs others' energy and emotion, I was usually amazed at how quickly they felt understood and known, as if I just described to them how they had been feeling their entire lives. They could often name the people whose energy they were absorbing who was causing this stress on their system. If you are feeling understood and known in this moment too, be sure to complete the exercises in this chapter to see if your aura is a contributing factor to your illness or state of mind.

Conversely, auras that are too small leave people feeling isolated, distant, depressed, and lonely. It can be hard to know oneself and to stand up for oneself when the aura is too deeply contracted. The world feels too intense because there is very little energetic protection surrounding the body. When clients come in depressed, it is not unusual to measure their aura and find it only half an inch wide. This can occur from a lack of heart chakra energy or from a tear in the auric field, which we will address later in this chapter.

An aura can range from half an inch to some reported cases of sixty-five feet or more in size, although in my practice I never experienced anyone with more than a six-foot-wide aura. A healthy aura helps us strike the proper balance between connecting with others and maintaining our boundaries. I have found a healthy and robust auric field to measure about eighteen inches from the body. This allows the people close enough to you to be felt within your energy field, without integrating lesser-known people or energy into your field. However, not all wide auras are necessarily detrimental. You can and should use your aura as one of your very best superpowers and sensing tools. If you are walking into a room and want to read the energy there, you can enlarge your aura and assess the energy of the place or people. You have probably already been doing this without even knowing it.

As mentioned in the last chapter, traumatic experiences can tear your aura and leave the energy draining from the auric tear. This type of energetic damage can be the result of physical, emotional, sexual, alcohol, or drug abuse, which leaves the body and spirit in shock. An individual with an auric tear feels everything everyone is feeling all the time and is powerless against its effect. As a result, they often experience social anxiety because it is too overwhelming to be around people. Because the energy is continuing to drain out of the aura, depression is also often experienced because there is little to no energy maintained for the body, mind, or soul. Also, the individual appears to have little or no healing response to energy work, homeopathic medicine, or acupuncture. The tear in their aura does not allow them to maintain their energy, as it is no longer contained within the auric field.

I think it's important to know about this condition. We can heal an auric tear by raising our vibration, and you will find all the meditations included useful for that, in addition to the tools in this chapter. But first, we need to be aware of what is happening. When we are aware, we can heal more strategically, and if you've been trying to meditate or use other forms of energy work and it hasn't been healing you, I hope this gives you an empowering possibility to consider.

By following the road map suggestions, you will heal your aura. If you've been implementing tools along the way, and building your own individual toolkit, you may be feeling considerably better. In addition, you can listen to the frequency of 432 hertz music (available on www.LoveHealThrive.com) while taking a saltwater bath with the oils that muscle test the best for you.

The Aura-Soma Etheric Rescue bottle is also a known healer for this particular energy condition, as it assists in healing the sacral chakra and helps the individual feel more emotionally balanced. It also helps heal resentment. If you have been struggling with severe depression and have experienced abuse in your past, take time to reflect on the sacral chakra chapters (chapters 13 and 16) and implement the suggestions into your life to heal any trauma in your aura.

People can also drain your aura through "excessive energy connections," which we'll address later. The more you learn how to control your aura, the more you will feel grounded, calm, patient, and empowered.

How does your aura expand?

- Do you often feel scattered and drained?
- Did you grow up in a traumatic environment as a child?
- Do you feel isolated, lonely, or depressed?

Children who grow up in an unsettling environment tend to have either large auras or overly small auras. Some children use their extra-large aura (I've seen up to six feet personally) to scan the room to determine if it is safe to enter, and if it is not safe, they leave. Growing up in a chaotic environment, the child establishes its aura at this overly wide size to maintain protection. When children have tantrums, it is often because they have taken on too much of other people's energy because their auras are so widespread. It is how they release their energy.

The opposite can also be true. If a child feels they need to be hidden because there is an abusive parent in the home, for example, their aura may retract and become so small that their energy cannot be felt or experienced. (They make themselves "invisible.") This can also happen if there has been an interaction that has caused great distrust, where the child feels they cannot trust anyone. This can result in a feeling of isolation and loneliness because they don't allow anyone to enter into the energy field. Without human interaction, we perish, though, so this condition needs to be addressed.

There are times where it is important and necessary to make ourselves invisible or, conversely, where we want our energy to be seen, but often childhood patterns remain in place and create many unwanted situations in an adult's life in repeated undesirable patterns.

Curious how big your aura is? Here are some great ways to determine your aura's size.

Seeing Your Aura

- Find a plain, colored, neutral background, such as a wall, curtain, or blanket.
- Hold your arm up twelve to eighteen inches (thirty to forty-six centimeters) away from your face, making your eyesight hazy. We see more of our aura from our peripheral vision.
- Begin to haze your eyesight by gently closing your eyes, leaving them open slightly. Now focus on the area a quarter of an inch (approximately six millimeters) from your skin.
- Continue to hold your gaze there and watch until it begins to illuminate. Typically, it will pop on like a light, and you will see what looks like a thin covering of energy at first. That is the first layer of your aura. As you stare longer, you may see this energy grow wider and wider and may even begin to see color.
- Continue to practice. You may see your aura grow and perhaps may even begin to see a color.

Determining Your Aura's Width

- Find a partner.
- Decide who goes first. This person stands with their back turned toward their partner, eyes closed. You should be twelve feet (just over three and a half meters) apart.
- On the count of three, the second partner begins taking small steps toward the first person, who should still keep their eyes closed. When the standing partner begins to *feel* their partner close, they should yell, "Stop."
- Now let the standing partner turn around and see how far their partner is away from them. Perhaps they are three feet away (around one meter), or six or seven (around two meters), or perhaps eighteen

inches (forty-six centimeters.). Remember this number. See how this aligns with what you have already learned about your aura. Both partners should take a turn walking toward the other partner.

Confirming What You Felt

Here is where you begin to trust your instincts and give yourself proof that what you felt was accurate. We can use dowsing rods to read the aura of the other person to confirm what you felt was accurate. If you don't have any, you can easily make your own dowsing rods with a DIY video online.

- Begin with you and your partner standing on opposite sides of the room.
- If you were the walking partner last time, now's your turn to stand still. Hold the rods and let the first partner (the one previously standing with eyes closed) walk toward you.
- You should find that the rods move when at the same distance as previously recorded, i.e. when the standing partner *felt* the second partner walk up. Once they move, feel free to move forward and backward and watch how the dowsing rods move back and forth with you as it detects your energy.
- Take turns with both partners walking forward and backward, watching how the rods move based on feeling your energy and watching the energy dissipate.

I love this exercise because it can provide physical proof of what you felt, allowing you to begin to trust what you are feeling and know you really are experiencing other people at that distance. It's a powerful place to start having an awareness of where your energy is.

CHAPTER 47

How We Empower Our Energy to Work for Us

BEGIN WITH DETERMINING who, what, why, when, and where your energy is depleted or energized. Cultivate your witness as you learned in chapter 37 and watch your thoughts. Are they *your* emotions or someone else's? When I'm in a Reiki session, I feel what the other person is feeling. Emotions, physical ailments—I also know if my client is sick or coming down with a cold because I will feel it, too. It may seem amazing, but we all can do it. It's a powerful (and useful) place to be when you can discern what your feelings are and what are another's feelings.

Bringing in Your Aura

Continue to fill your body with positive energy through your breath. Be sure to breathe in relaxation and breathe out relaxation throughout your entire day, especially when doing energy work. With each breath, set intention for any energy that is not yours, which may have been absorbed from someone else, to be dispersed to your pelvic floor to be released into the center of the Earth for transformation and rejuvenation.

Ground your energy by drawing a root from your pelvic floor 90 percent of the way toward the center of the Earth, inviting Mama Earth to draw it in the rest of the way. Give Mama Earth much gratitude and then release the stagnant energy from your pelvic floor, and any energy that does not serve you, into the center of the Earth to be transformed into power and strength. Draw the healing Earth energy into your pelvic floor, the base of your spine, and your perineum.

Then pull in your aura. I like to imagine energy cords attached to my aura flowing through each chakra and from my center and all the way out to the edges of my aura. When I want to pull in my aura, I see myself drawing my aura in, almost like pulling an umbrella closed down its handle through each chakra. Then I take that cord, pull it all the way to my center, and send it into the center of the Earth 90 percent of the way and then invite Mama Earth to attach and draw it into the center of the Earth the rest of the way, like a seat belt and pulled taut to the center of the Earth, making the aura tight and secure. You can do this in an instant in the middle of a conversation, crowded room, or your car before heading into work, school, or home.

Energy Elevation

Once your energy and aura is pulled in tightly, use energy elevation to raise your energy. To elevate your energy, apply an energy screen around yourself that elevates your energy higher than your surroundings so you no longer absorb that energy. The screen can be two to three feet (up to around one meter) around, above, and below you. To clarify, I envision a window screen that breathes, not an electronic device screen that would be reflective, not connective. You can place different energies around you to assist with different challenges. While some teachers have recommended energy shields, I prefer teaching this as a screen that allows for the energy to breathe in and out. You do not need to be afraid, or to feel you need to protect yourself, from someone's energy, because we are all connected. You simply need to elevate your energy to a higher vibration. Sometimes to do this we need the help of a screen.

A white screen is great for being in large crowds. A pink screen is energy influence to help everyone feel love energy emanating from you. An indigo screen helps you feel hidden and protected. Once the screen is secure, you may place a bowl outside the screen to hold the energy and emotion of whomever you are listening to. This is an incredible way to remain present for a loved one or client without taking on their energy. Beloved Buddhist spiritual leader Thich Nhat Hanh said one of the best things we can do for another is to allow them to empty their hearts. So I let them and even encourage them to empty their hearts, inside the bowl yet outside my energy field. They feel the presence and intention held, and my energy is not infused with their energy.

If you are around a really toxic person, you can choose whichever screen you prefer and ask for a protector to patrol around you, such as Archangel Michael and his mercy of angels with swords and shields, Jesus, or someone who translates to safety or security for you. But you place them out front so you can feel safe and secure.

I taught my daughters this long ago. Now they know, white screen for the state fair and pink screen around friends, or as you read earlier, blue for invisible protection. Kids are so sensitive, and these conversations, much like many of our parenting conversations, can be easy. Make it matter of fact, and it will help everyone have a better day. They will love feeling empowered—and it works. No more tantrums! I saw such a shift when I first taught them this technique.

Now I often remind them before we enter a crowded venue and they respond, "Yeah Mom, I know. Already did it!"

So great!

Energy Cleansing

At the end of a draining event or busy day, it helps to know some techniques to cleanse and revive yourself.

- Carry a black tourmaline crystal to help clear and protect your energy.
- I like to take a chakra shower, which we detailed earlier, to help clear my day, setting the intention I am clearing and releasing stagnant energy, stresses, and negative energy that do not serve me.
- On leaving a volatile energy situation, scrub out, just like a doctor. Wash your hands with cold water up to the elbows to wash off that energy and cleanse yourself as you detach from the energy of the experience. This is important for any and all bodyworkers to do before and after every client and anyone who has just endured a frenetic or toxic energetic experience. Just like a doctor, you are maintaining energetic hygiene.
- Grounding clears your energy as well as the people you encountered throughout your day. It is one of your most important energy clearing methods.

When you get home . . .

- Wash hands immediately.
- Ground.
- Spend two minutes in the dark and quiet. This helps to reset your energy.

CHAPTER 48

Excessive Energy Connections and Connection Clearing

WE HAVE LEARNED MANY WAYS to keep our energy clear, clean, and vibrating high. We are all connected, we are made up of energy, and we are connected by energy cords. There is an abundance of Divine positive energy flowing through these cords at all times.

When we are in a loving, high-vibrational space, these cords connected to everyone feel luscious and feed our soul and theirs. Sometimes, though, our thoughts trigger our emotions that create a toxic energetic buildup in our energy cords connected to certain people in our lives. This is what has traditionally been called "cording in." However, rather than calling it being corded (which I believe has very negative connotation), I prefer to call it being connected. I believe every one of us is connected, and the "cording" experience is when there is toxic energy built up between two people and their connection has become a drain rather than a source of nourishment, typically when our energetic frequency is low.

We encounter this excessive energy connection when we feel someone is trying to take our power away or that, through our actions, we've given our power away. Toxic energy can build up as a result of an argument or an emotional entanglement, obsession, or a feeling of lack. However, it's not the entanglement that causes this toxic buildup. It is the emotional dissonance within *you* that triggers the stagnation.

Are you feeling jealous? Insecure? Did this person fill a place within you that made you feel complete? Did you get upset when they left? Did you lose sight that you are unique and special because you are one with the Divine, as we all are?

The symptoms of these connections being filled with toxic energy will look a lot like how we feel when our physical body is toxic—exhausted, irritable, drained.

There is always a moment when we allow an excessive energy connection to happen. This outside energy fills us somehow. Our ego gets a boost from the attention we receive, or we feel important about how we are helping others. We are filled energetically by the person, so we welcome the excessive energy connection. But the long-term drain on our soul of this person's energy draw leaves us depleted and exhausted.

Excessive energy connection also happens when someone sees the light in you and wants it for themselves. Instead of going to the direct source of the Divine, they draw more energy from you through your shared energetic connection, which would typically be balanced and healthy. When this happens, this excessive confiscation of your energy leaves you feeling spent and drained.

Here's a great example of how this works. I had a new client who came to see me feeling depleted and exhausted, much like the description above. She was a physical therapist and helped many struggling patients. She had one morbidly obese patient who just wanted her to do "all the work." Her patient didn't have the drive to heal herself.

After our first session in learning how to cleanse cords, my client reported back she could not believe it. She had tons of energy and felt great, but the best part was that as soon as she cleared the energy connection, her patient—all of a sudden, after months of apathy—wanted to get up and move for herself.

The patient saw the incredible light in my client and wanted it for herself. She had excessive energy connected into my client and was exhausting her own energy. By cleansing the connection and allowing her patient to find her own Divine connection, my client found her patient was inspired and connected to the Divine directly, resulting in energy and a drive to get healthy. Both parties always benefit from connection cleansing.

For those on social media, I have found myself drained after I've posted a moving story that inspired many people. Once, I felt thousands of cords drawing excessive energy from me, and I was exhausted. This can be looked at in two ways:

1. People wanted my light for themselves instead of going to the Divine.
2. I contributed to the toxic energy because I wanted them to benefit and love the post.

Together, we created an energy that exhausted me. Once I cleansed my connections using the following technique, I felt energized and was able to respond to all of the online responses.

If you are online, be aware of this potential energy hazard, and post because you feel called to post without any attachment to outcome. As quoted earlier, you have a right to the work alone, not to the fruits of your labor.

This process has traditionally been separated through energetic cord cutting, where one brings in Divine scissors or a sword to cut the cord between two people. The intention is to remove the energetic cord and, ultimately, the energetic draw from the other body. This cord cutting allows the cord, and the other person, to be reconnected with the Divine because it severs the cord from the human and redirects it to the Divine.

The exception is that we are all connected. Many spiritual teachers will say that we are connected and at the same time advocate for cutting the energy cord to those who hurt us. How can we say that we are all connected except to this person who wronged us or hurt us? It's not possible. We are all connected. As such, we need to start clearing our connections differently. We need to clear them, not cut them.

In the following excessive energetic cord clearing I will describe, the person who may be drawing energy is being redirected back to the Divine but without cutting the energetic connection between each other. You are flowing Divine energy toward them to redirect the energetic draw, so they draw directly from the Divine. The result is a connected world with each other and the Divine.

We live in a world where we are so disconnected, both from each other and from the Divine. Will we have more compassion for each other as we clear our connections rather than cut them? If we are truly all connected, does cord cutting ultimately cut us off from a version of ourselves? Will we be more loving to each other if we clear instead of cut? Will we begin to feel less isolated and more connected? That's a world I can't wait to experience.

Part of me wonders if this global disconnection we experience is the result of traditional cord cutting, which severs links between people in a way that can sometimes seem brutal, rather than cord clearing where we allow ourselves to remain connected yet flowing with mutual Divine power.

Be on the lookout. If you are extremely exhausted, it may be time to cleanse some connections and flood yourself with Divine upleveled energy. It's a great idea to make this a nightly ritual.

How to Clear Your Connections: Brief Instructions

Scan your body and see where you may feel a negative buildup of energy within your connection points. Perhaps you know who this person is or you may not. It doesn't matter. You are doing this to purify your energy system.

Often, excessive energy connections are found below your belly button but not invariably so. (This step can also be skipped because the specific location ultimately does not matter. The intention to cleanse is more important.)

Ground your energy by connecting your tree root to the Earth 90 percent of the way and inviting in Mama Earth to connect and draw it in, clicking in and pulling taut to the center of the Earth, giving Mama Earth some gratitude first and then drawing up

Mama Earth's energy, filling in your pelvic floor, the base of your spine, and your perineum.

Invite that beautiful golden energy to flow through your spine and up to your Divine source, basking in the connection with the Divine, seeing this beautiful golden light flowing through you from the Earth to the Divine.

From here, you can cleanse your connections by welcoming golden light in through the crown of your head and through each of the chakra centers, through the front and back, flooding them with this beautiful golden light. This downpour of light allows for a cleansing flow of energy throughout all the energy connections within you and with connections to other people. Be sure to set intention that the energy found within these cords is transmuted into the highest Divine love energy so that you flow positive energy to everyone and do not take on their negative lower-vibe energy. Be the bright light and flood the room and energy around you with positive energy.

When it reaches the other person, you can set intention for the golden light to carry through to their Divine sources if that is what they feel serves them best, clearing the entire connection between you two completely to the Divine, or for the energy to dissolve into Divine energy. However, you do not have permission to enter someone else's energy field, so you can set intention for the complete cleansing, and if the other person's higher self chooses to welcome it, it will be. They may need to heal their emotional state before they are ready and willing to clear the rest of the energy connection, but that is not your concern, nor does it detract from your process. You are flowing Divine energy that is blessing, healing, and clearing the toxic energy from your system with the intention that it is cleared for all.

Connection clearing will encourage a sense of peace within yourself and all the people to whom you are connected. They may feel a shift in their own energy and will reach out to you by text or a call because they notice this, regardless of whether or not they recognize it to be an energetic shift.

I once met a woman at an event who hadn't talked to her brother in years. We completed this exercise, and she called me the next day to let me know he had been texting her all day. She couldn't believe it.

This incredible clearing eliminates the toxic energy in your connection and gives your loved ones the gift of going directly to the source for themselves.

Be filled with GRACE Technique

I used to host many grief workshops, and people would feel really connected to me. Afterward, they would share their most intimate and painful stories with me. I felt so honored. However, after my first event, I was in bed for two full days because so much heavy energy had been dumped on me. I wasn't sick, I just had zero energy. I was suffering from excessive energy connections. I had to come up with a good system so this didn't happen again because I wanted to continue to serve. I met with every spiritual counselor I knew, read books, and came up with this shortcut to protection because it was a long haul for me. I want to save you the pain I endured pulling this together.

This can be remembered easily: fill yourself with GRACE.

- G: Ground with gratitude
- R: Retract your aura
- A: Attach to the center of the Earth,
  with Mama Earth's assistance.
- C: Cover with an energy screen
- E: Empty the bowl you placed out for others once
  they are finished emptying their hearts into it

This is how I personally make use of what has been discussed:
- Ground with gratitude.
- Retract my aura and energy with arms pulled in and
  energy down, connecting all the way down to the
  center of the Earth, imagining the umbrella closing.
- Attach to the center of the Earth with Mama
  Earth's assistance.

- Energy screen three feet above and below and around my body.
- Place a bowl outside of my shield when holding space for someone else and empty it out once they have emptied their heart.

Protecting Your Home

- **SAGE.** White sage is traditionally used for healing. In a process called smudging, the smoke is used to bless, cleanse, and heal the person or object being smudged. Sage is used to "wash off" the outside world. Native American tribes used it for spiritual house cleaning.
- **PALO SANTO.** This means holy wood. Traditionally burned by the Incas, Indigenous people of the Andes, for spiritual purifying, energy cleansing, and healing, the smoke is believed to have both medicinal and therapeutic healing power.
- **WHICH TO CHOOSE?** Use your instinct to decide what is best suited for you. Both are powerful, healing, and purposeful. Muscle test for yourself what tool will work best for you. Both are incredible healing and cleansing agents.
- **SMUDGING PROCESS.** While holding the sage in your hand, bless the dirt the foundation rests upon. Bless the foundation. Begin at the front door, moving left around the home or at the farthest back corner of the house. Muscle test to decide which beginning location is best for you and your home. Burn the sage and allow the smoke to float into all four corners, across the room, under furniture, and in closets. While smudging the doors to the outside, move the sage in a circle in a counterclockwise direction and state, "I only allow love and light to enter here." You may use the smoke to draw an emblem on each of the four walls (not actually

touching the wall, just the essence of the smoke near the wall) of your home. You may use the sign of the cross, a heart, Reiki symbols, or any symbol that calls to you. This sets intention for the room and raises the vibration of the energy within it.

- **PRAYER.** This is the prayer I use every night before I go to sleep. This has changed my home's energy dramatically. I invite you to use this daily prayer, too. "Archangel Michael and your mercy of angels, thank you for standing at all four corners, all windows and doors, and at the foot of every bed. Thank you for your golden dome of protection and your platinum net of protection. Thank you for removing all negative or imbalanced energies from this space and, upon doing so, thank you for filling this space with love." You can add on to or replace *love* with what you want in your home—connection, peace, joy, laughter, etc. I typically list a number of intentions every night.
- **FRONT DOOR SCREEN.** At the end of my saging, I set intention with the sage to create a cobweb-like film at the front door that will catch anything not of love and light. It is caught in the web and unable to enter my home. This is a great technique if you often have people coming in and out of your home or before and after and large get-togethers.

Empath meditation: Join me online for a powerful empath meditation at www.LoveHealThrive.com.

———————

Many of my clients experience social anxiety and feel anxious in crowds. These techniques have empowered them to understand why they are experiencing their symptoms from an energetic perspective and have used these tools to successfully engage in social situations without feeling threatened, anxious, or upset.

I once stood in line for lunch at a town fair, surrounded by people. Suddenly, I felt anxious from all the frenetic energy around me. I used this method precisely as stated in the middle of the fair, while standing in line. Instantly, I felt calmer and empowered. It was as if I were in my own protective bubble with the world passing around me. I felt safe and secure in my space.

I don't want you to make this difficult. I've attempted to make every tool I've placed along this road map available immediately for you that can be used in a second. Mantras can be said in your head. Energy techniques can be completed while standing in lines. Your work lunch can be packed to nourish your energetic needs for the day. Build these tools into your day.

Utilize this GRACE technique before going into crowds or before a tough conversation. If you're in a crowd and you feel anxious, complete this protection then. As you practice, you can begin to do this really quickly. You will feel you are in your own protective cocoon, and it will help you manage crowds in ways you've never expected. You will find yourself less anxious and full of more energy after being out.

CONCLUSION

Your Divine Connection

THIS IS HOW MY DAY STARTED once many years ago on a beach in Maui and continues to start this way every day. This is what I want for you, too.

The sand presses into my skin as I witness the ocean's foam find its perfect resting place, effortlessly making its way out of the ocean. I experience my body and thoughts as something separate from me. As I sit there at daybreak, greeting the sun to its day, I mentally scan through each of my energy centers and clear, clean, and balance each one. Once all of them are harmonized, I then begin to meditate.

But my focus and meditation somehow now feel different. I realize I am an energy body and the stories that I have told myself are what are slowing my energy up. This slower energy is the same place I have physical challenges. As I clear the belief and the story, the pain disappears. I then sit in a delicious, connected meditation feeling as though the gentle wind is kissing my cheek and the ocean is taking away every thought that does not serve me.

I am connected and energized and continue to feel this great all day as miracles continue to manifest moment by moment.

By utilizing the tools and techniques of this road map on your journey, you will find your root cause for healing and your true inspiration for happiness. You've cleared and balanced your energy centers and now you can hand over any other worry or stress to the Divine every time you connect into the Divine and release what no longer serves you. Your only job is to connect with the Divine and let all that is intended settle into its assigned place in your life.

Our thoughts trigger emotions, emotions move energy,
and energy manifests physically.
What we do with our energy matters.
If our energy isn't weak, our body doesn't weaken.

Honor the place in you that is ready to heal. Honor the parts of you not quite there yet, but more than anything, honor the partnership. It is only our humanness that wants to rush and force the process. The Divinity within us knows the perfect time, the perfect way, and the perfect partnership. Trust and know that as you complete one lesson, it opens the gateway to the next level of healing. Somehow you will find yourself ready to move forward and heal when you hadn't felt ready before.

Do something every day. Ground your energy. Choose a breathing technique. Chant a mantra. Just as you would brush your teeth every day for dental hygiene, cleanse your energy every day for energetic and spiritual hygiene. Get quiet and listen. Your body will speak to you loudly and now you will know where to look to find the true answers.

Emergency Technique Reviews

You've finished reading *Establishing Equilibrium*, but your journey is just beginning. My hope is that as you have integrated a few of these tools into your life, your illness and its symptoms have begun to dissipate while you've strengthened your energy and your connection to yourself, others, and the Divine. If you are panicked or upset, you can always lean on this emergency technique. Bring your full focus and attention down to your pelvic floor, the base of your spine, and your perineum. Send your energy root down into the center of the Earth 90 percent of the way and ask Mama Earth to do the rest to click it in and pull it taut (you may offer gratitude if you like here, but Mama Earth's compassionate heart knows you are in a state and will make allowances if you do it later). Now, draw that beautiful Earth energy up and fill in your pelvic floor, the base of your spine, and your perineum. Allow this energy to nourish this center. Chant the mantra LAM repeatedly in a low tone, out loud, or in your mind. Bring presence back to this space within your body until you have nourished your root chakra and the episode passes.

Ongoing Healing Using the *Establishing Equilibrium* Road Map

As you make a lifestyle of responding to your physical symptoms and addressing the corresponding emotional healing they need, you may notice you have fewer and fewer days riddled with illness and stress. As you strengthen your foundation first and build from there, you will experience a life that feels more empowered and joyful. Begin your day with grounding when you wake up, when you stand up out of bed, and when you brush your teeth. Even while standing, you are still grounding from your pelvic floor.

You can choose one root energy cord to lead from the center of your pelvic floor down into the center of the Earth, or you can see that energy going down both your legs and connecting both energy cords into the center of the Earth. But the source of your tree trunk's root is always your root chakra at your perineum. Do this grounding exercise on a daily basis, and you will find your life becomes a joyful and present experience.

The Establishing Equilibrium Road Map

Use this map daily for maximum effect, adding in the tools you

✧ *Establishing Equilibrium Roadmap*

**You
Are
Here**

I'm so lost.

I feel terrible.

Where should
I go?

What should
I do?

Am I . . . ?

CROWN CHAKRA
Experiencing Pineal gland issues, seizures, nausea • Overthinking • Struggling with migraines • Worrying. **Solution: Move to MARKER 3—SOLAR PLEXUS**

THIRD EYE CHAKRA
Hallucinating or believing false stories • Feeling extra sensitive to energy • Experiencing overwhelming Sixth sense and seeing uncomfortable flashes of images or hearing guidance. **Solution: Go to MARKERS 1–5 and bring attention to your physical body to reconnect your third eye with your physical senses.**

THROAT CHAKRA
Burdened by situation from 28–35 years old • Overtalking • Always challenged to speak up for self • Having ear and mouth problems • Having hearing problems • Struggling with thyroid issues. **Solution: Move to MARKER 2—Sacral**

HEART CHAKRA
Burdened by situation from 21–28 years old • Envious • Attached to people and ideas • Jealous • Struggling with skin issues • Nervous about people touching me • Healing hand problems. **Solution: Move to MARKER 1—Root**

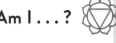

SOLAR PLEXUS CHAKRA
Burdened by situation from 14–21 years old • Controlling • Angry • Power-hungry • Lacking self-will • Struggling with eye and sight issues • Managing Pancreas, stomach or liver issues. **Solution: Move to MARKER 7—CROWN**

SACRAL CHAKRA
Burdened by situation from 7–14 years old • Blaming • Codependent • Struggling with tongue issues • Challenged with taste issues • Experiencing sexual organ challenges. **Solution: Move to MARKER 5—THROAT**

ROOT CHAKRA
Burdened by situation from 0–7 years old • Distracted • Losing my keys? • Struggling with hemorrhoids • Challenged by smell issues • Exhausted by adrenal issues. **Solution: Move to MARKER 4—HEART**

MARKER 7: CROWN—Ground. Visualize gold cleansing energy pouring down from the Divine into the space in between your right and left brain hemispheres. Cultivate your witness, exhale, let go and trust in the Divine plan. Envision OM symbol above head.

MARKER 6: THIRD EYE—Either go into the sun or envision the sun's healing warm light shining into your third eye, bringing warmth and balance. Chant OM.

MARKER 5: THROAT—Inhale and visualize ether flowing in through the space above the V-shaped area of your collarbone and open your mouth in lion's breath to exhale and release stagnation. Journal or share your feelings. Chant HAM.

Destination: Equilibrium

MARKER 4: HEART—Inhale and fill your lungs and heart. On the exhale, release attachments and what no longer serves you. Bask in human connection and love. Chant YAM.

MARKER 3: SOLAR PLEXUS—Build an inner fire under your rib cage and use it to burn up anything that does not serve you or that is holding you back. Build healthy pragmatic structure and routine. Chant RAM.

MARKER 2: SACRAL—Visualize water slowing down or speeding up emotion to reach emotional equilibrium and find the balance to speak your truth. Chant VAM.

MARKER 1: ROOT—Grow your tree root, allow Mama Earth to grab it and infuse you with earth energy into your pelvic floor, creating a three-vertebrae tall garden of soil to nourish your pelvic floor. Know you are safe and secure no matter what. Chant LAM.

personally need for each day to create the most powerful, empowered, healthy life you ever dreamed of living. As a symptom shows up in any space, get to the root cause quickly. Look to the silent partner and give it the attention it needs to bring balance to the partnership. As you continue to respond quickly to your body's signals, the healthier and happier you will find your body becomes.

This is a daily map and will help you draw in health, happiness, and joy.

Repeat your mantras, guide your energy, and honor your journey. It has brought you to this place and you are doing brave work in order to know the deepest parts of you. In doing so, you will no longer have to imagine a life of ease, health, and happiness, because you will be living it.

Our time together was just the beginning of your journey. Take your road map and find your way back to you. I hope you experience the undeniable resonance of your soul and hear your soul's sacred ring of truth as you continue to grow more connected to all that is You in your pursuit of establishing equilibrium.

APPENDIX

Sushumna, Ida, and Pingala

There is an even deeper connection to our autonomic nervous system detailed in ancient Sanskrit texts called the Tantra. It is believed we have seventy-two thousand *nadis* (channels of energy) where energy flows. The three most significant channels are the *sushumna*, *ida*, and *pingala*. *Sushumna*, which is pure energy of consciousness, runs from the base of the spine parallel to the spinal column to the crown of the head. *Ida* and *pingala*, residing on either side of *sushumna*, weave back and forth and meet at each chakra. When these channels meet together with *sushumna* in three specific chakras—*muladhara* (root), *anahata* (heart), and *ajna* (third eye)—this person experiences a *ganthris*, or psychic knot, a spiritual challenge to overcome that brings them closer to their center. It is in each of these knots where great spiritual awareness is achieved, leading to deeper awareness and clarity and spiritual connection.

Pingala is to the right of the central energy line, *sushumna nadi*, and embodies our masculine energy. *Pingala* is connected to the sun's energy and coincides with our sympathetic nervous system. It ignites our fire when we need it to respond to an external threat. This energy channel moves us forward and helps us take action.

Ida receives and is located to the left of the central energy line, *sushumna*, is connected to the moon's energy, and is associated with the parasympathetic nervous system. It feels its way to healing. In order to feel, we must move slowly enough to feel our feelings. As such, *ida* activates our parasympathetic nervous system and slows our heartbeat and breathing so we can feel into our solution.

Bija Mantras

We are going to use mostly *bija* mantras to bring your energy center back to its original and most vibrant frequency. The word *mantra* is derived from two Sanskrit words—*manas* (mind) and *tra* (tool). *Bija* means seed. Together, this powerful small little mantra, the *bija* mantra, has the power to transform your energy and your life by balancing and invigorating each of your energy centers. The *bija* mantra resonates at the frequency of each chakra. As you chant the mantra, it brings your energy center into alignment with that frequency and brings balance and health to the chakra.

Each of the energy centers will embody the same seed sound AUM. We can think of this as a three-part AUM, although it sounds more like A-U-N-M. The first sound (A-U) begins in the base of your spine as low and as deep as possible. The middle portion begins to rise in frequency and sound up your spine and encourages a nasal vibration to activate the third eye through the use of the sound (N). The final sound is the highest in sound and vibration, continuing to create vibration and bringing your energy into your crown chakra with the final sound (M).

AUM is the base seed sound of each chakra but is often used on its own for prayer, connecting to the Divine and cleansing of the spirit. Each chakra vibrates to a seed sound, also known as a *bija* mantra. Each *bija* mantra will begin with a different sound according to each chakra addressed in each chapter. __ + AUM = LAM, VAM, RAM, YAM, HAM, OM.

Begin with the keynote and frequency of the particular chakra and remain in that frequency until your chakra feels balanced and powerful. If it feels right to you, you may then continue onto the three-part AUM and bring that energy upward through your *sushumna* that runs parallel to your spine to connect with the Divine. Always begin and remain in the chakra frequency until it feels balanced. In the depiction of each chakra, each seed sound is carried in by a particular animal that embodies the energy of each chakra.

ACKNOWLEDGMENTS: FILLED WITH GRATITUDE

1. **JOSH**—My brother from another mother, mentor, and most importantly friend. So grateful for you and for helping me bring book #1 to life, so you are #1; unfortunately, your guacamole is not.

2. **SARAH**—Never #2 and always my #1 phone call, confidant, and sounding board. Words cannot express my infinite gratitude and love for you. "To be continued."

3. **TO MY EDITORS**—You know who you are, and I will be forever grateful for all the insight and cohesiveness you provided to me, for the way you pushed me farther than I ever thought possible, and for being the ultimate grammar police. Great-FULL!

4. **MILLIE**—From the download of my logo, you were all in and I could not be more grateful for the love, support, wisdom, insight, and labyrinths we have shared. So good!

5. **ASHLEY**—Your tough questions pushed me beyond my comfort zone, and I could not be more grateful. Here's to getting there 10K steps at a time.

6. **TAMI**—We are always 0.9 miles apart by heart and am so grateful for all the genuine love, honest advice, and shared learning of new ways to heal all the time.

7. **JIMMY!** So grateful for your years of true friendship and the most incredible artwork! You are so talented and so grateful for all your support and help along the way!

8. **ALEX AND ROXANNA**—I am so grateful for all your continued love and support and Days of Decadence for all of these years. I love you more.

9. **BARBARA (BP)**—Your accountability has kept me moving the needle all these years. Grateful for your love, support, and beginning every week with the sound of your voice.

10. **SUSAN**—Your making-dinner phone calls have offered support and advice that is more immeasurable than our ingredients. I am forever grateful for the support, love, levity, and advice you've offered at all hours of the night.

11. **CHRIS**—So grateful for your loving, honest sounding board and fantastic advice. May you always *Live on a Prayer.*

12. **ALL MY TEACHERS ALONG THE WAY**—I am so grateful for every moment, every insight, and every step we took together.

13. **ELIZABETH**—Thank you for your years of guidance and love and feeding me through all this hungry work. Podium, here I come!

14. **SAMMY**—So proud of all the ways you are expanding and growing and so grateful we get to journey there together. Love you so!

15. **JESSICA**—From preschool to the center to walking sessions, I am grateful we have each other every step of the way on the many roads we are traveling together.

16. **TIM**—To my brother from the same mother and my favorite chakra series student, may you continue to learn and grow. So grateful you now know my class is not, in fact, about Chaka Khan.

17. **LORI**—My sista! Grateful for all of our shared decadence and all your support through the decades. May your ice cream cake and huge heart forever bless this world.

18. **CAL**—*Om Mani Padme Hum.*
19. **PAYTON** (Beetlebug)—Keep saying yes and the world is yours.
20. **TO MY MANIFESTING** through Gratitude Queendom— Grateful for you honoring and witnessing my gratitude and growing our energy and dreams bigger and bigger together every single day. Oohh lala! Cha cha cha!
21. **ALLY**—You are a powerful manifestor who has the world in the palm of her hand. I love you so much and love seeing you learn, understand, and own your energy as you bless this world with your charm, drive, and immense talent.
22. **KELSIE**—To my first editor and portrait of a lady. Thank you for your incredible insights! Way to be the example of how to remain high-vibe to manifest whatever you want. So proud of you for blessing this world with your charm, joy, and love for life. I love you so much.
23. **E**—my soulmate, best friend, hubby, and partner. I am so grateful for all of your love and support and encouraging me to keep going even when I doubted myself. Love that you have become your own amazing manifestor. I love you so much! Fight on!

BIBLIOGRAPHY

Chapman, Gary, *The Five Love Languages: The Secret to Love That Lasts,* Northfield Publishing, 1992.

Dale, Cyndi, *The Subtle Body: An Encyclopedia of your Energetic Anatomy,* Sounds True, Inc. 2009.

Dispenza, Dr. Joe, *Breaking the Habit of Being Yourself: How to Lose Your Mind and Create a New One,* Hay House Inc., February 15, 2012.

Eden, Donna, *Energy Medicine,* Penguin Group, 1998.

Falcone, Vickie, *Buddha Never Raised Kids & Jesus Didn't Drive Carpool—Seven Principles for Parenting with Soul: How to Create More Peace at Home,* Jodere Group, July 1, 2003.

Goldman, Jonathan, *The 7 Secrets of Sound Healing,* Hay House Inc., January 10, 2017.

Gottman, Dr. John M., *The Relationship Cure,* Random House, May 15, 2001.

Hay, Louise, You Can Heal Your Life. Hay House Inc., January 1, 1984.

Khalsa, Narayan Singh, *Illnesses and Ailments—Their Psychological Meaning, February 1991.*

Len, Ihaleakala Hew, and Joe Vitale, *Zero Limits,* Wiley, December 9, 2008.

Lipton, Bruce H., *The Biology of Belief 10th Anniversary Edition: Unleashing the Power of Consciousness, Matter & Miracles,* Hay House Inc., January 1, 2008.

Ratan, Dr. Minoo, and Dr. Ravi Ratan, *Journey through the chakras*, Mumbai, India, 2009.

Sharma, Robin, *The Monk Who Sold His Ferrari: A Spiritual Fable About Fulfilling Your Dreams & Reaching Your Destiny*, Bolinda Publishing Pty Ltd., 1997.

Silverstein, Shel, *The Giving Tree*, Harper & Row, October 7, 1964.

Three Initiates, *The Kybalion*, Yogi Publication Society, 1908.

Websites

Askinosie, Heather, and Timmi Jandro, "The Power of Gemstones," https://energymuse.com/pages/about-gemstones.

Berkovich-Ohana, Aviva, Meytal Wilf, Kahana Roni, Amos Ariell, and Rafael Malach, "Repetitive Speech Elicits Widespread Deactiviation in the Human Cortex: the 'Mantra' Effect?" May 4, 2015, https://www.ncbi.nlm.nih.gov/pmc/articles/PMC4511287/.

Cai, Xiaomei, L.A.c., Ph.D. and Qineng Tan, L.Ac., Ph.D., "How to Treat Allergy with Acupuncture and TCM," November 27, 2020, https://myartofwellness.com/how-to-treat-allergy-with-acupuncture-and-tcm/.

Casperson, Erin, "The Ayurvedic Art of Cooking Water," www.kripalu.org/resources/ayurvedic-art-cooking-water.

Diamond, Marie, https://www.mindvalley.com/fengshui.

Dibdin, Emma, "The Mental Health Benefits of Journaling," March 31, 2022, https://psychcentral.com/lib/the-health-benefits-of-journaling/#:~:text=Scientific%20evidence%20supports%20that%20journaling,to%20create%2C%20intuit%20and%20feel.

dōTERRA Essential Oils, "Bioactivity of Essential Oils," https://www.doterra.com/US/en/blog/science-research-news-bioactivity-essential-oils.

Drobena, Darcy, and Duncan Harte, "Aura Definition, Aura Size and Aura Patterns . . ." www.The-auras-expert.com/aura-size.html.

Groot, Peter A., and Jay A. Gottfried, "Titrating the Smell of Fear: Initial Evidence for Dose-Invariant Behavioral, Physiological, and Neural Responses," 2021, https://journals.sagepub.com/doi/full/10.1177/0956797620970548.

Halpern, Dr. Marc, "The Five Elements in Ayurvedic Medicine," October 7, 2013, https://www.ayurvedacollege.com/blog/five-elements-ayurvedic-medicine.

Huberman, Dr. Andrew, *Huberman Lab Podcast,* 2021.

Hughes, Aimee, "Shiva and Shakti: The Divine Energies within Us All," https://www.yogapedia.com/shiva-and-shakti/2/6052, February 27, 2020.

Lipton, Dr. Bruce, "Dr. Bruce Lipton Explains How to Reprogram Your Subconscious Mind," https://www.youtube.com/watch?v=OqLT_CNTNYA, July 9, 2019.

Lipton, Dr. Bruce, "What are the volts of electricity in your human body?!" https://www.brucelipton.com/what-are-the-volts-electricity-your-human-body, September 12, 2022.

McColm, Jan, A Hug a Day, https://endeavors.unc.edu/win2004/hugs.html, January 1, 2004.

Mohata, Vandana , "An Interview with Jonathan Goldman," https://www.healingsounds.com/mantras-an-interview-with-jonathan-goldman

Nicole, Gina, http://school.ginanicole.net/chakra-feng-shui

Orloff, Judith, "The New Science of Empathy and Empaths," https://drjudithorloff.com/the-new-science-of-empathy-and-empaths.

Shmerling, Robert H., MD, "Wondering about goosebumps? Of course you are," https://www.health.harvard.edu/blog/wondering-about-goosebumps-of-course-you-are-2020080320688, October 2, 2020.

Tantra-Kundalini, "Chakras," https://Tantra-Kundalini.com/chakras.

Tickell, Josh and Rebecca, *The Earthing Movie,* https://www.earthingmovie.com, March 2, 2019.

UC Davis, Law of Conservation of Energy, https://energy education.ca/encyclopedia/Law_of_conservation_ of_energy

Van der Kolk, Bessell, KripaluVideo, "Overcome Trauma with Yoga" (interview), September 5, 2018, https://www.you-tube.com/watch?v=MmKfzbHzm_s&feature=share&fb-clid=IwAR0SkmsZPTb36XCBJMsLGN6XrJwwv0OJ-EL-M3S-O_10SrBrZILLKUQDWZC0.

Yogani, "Spinal Breathing Pranayama," https://Aypinternational. com, Advanced Yoga Practices International, https://www. aypinternational.cpom/lessons/41-spinal-breathing-pran-ayama, December 11, 2003.

ABOUT THE AUTHOR

ERIN GARAY is an intuitive, Reiki Master, hypnotherapist, certified enneagram and meditation teacher who loves unearthing behavior and energetic patterns to bring health and healing to clients. She leans on her decades of learning and experience to offer tools and techniques to audiences to manifest a life that feels richer and more connected. She hosts a weekly podcast and teaches mindful leadership to corporations and universities. You can join her community at www.LoveHealThrive.com where you will learn to love yourself enough to heal and heal yourself enough to thrive.

Made in United States
Troutdale, OR
09/26/2023

13207023R00209